THE
COMPLETE
VEGETABLE
GARDENER

The publishers are indebted to Floraprint Limited
for the majority of color transparencies in this book.

First published 1976

Published by arrangement with Intercontinental Book Productions,
Berkshire House, Queen Street, Maidenhead, England

Library of Congress Catalog Card Number: 76-49709

ISBN 0-89104-059-5 (paperback edition)
ISBN 0-89104-069-2 (hardcover edition)

THE
COMPLETE
VEGETABLE
GARDENER

by Peter Seabrook

Illustrated by Brian Edwards
Andrew Farmer and Martin Holbrook
Designed by Nicholas Maddren

A&W Visual Library

Contents

Introduction

My British friend, Peter Seabrook, has honored me by asking that I write an introduction to the American edition of his classic book THE COMPLETE VEGETABLE GARDENER. Many years ago it was my privilege to work and study under an English gardener, which accounts for my respect for the depth of horticultural knowledge it requires to teach gardening in a nation of gardeners.

Like myself, Peter Seabrook hosts a nationwide television program devoted to gardening. His name and reputation are without equal in Britain, and it is time he should be better known in this country. I can say without reservation that every serious gardener, novice or experienced, can deepen his understanding of horticulture and have a more abundant harvest by studying Peter Seabrook's book.

In America as in Britain, growing vegetables in the garden used to be an accepted part of life – something that everyone did and no one thought a great deal about. In the mid-decades of this century, this practice became somewhat superseded by the cultivation of ornamental, rather than edible plants, but ever-rising prices and current economic problems have brought it very much back into the limelight. Now, people are anxious to know how to make the most of the land available to them as well as how best to cultivate different types of vegetables for maximum yield and greatest variety.

This book is divided into several sections covering all the major aspects of vegetable growing, among them the siting of the vegetable plot in the garden, necessary tools and equipment, how to recognize and improve soil, raising seeds, the importance of crop rotation (particularly in the small plot), some hints on the use of cloches, frames and simple greenhouses, and how to recognize and control weeds, pests and diseases. The principle and workings of a 10 ft × 12 ft plot are explained with various plans to show how best to use the plot for your own requirements. Several charts show you at a glance the economics of growing vegetables, how long seed will last before losing its germination factor, exactly when to sow and harvest each vegetable so your land need never be unproductive, and how to store and keep them. It is worth spending time perusing these sections before studying the book's largest section, from page 40 onwards, in which the individual cultural requirements of each vegetable are described.

The practical and economic aspects of vegetable cultivation have been overriding concerns in the writing of this book, for there is undoubtedly great pleasure and satisfaction in producing succulent, fresh vegetables throughout the year at a fraction of the cost of their older, less flavorful supermarket counterparts. In addition there are few people who do not find enjoyment in seeing things grow – and the physical exertion of gardening, even in the small doses we recommend, is therapeutic to both the body and the mind.

James Underwood Crockett

The Vegetable Plot in your Garden

When professional landscapers talk about garden design, it should be remembered that they have a background of training and experience in the artistic use of plants and garden accessories on both a large and small scale. For most of us, however, gardening is a series of compromises. The average family will make a number of demands on the immediate area surrounding their house – at least on that which constitutes their 'territory'. It is necessary from the point of view of property value, as well as for aesthetic reasons to keep the garden tidy and attractive all the year round. Hedges and fences are needed to establish boundaries, as well as giving protection from wind and providing some degree of privacy.

Children and adults will have different requirements from a garden, but both needs can be considered at planning stage. Children will doubtless want some grassy area for playing and

Left; Many features have been fitted into this small suburban garden.
Right: Vegetables growing in the author's garden.
Below: Figure 1: Vegetable plot featured in the patio area. Figure 2: Vegetable plot in full view of the house.

Figure 1.

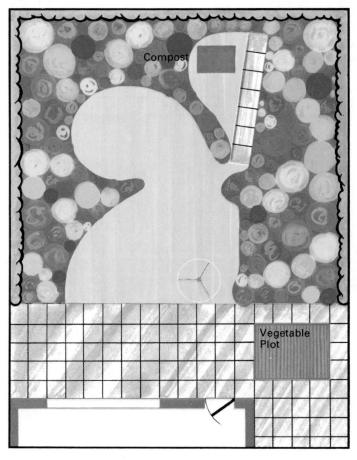

Compost

Vegetable Plot

Figure 2.

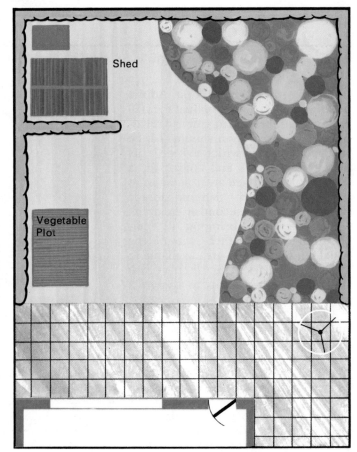

Shed

Vegetable Plot

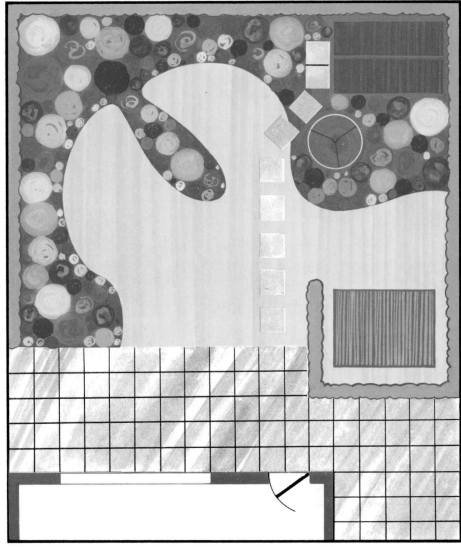

Figure 3: Vegetable plot is close to the house, but is screened by a hedge.

draw up a list of all the features and utilities you want to include and then cut each out to a scaled size. Mark out the total garden shape and size to the same scale on a large sheet of paper and then try a variety of combinations and arrangements to see how you can fit everything together in the most pleasing way.

Whether making a new start in a new garden or revamping an old one, first establish the boundaries, by planting hedges and erecting fences to give protection as soon as possible; next, cultivate the garden, making it level before sowing grass seed, laying paths and paving. After seeding, it is easy to cut out the beds, borders and vegetable plot area.

The Vegetable Plot
If you have a modern, virtually square, garden and wish to fit in a 10 ft × 12 ft (3 × 4 m) vegetable plot for example (see page 22), there are a number of ways of doing so (see figures 1, 2, 3 and 8). You could either site it so it is hidden away or so it is in full view from the house or patio area, and this will depend on how you feel about it individually. I find great pleasure in looking at a vegetable plot packed full of vigorously growing rows of plants in June, but the sight of overwintering greens, I find less appealing. On the other hand I love to see beautifully dug earth – all neat and level in a winter plot.

perhaps a swing and sandpit. Adults are likely to be happy with just a grassy area for summer sitting-out and relaxation! Then provision should also be made for a shed in which to keep tools and garden tables and chairs; for a compost and service area; perhaps an ornamental pool for fish and storage space for a boat or second automobile. To most people, bringing all their requirements together within the strict confines of the area available to them, particularly when that is minimal, stretches an ability to 'design' a garden to the limit!

Great improvements can be made to an existing layout, however, with just a little careful planning. At a time of reorganization, whether it be that you are faced with what is a completely new garden to you, or whether you merely feel it is time to make a few major changes to your existing garden, do allow yourself time to really *plan* the future arrangement. Ideally,

Figure 4: Some typical garden shapes.

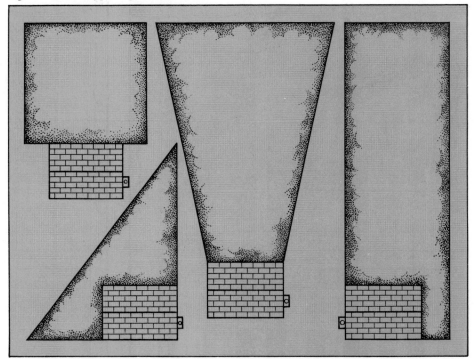

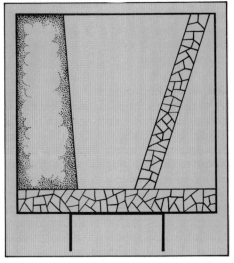

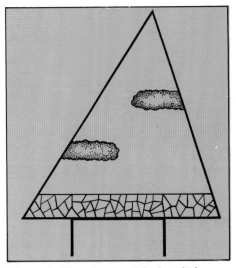

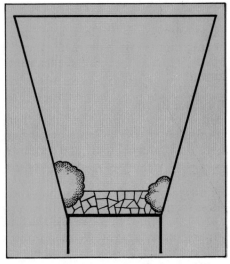

Figure 5: Paths and borders help to make a square garden look longer.

Figure 6: Cleverly placed hedges hide converging lines of a triangle.

Figure 7: Shrubs close to the house hide closely fenced boundaries.

Generally speaking there are three basic garden shapes; square, rectangular and triangular (see figure 4). Having the vegetable area in sight or out of view can be alternatives whichever basic shape you have. It is important, however, to watch and plan the angle of paths and screens in the extreme cases.

If a garden is completely square you can make it look longer by placing two paths or a path and border so that they slant away from one another to give diverging lines instead of converging lines (see figure 5). Similar treatment will help to broaden the appearance of a narrow garden.

The definite outer lines of triangular gardens can be softened by strategic planting of evergreen shrubs and screens. Where the house is at the base of the triangle, as it were, a screen jutting out from one side (see figure 6) will help hide the converging sides. If, on the other hand, the wide part of the garden triangle is at the bottom of the garden, planting bushy shrubs close to the house will help to hide the closely fenced boundaries (see figure 7).

Lawns and Paths
When you are planning to sow or lay turf for a lawn, aim to keep it in one area of garden only. It is not only then easier to mow, but gives the largest area for adults to sit in and children to play in and also helps prevent the garden from looking fragmented. Paths are important, especially close by the vegetable plot for you will want to be able to get to the vegetables in wet weather without getting your feet muddy. If there is a path surrounding the plot, it is also easier to cultivate –

you can hoe and weed from either side with a minimum of trampling over wet soil.

The siting of clean, dry paths must also be included in your plans, so that clothes lines, compost heaps, etc., are all easily accessible.

Don't discard the possibility of growing vegetables to form temporary summer screens. Obvious and attractive examples are runner beans grown up poles, with their scarlet, white or combination-colored flowers and the Jerusalem artichoke.

Figure 8: Vegetable plot placed at the end of the garden. Both here and in Figure 3 a compost heap could be made close to the hedge.

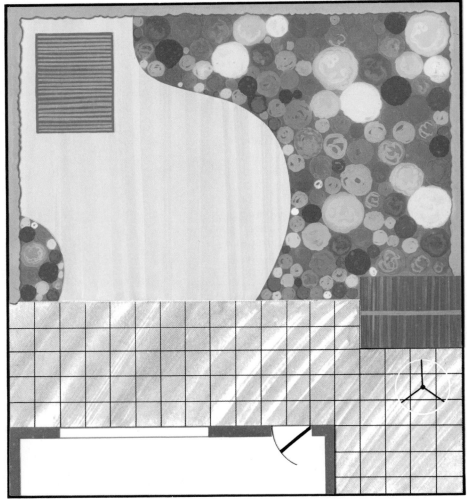

Essential Gardening Equipment

Lack of sophisticated gardening tools is no obstacle when it comes to vegetable growing – in fact your basic requirements are no more than a spade, a piece of wood and a length of string!

Buy the Best
Although a spade is the bare minimum, I am in no way against owning a range of tools and certainly, for the new gardener, having the right tool for the job will make things easier. You must, however, always buy good tools – cheap inferior ones are invariably a bad buy. I can assure you, in buying tools, it is your economies you will regret, never your extravagancies.

Working through a list of tools in a rough and ready order of priority, as I have already made clear, the spade comes first. The range of different types is formidable. Choose the type of spade which suits you personally – as a traditionalist I prefer those with wooden handles, but admittedly the new plastic handles are much more resistant to wet and other climatic conditions. Heavy, wet soils are easier to dig using a very shiny stainless steel spade, as the wet soil slips off the blade, but bear in mind that stainless steel tools are more expensive than those made of ordinary steel. If an ordinary steel spade is wiped clean after use and perhaps rubbed over with an oily rag to retain the shine, it will be quite as easy and comfortable to use.

Comfort is Important
Note the word 'comfortable' for that is the important thing to bear in mind when choosing tools. Generally speaking, although the stainless steel types are more expensive, they are usually more comfortable to use and easier to keep in clean working order.

One point to watch when buying a spade is the finish on the 'tread' (i.e. the spot where you push the spade into the ground with your foot). Many modern designs have a straight edge at the tread, while others have a small flat piece of metal. Although wet soil may stick to this as you dig the soil, it does protect your instep, but it may be that you will find a spade with a metal tread most useful when gardening on lighter soils.

Since we are talking about *essential* gardening equipment, it may seem like going from the sublime to the ridiculous to mention power tillers or cultivators. A power tiller (rotary cultivator) can speed up soil preparation

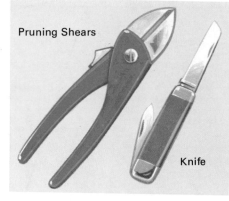

Pruning Shears

Knife

Figure 9.

in spring and fall and it's especially useful in breaking new ground for vegetable plots, new lawn areas and shrub and flower borders. The rest of the time the power tiller will probably sit in the tool shed or garage, simply because the tiller can not be used for cultivating between vegetable rows safely unless the rows are spaced from about 2½–3 ft (75–90½ cm) apart.

Most power equipment can now be rented from local dealers and garden centers.

Figure 10.

A garden line, comprising just two sticks with a piece of string tied between them, is useful to keep rows of vegetables straight at sowing and planting time.

Irrigation Equipment
A watering can is a fairly essential piece of equipment; generally the thing to remember is that the longer the spout, the lower the angle of the spout to the ground when you are watering. This means you can give a slower, less heavy delivery of water, which causes less damage to, and interference with, the soil. In addition, the lower the spout, the easier it is to apply the water accurately.

Next on my list comes the hoe, and although again there are many different designs, they may be divided into two groups – those you pull towards you (either drawing out a drill or in a drawing, chopping action to control weeds) and those you push, known as Dutch or scuffle hoes. Ideally you should use the draw hoe for seed drills and to earth up crops like potatoes and the true Dutch hoe to control weeds

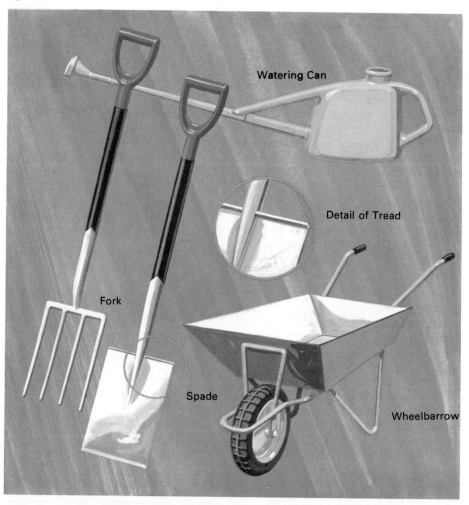

Watering Can

Detail of Tread

Fork

Spade

Wheelbarrow

and leave a nice fine tilth. The draw hoe can be used to control weeds, but you have to work forward with it which means you not only tread on the soil you have just worked, but in damp soil conditions you will also tread back weeds as well as consolidating some of the newly made tilth.

While the traditional Dutch hoe has the blade supported on a 'Y' frame a number of makes now have either a 'T' or 'L' shaped head. These more recent designs make it possible to get right up to plants for weed control or to thin out seedlings. Care is needed, however, because the outer edges of the hoe will be out of sight under the soil, in a position to slip easily through the plant root by mistake.

Pruning shears are useful to all gardeners and the vegetable gardener is

choice of a short cranked handle design or a long straight handle. In my experience, you need a strong wrist to cope with the longer handle. Hand trowels are usually offered as a pair with small hand forks, but the latter have little use other than on a rockery.

Garden forks come quite low on my priority listing because the spade can be used in most instances and is also more adaptable. If a garden has a large proportion of stones, however, a fork will penetrate the soil more easily than a spade. The fork can also be used as a mixture between rake and cultivator if turned with tines down towards the soil and pulled towards the operator. A good rake would however, be better to prepare a fine level tilth before seed sowing or when filling in seed drills,

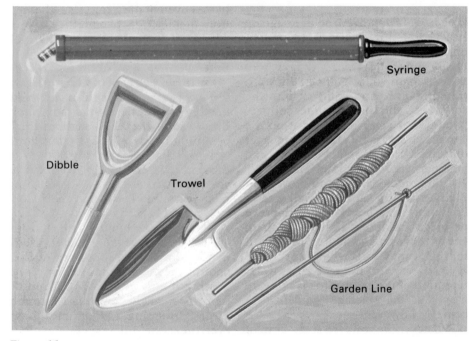

Figure 11.

deners and the vegetable gardener is no exception. They may be used for preparing sticks for peas, gathering peppers, squash and so on. Pruners with replaceable working parts will give a very long working life and are easily sharpened. Do buy good quality pruners, cheap designs will very soon lose their edge or become twisted at the axis.

Transplanting
Most vegetable transplanting can be done with a dibble, easily made from an old, broken tool handle, but a trowel will also make things easier for you. Top quality and the highest priced are the stainless steel ones, but whatever price you pay, you have a

for example. A long-handled cultivator is also useful on a larger plot where a sizeable area of soil needs regular light surface cultivation.

Other useful pieces of equipment include a light wheelbarrow (with as wide a wheel as possible to make it easier to use on wet soil), a sharp pocket knife and some form of syringe or sprayer for insecticides and fungicides. The relatively cheap plastic hand sprayers will give adequate service for a number of years if used carefully and not abused by dropping or leaving filled during frosty conditions.

Even more practical for the small garden is a simple sprayer. When pests strike, filling and using the duster is quick and easy – and effective.

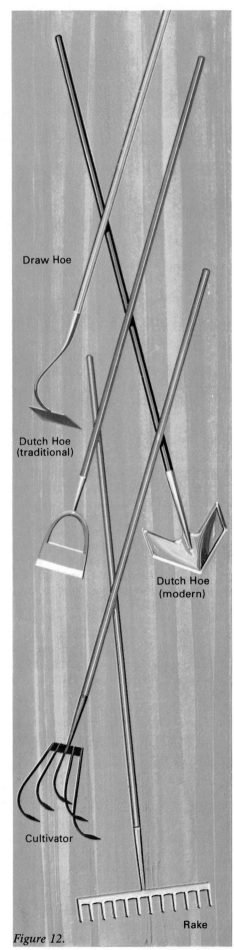

Figure 12.

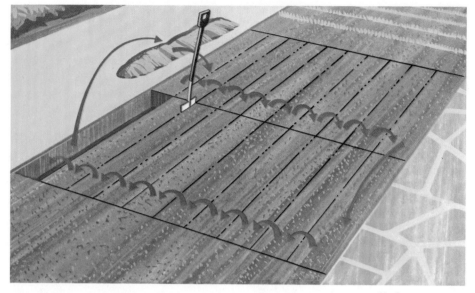

Figure 13: Single digging. There is no need to divide the area on a small plot.

DIGGING THE SOIL

There are four general types of soil – light and sandy; medium loam, (generally referred to as good garden soil); heavy clay; and alkaline. All types of soils will be improved by the addition of well-rotted animal manure, composted vegetation and peat. Heavy clay soils, for example, become much easier to dig, hoe and rake if you work peat moss and compost into them. When you do this, concentrate the application in a small area, spreading a layer 3 in (7·5 cm) deep or so and then cultivating it. When economics allow treat another area and so on, until you have improved the whole plot. Don't scatter a little peat over a big area – this way the real value is lost and you will never see any benefits.

The same advice goes for well-rotted organic matter although here the limitations are those imposed by just accommodating and rotting down sufficient waste vegetation, rather than buying the peat. Sphagnum peat moss is the most universally available source of humus and it is as close as the nearest garden center. But peat moss can be expensive for use in large gardens. Shop around for the best prices and try to buy several bales at once at a lower price.

Although sometimes recommended as a mulch, peat moss is better used as a soil additive. As a mulch, it tends to blow away or forms a velvety surface that sheds rainfall and water. Instead use straw, hay, wood chips, rotted sawdust or black plastic.

Organic matter dug and worked into the soil in whatever form has many functions. It helps light soils retain moisture; it improves the drainage on heavy soils; it tends to reduce or eliminate the extreme alkalinity of chalk soils and it encourages root growth in all soils. You can dig well-rotted manure and compost into the soil during the fall and winter soil preparation, or you can spread it on the surface as a mulch (a blanketing layer of material used to retain moisture and smother weeds) to dig in later.

Other methods of soil improvement include mixing sand and well weathered ashes into heavy soil to improve drainage qualities and make them easier to work; and adding heavy soil to light, sandy soils which works in a reverse way to improve the water retention of the sand. This is not very easy for the average gardener to achieve, however.

Whatever the soil type some form of annual cultivation is necessary and one of the attractions of vegetable growing for me is the opportunity of burying any mistakes once a year, thus having a perfectly clean start for the next season. Digging need not be the painfully hard job some people make it out to be. The tricks are to use a comfortable spade, (the blade of which should be kept shiny and clean) and not to lift too much soil at a time.

Follow these simple step-by-step digging instructions to prepare your vegetable plot. First take out a trench the width and depth of a spade at one end of the plot (see figure 13). Pile the soil in a heap at the other end. Turn over a 3–4 in (8–10 cm) wide strip of soil, one spade full at a time, across the plot. Move back over the next 3–4 in (8–10 cm) strip, and so on, until you have covered the plot. Use the soil from the first trench to fill the last one. Always lift a smaller spadeful than you think you can manage and take your time.

Put down a layer of hay on wet heavy soils to keep your feet clean and make the digging easier. Bury any short lived weeds (the kinds without thick perennial roots) as you dig but don't miss the chance of picking out any of those thick perennial weed roots as you go. It will save you a lot of hoeing next year (see Weeds and their Control, page 117).

When you are digging in the fall and early winter, leave the spadefuls of soil in big lumps. The processes of frost cooling the soil and then thawing, rain wetting it and wind drying it out all help to break it down into crumbly pieces. In spring and summer, however, break the soil down as you dig to

Figure 14: Double digging involves cultivating the lower soil as well as the top soil. It is useful for deep rooted vegetables and crops like asparagus.

Figure 15: Don't take too much soil at each spadeful . . .

Figure 16: . . . a smaller amount is easier to lift. Don't hurry digging work.

Figure 17: Leave heavy soils in lumps, the winter weather will break them down.

prevent it drying into large lumps and thus losing a lot of moisture. Try to dig when it looks as if you are in for a few hours of dry and drying weather. This is particularly important on heavy soils as rain on the freshly dug soil will destroy the crumbly structure you have been working so hard to create.

MANURES

Animal manure is a very good soil improving material, but is best rotted down with other organic matter such as straw, peat and wood shavings before use. Its goodness stems from the fact that it provides the basic plant foods, (also supplied by chemical fertilizers), as well as composted organic matter which improves the physical crumbliness of soil.

You should apply animal manure in moderation, as too much of it, particularly if it is not well rotted down can cause temporary 'scorch' damage to plants. It is fairly unlikely that the average gardener will have too much manure to add, however, and it is well worth remembering that all natural and organic materials, even if added to excess, will do no permanent damage to the soil. This is not the case with chemical fertilizers which, if too heavily applied, can damage crops and soils for a number of years. Natural liquid manure can be made by soaking sheep and cattle manure in water – diluted to just color the water.

The combination of peat and animal manure is 'perfection' for gardeners as it provides plenty of organic material to improve the soil as well as

food for the plants. When buying any form of animal manure, go simply for the greatest bulk you can get for your money. Where manures have been used to grow a previous crop, (for example horse manure and peat used for mushrooms), they remain valuable for the supply of organic matter but will have had the plant foods depleted.

Occasionally the term 'green manuring' is used and it refers to the cultivation of a rapidly growing plant like annual lupin and mustard to produce masses of foliage which is then dug into the soil. The leaves and stems of these plants provide the soil with improving organic matter. Although in fact lupins and similar legumes also add nitrogen to the soil, extra nitrogen fertilizer has to be added when digging in most green manure crops. It should be sprinkled over the land to speed the rotting down process. If it is not applied, the following crop may be starved of this basic plant food. Lawn

grasses and clover are excellent green manures so if you are digging up a piece of old lawn don't discard the turf – instead dig it well into the soil to improve future crops.

COMPOST
Rotted-down Plant Remains

Gardening provides great opportunity to be virtually self-sufficient – a trend currently much in favor. All the goodness taken from the soil by growing vegetable crops can be replaced by rotted down old leaves, stems, lawn mowings and so on which accumulate in the garden. Well rotted down, or 'composted', plant remains are a perfect soil additive, and provide plant food and organic matter to improve the crumbliness of the soil. There are many involved and detailed descriptions of compost making and compost gardening but like everything else, it is really only the general principles you need to remember. The system I like

Figure 18: Large lumps (left) must be broken down, either by the weather or further digging, to provide crumbly textured soil (right) for planting.

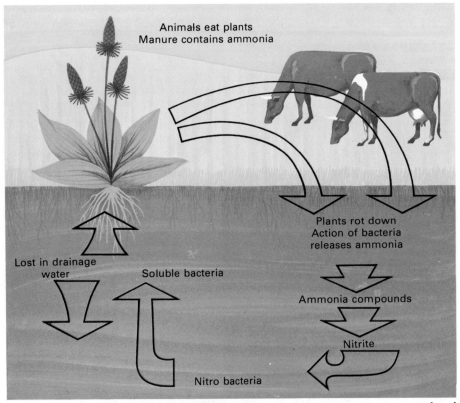

Animals eat plants
Manure contains ammonia

Plants rot down
Action of bacteria
releases ammonia

Ammonia compounds

Nitrite

Lost in drainage
water

Soluble bacteria

Nitro bacteria

Figure 19: The process of animals grazing and plants growing promotes a perpetual cycle of nitrogen and mineral extraction and replacement in the soil. This 'cycle of life' is of vital importance in the growing of vegetables.

best uses four posts 4 ft (120 cm) long driven 12 in (30 cm) into the soil to mark out a rectangle 5 ft × 3 ft (150 cm × 90 cm). Wind wire netting round the stakes to form the compost bin, and line it with plastic. Alternatively use plastic sheet and other materials such as old pieces of board and corrugated sheet to form the sides. You can of course buy and use one of the various factory made compost containers, but obviously the more sophisticated they are, the higher the price will be.

All the non-woody plant remains – pea and bean stalks, cabbage leaves, weeds and lawn mowings, raked up tree leaves and kitchen waste – can all be tipped into the bin. Once you have accumulated a fair heap, pull out the stakes and re-erect the bin on an adjacent site. You can then make a new heap by placing the least well decayed material from the top of the first heap at the bottom of the new one, and so on, until you have completely turned the heap (see figure 20).

Shake the material out a bit as you go because air is needed to speed the decomposition. Two other commodities are needed for the most rapid rotting down – namely moisture, (so have a nearby can of water to use on dry spots as you turn the heap) and

some form of nitrogen. If you have rabbits or similar pets then their hutch cleanings will help provide the nitrogen. If you have no animal manure a good sprinkling of a complete fertilizer may break the self-sufficiency rule but does a really good job!

Start to accumulate rubbish in summer and fall so as to get a full heap which you can turn early the following spring. It will then rot down fast enough to provide a good site for squash growing in the summer. After the squash crop, dig the remaining heap of good friable brown compost into the soil in the fall. A winter and spring accumulated heap will also be sufficiently rotted down after early summer turning to dig in during the fall and winter.

Try to mix the waste at all stages as this helps to get the most rapid rotting down. Hard corn stalks will rot down more quickly when mixed with lawn mowings, for example, while lawn mowings on their own tend to pack down tightly, excluding air and therefore being slow to decay fully. Beans and other items keep the mowings opened up, and everything rots down more quickly as a result.

Useful organic sources of plant food such as blood from the butcher, fish bones and such like can also be

thoroughly mixed with garden waste to enrich the ultimate compost, but keep a look-out for vermin which may be attracted if too much waste food is added to the heap.

FERTILIZERS

Nitrogen, phosphates and potash are the three major chemicals supplying plant foods. They can be purchased in natural organic form or as inorganic chemical fertilizers. Nitrogen, the main food in organic dried blood and inorganic sulphate of ammonia, encourages rapid leafy growth and should predominate when applying

Garden-produced compost is of great value to the vegetable grower.

top dressings to crops like cabbage in spring. Plants which have had a check to growth or those suffering hot dry conditions can be given a new spurt of life with nitrogen-rich fertilizers.

Phosphates, the main constituent of organic bone meal and inorganic superphosphate, are seldom applied alone except perhaps as a dusting over seed beds. This chemical's main function is to aid root development generally and it also becomes necessary at the seed ripening stage.

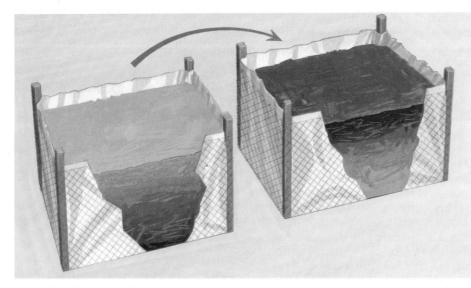

Figure 20: Turning and mixing compost helps to speed the rotting-down process.

Potash, found in wood ash as well as sulphate of potash, is the counter balance to nitrogen. When plants have excessive leaf growth, either from too many moist, warm, sunless days or excess nitrogen, potash will harden up the growth. This helps to make the plant fruitful and improve the flavor of the vegetables.

Compound fertilizers, a mixture of all three, are the easiest to use and are the most frequently bought and applied. The general fertilizers tend to be a balanced mixture of Nitrogen (N), Phosphates (P) and Potash (K), often referred to as NPK. If anything they have an emphasis on nitrogen. Tomato and rose fertilizers, on the other hand, tend to have the emphasis on potash, which gives more flavor to the tomatoes and more color and greater disease resistance to roses.

Apply a general fertilizer at one handful, 2 oz per square yard, (56 gms per 0·8 sq m) before sowing and planting to increase yields. This will actually do all that most gardeners require but to get even better results, you really need a general fertilizer for initial soil preparation, a higher potash fertilizer for top dressing and one quick acting nitrogen fertilizer like dried blood or nitrate of soda to give plants an occasional 'boost'.

The compound fertilizers are available in dry forms (which may be sprinkled on the surface and hoed in), as well as in soluble form for liquid feeding. Top dressing with dry fertilizer is usually at the lower rate of 1 oz per square yard (28 gms per 0·8 sq m) and you can give more than one application in a season.

Continual cropping and the addition of compost and manure may make the soil a bit acid and to counteract this apply a dusting of lime in winter to dug soil. Avoid applying too much lime as this will not help growth. The only way of checking the lime content is to test the soil, which you can have done by a specialist or do yourself with a soil testing kit. The figure which indicates the correct amount is pH 6·5. Soils with figures lower than this will need 3 oz lime per square yard (85 gms per 0·8 sq m) or even more to reduce the acidity and raise the pH figure. Lime applied to heavy soils also improves the texture in that it helps the fine clay particles to stick together to form a crumbly structure.

Minor plant foods, often referred to as 'trace elements', include chemicals like magnesium, iron and boron, but as most soils have ample supplies of these it is seldom necessary to apply them. Very occasionally single crops may not grow well because of the lack of a trace element.

A deficiency of magnesium when growing roses and tomatoes, for example, (indicated by leaves turning yellow between the veins) can be rectified by watering with epsom salts. Cauliflowers which develop narrow leaves (known as 'whiptail') may occur when grown in soils lacking in molybdenum, but the conditions can be eliminated by watering with one dessertspoonful of sodium molybdate in one gallon (4·5 liters) of water per 5 square yards (4 sq m) of soil.

In general, however, a little care in the planning and rotation of crops coupled with good husbandry in the form of organic matter, such as well rotted compost applied liberally when digging, is all that is needed for good vegetable crops. The addition of a little fertilizer will just increase the yield. The immediately available plant foods are, of course, soluble and taken up by the plant with moisture. Thus it naturally follows that light sandy soils, being free draining, are the most quickly leached, so apply fertilizers little and often on such soils.

Foliar fertilizers are the most quick acting of all – the plant foods in this case being taken up by the leaves. They are either sprayed or watered on to the foliage and will give results in a matter of days if the temperature is warm enough for growth. All leafy crops, roots like carrots and beet, as well as peas and beans, respond to foliar feeding, especially in hot dry weather conditions.

Figure 21: Plants such as squash grow well on rotted-down compost. Plant two seeds on an average sized heap.

Crop Rotation

It is good, basic gardening practice to rotate crops with one another around a vegetable plot to avoid cropping the same site with the same vegetable or same type of vegetable year after year. Vegetable crops are generally divided into three main groups: root crops, brassicas and the 'others'. The importance of rotation can be demonstrated by taking 'greens' as an example. Greens fall into the brassica group and include broccoli, brussels sprouts, cabbage, cauliflower, kale and cress. If these crops are grown year after year in the same soil, diseases such as club root will multiply rapidly. If, on the other hand, they are only grown in any one site, one year in three rotated with the other two groups, then the disease is denied its host plant and cannot build up in the soil. The disease club root is a classic example, but the same goes for many diseases and vegetable pests.

Apart from pests and diseases, the plant food requirements of the various groups of vegetables are different. The peas and beans, technically called legumes, grow with the help of bacteria which take nitrogen from the air and convert it into nitrogenous plant foods. They do this so efficiently in fact that they leave more nitrogenous material in the soil after growing than was there at the outset. Planting brassicas to follow the legumes allows the green vegetables to use this extra nitrogen, thus considerably helping their growth as well as saving the trouble and cost of additional nitrogenous fertilizers.

Use of Manure and Compost

Crops such as celery, potatoes and lettuce revel in soils which have plenty of freshly dug-in, well-rotted animal manure and garden compost. Soils recently enriched in this way are not ideal, however, for root crops such as carrot, chicory and parsnip because the roots tend to divide up and go several ways in search of the manure. It is much better to allow crops like beans to take full advantage of the freshly prepared land and then follow with carrots a season later. Carrots will grow faster and to a larger size in richer and more moisture-retaining soils which contain very well-rotted down organic matter.

Although fertilizers can be added to soil at any stage, it is a good idea to apply lime (if it is needed) ahead of brassicas. In a normal rotation scheme

Potatoes in the root crop section of the author's garden, growing alongside the pea and bean section.

this will give the greatest period of time between the application of lime and the planting of potatoes, which are more likely to get their skins marked by the disease scab in alkaline soils.

Where gardens are large enough the whole rotation scheme can be expanded by separating peas and beans (the legumes) from the 'other crops' group to give a four-year or four-season rotation. Although the real professionals may work their cropping schemes to this level of perfection, for most of us it is quite sufficient to arrange things so that the same crop is not grown on the same site two years running.

The commonly recommended rotational plans have been worked out over many years and are not only very practical, but also labor-saving. Fall, winter and spring maturing brassicas can often be planted to follow early crops of peas with no more cultivation than hoeing or tickling over the surface of the soil with a fork or spade. If soil is dug as early potatoes are lifted, it only needs knocking down to a fine tilth before the August lettuce sowing. Two main crops can often be grown, therefore, without thoroughly digging over the whole plot a second time, but it is necessary to keep the surface of the soil well hoed and of a crumbly texture, (particularly avoid trampling over it when wet) to achieve this work saving. It will usually be necessary on all but the lightest soils to dig the ground thoroughly for the third crop.

It is also possible to get two main crops within one rotational group in a season. Early peas and broad beans can be sown, harvested and cleared in time to set out leeks for winter harvest,

Peas and broad beans growing alongside spring cabbage with lettuce and radish grown as an intercrop.

First Year	Second Year	Third Year
OTHER CROPS Beans Peas Celery Peppers Eggplant Spinach Leeks Squash (Summer) Lettuce Sweet Corn Onions Tomatoes	Broccoli Kohl-Rabi Brussels Sprouts Radish Cabbage Rutabaga Cauliflower Turnip Chinese Cabbage Turnip Greens Kale Savoy	Artichoke, Jerusalem Beets Carrot Chicory Parsnip Potatoes
ROOT CROPS Artichoke, Jerusalem Beets Carrot Chicory Parsnip Potatoes	Beans Peas Celery Peppers Eggplant Spinach Leeks Squash (Summer) Lettuce Sweet Corn Onions Tomatoes	Broccoli Kohl-Rabi Brussels Sprouts Radish Cabbage Rutabaga Cauliflower Turnip Chinese Cabbage Turnip Greens Kale Savoy
BRASSICAS Broccoli Kohl-Rabi Brussels Sprouts Radish Cabbage Rutabaga Cauliflower Turnip Chinese Cabbage Turnip Greens Kale Savoy	Artichoke, Jerusalem Beets Carrot Chicory Parsnip Potatoes	Beans Peas Celery Peppers Eggplant Spinach Leeks Squash (Summer) Lettuce Sweet Corn Onions Tomatoes

The above chart gives a suggested crop rotation plan for a three-year period.

or a quicker-maturing crop such as snap beans or summer squash can be sown instead.

Vegetables which need considerable space and a long growing season – melons and winter squash – are usually not included in small plots. Some gardeners locate them on the edge and train the vines to grow outside the plot, but this is untidy and a nuisance in mowing. Cucumbers, so vital for summer salads, bear very well when trained up a trellis, not so easy with the heavier-fruited vines. Most summer squash, including zucchini and patty pan types, are bushes rather than vines. Although each plant requires from 3–4 ft (90–120 cm) each way, most plots have space for at least three or four plants.

Perennial crops – globe and Jerusalem artichokes, asparagus, rhubarb – are best grown outside the plot or at one end, as they remain in place for years.

Spacing and Rotation Charts
The colored squares included in the 'Growing your own Vegetables' section – pages 40–111, and shown right indicate the group to which the various crops belong, which will help you to plan your crop rotation, purple indicates brassicas, yellow – other crops, brown – root crops and bright orange – perennials. The last group are obviously not included in the crop rotation plan. The measurements within the square refer to the spacings between the plants and rows and wherever possible these have been shown approximately to scale.

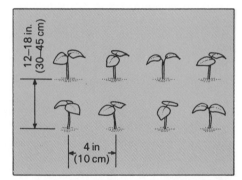

Right: Example of a planting diagram.

The same spot shown opposite, photographed a few weeks later.

Seed Raising

SEED COMPOST

Good seed germination basically depends on three things – oxygen, moisture and temperature. If there is no oxygen in the growing soil, if there is too much or too little moisture, or if temperatures are too high or too low, the germination of seeds will be erratic. Obviously we have little control over seeds sown outside in the garden, but this is not the case with seeds raised under cover.

The best results indoors come from warmth, adequate light and the right growing medium, known as compost. Seed compost is used to germinate the seedlings and potting composts are used to grow the seedlings on into larger plants. The word 'compost' used here as a term to describe a growing medium may be somewhat confusing, after having used the same word to describe rotted down vegetable waste for soil improvement.

Seed and potting composts probably get this name from the fact that good turf was cut, stacked and virtually 'composted' before being chopped up and sieved to form the basis of all growing composts in the past. At one time skilled gardeners had many recipes to make growing composts, and they used different ones for nearly every crop. Things are much simpler today, and there is really only one 'recipe' for all seed composts, and one for potting composts.

The John Innes Institute of England did much of the basic research which brought about the reduction in the number of seed raising composts. It was followed by the University of California, which produced the UC mixes, and subsequently several commercial companies.

Loam-based and Soilless Composts

The major difference between England's John Innes (JI) composts and most commercial American mixes is that the Innes composts are based on steam-sterilized loam (loam here meaning good soil from stacked turf) while the American mixes use no soil and are called 'soilless' or 'synthetic.' Both give excellent results. If you have access to good loam that you can sterilize, you can make a mix similar to the John Innes compost. One formula might be 2 parts loam 1 part peat moss, 1 part coarse sand. To each bushel (36 liters) add 1½ oz (42 gr) of superphosphate and ¾ oz (20 gr) ground limestone. This mixture is fine for seed sowing. To enrich it for seedlings and older plants, add per bushel (36 liters) 4 oz (120 gr) of 5–10–5 complete fertilizer or about 2 quarts (2 liters) of dried manure. Mix all ingredients thoroughly.

The soilless composts or mixes (also called synthetic soils) available to Americans through mail-order houses or local nurseries and garden centers have eliminated much of the grief and fuss formerly associated with indoor seed sowing. Perhaps most important is that they are sterilized and free from weed seeds; secondly, they are light in weight when compared to true soil composts so are ideal for containers in which many city-bound and space-short suburban gardeners must now grow their vegetables.

However, everything has its drawback or price – and in this case, it *is* the price. The soilless mixes, although 'a good buy,' may not be within everyone's budget. You can mix your own which will result in some savings, but since mixing the necessary fertilizer ingredients into the soilless mix, usually peat moss and vermiculite or peat moss and sand, is a rather critical operation, it is really better to buy the factory mixes. (If you wish to try mixing your own, consult your local extension agent for a suitable formula – he is listed under the County Government in the telephone book.)

A few of the packaged soilless mixes which should be readily available are Jiffy Mix, Redi-Earth, Pro-Mix and Super Soil.

Moisture content of composts is important particularly at seed sowing and seedling transplanting stages. For the soil-based compost, moisture content is correct if a handful squeezed in your hand cracks open in one largish crack when you release your grip. If the compost just crumbles when you release the pressure, it is too dry and if the lump remains in the shape of your hand without cracking at all, it is too wet. The peat composts are at the right moisture content if moisture just oozes between your fingers as you squeeze a handful.

Containers just 1 in (2·5 cm) deep can be used for raising many fine seeds, and will use less compost than deeper types.

When transplanting seedlings into new containers, handle by the leaves, not the stem.

Figure 22: Loosely fill container with compost and firm evenly.

Figure 23: Cover seeds with soil-based compost.

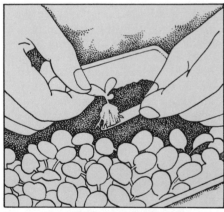

Figure 24: Lift seedlings with stick.

Figure 25: Prick off into boxes.

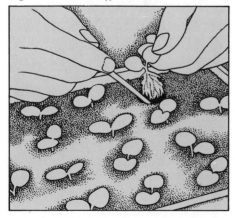

Figure 26: Warmth at the base speeds germination and growth in a simple propagator.

SEED RAISING INDOORS

Raising a few seeds on the window sill or under fluorescent lights can be a profitable occupation with a number of vegetable seeds. Beat the rough winter weather and get a good growing start by sowing hardy plants like peas, cabbage, lettuce and cauliflower indoors in January and February to plant out later. Follow these (still indoors) with the more tender vegetables like cucumbers, peppers, runner beans, eggplants and tomatoes.

If you have a garden frame or greenhouse, you can greatly increase the number of plants you can raise.

Indoor seed raising is however a simple step-by-step operation. The peat pot – and Jiffy 7 pellet – have made it even more simple, and often a one-step process. One or two seeds are sown in the Jiffy 7 pellets, inflated to pots by soaking in water. At a later date both plant and pot are set in the ground.

Small quantities of seeds can be sown in flower pots, seed pans (the equivalent of flower pots but half the depth) and/or seed boxes. Loosely fill the containers to the brim with moistened seed compost, gently firming it with your fingers at first and then using a flat object such as the bottom of another pot or piece of board. This will leave the firmed compost level and about ½ in (1 cm) from the top of the container. (Make sure the corners of boxes are 'finger-firmed' before firming over the whole surface).

Space the seed over the surface and then just cover it with a further layer of seed compost. You can sprinkle the all-peat composts over by hand but you should spread the soil-based composts by passing them through a sieve. Cover the sown containers with glass to help retain moisture and newspaper to exclude light or place them in plastic bags. A temperature of 55°–65°F (13°–18°C) is needed for speedy germination.

Keep a watch on the sown pots and as soon as you see the first signs of emerging shoots, remove the covers and move the pots close to the glass to give the young seedlings as much light as possible.

As soon as the seedlings are large enough to handle they are ready for spacing out singly in other containers – a practice known as 'pricking off' and 'pricking out'. Use a pointed label or sharpened stick to lift the seedlings up from under the roots and to separate them. Then plant them out singly in pots or space them out in boxes. Always handle seedlings by the leaves, *not* the stem. A damaged leaf will soon be replaced by a new one, but there is only one stem. The earlier you prick off seedlings the less likelihood there is of checks to growth.

Larger seeds like those of broad beans, peas, sweet corn and beans can either initially be sown singly in peat pots or planted two seeds per pot, which are thinned back to one plant as they germinate.

Figure 27: Rake soil to a fine tilth.

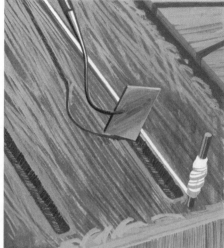

Figure 28: Draw shallow drills for seed.

Figure 29: Space seeds down the drill.

Figure 30: Thin seedlings as recommended.

SEED RAISING – OUTDOORS

A nice crumbly soil is the key to easy and successful outdoor vegetable seed raising. Winter frosts break down fall and winter-dug soils, so they automatically form this required crumbly structure – called tilth – in spring. If you have lumpy, hard soil however, try mixing a good layer of well moistened peat in with the surface soil. This helps to produce reasonable seed sowing conditions.

When you are preparing the ground for actual sowing, knock down all dug soil with a cultivator, fork or spade and tread along the line of the row once with your feet to firm. Finally level the soil with a rake or spade to achieve the desired tilth.

When the soil is prepared stretch a garden line across the plot to mark out the position of the row and then make the seed drill with a draw hoe, dibble or piece of wood. If the soil is very wet stand on a board to prevent pressing the soil down hard with your feet.

The depth of drill may vary but most seeds require a drill no more than 1 in (2·5 cm) deep. In practical terms this means sufficient depth to cover the seeds well with soil after sowing. The seed must then be spaced down the drill, and this is best done by sprinkling it along the row from between your fingers. Hold the supply of seed in the palm of your hand and feed it through your thumb and forefinger, to roll the seed into the drill. Alternatively, take a pinch of seed and sprinkle it into the drill.

Cover the seed with soil by shuffling down the row with a foot on each side of the row. Finally firm the soil either by gently treading once or using the back of the rake. Then 'scuffle' the surface to remove footprints and ruffle any smoothed areas which will otherwise go hard after a fall of rain.

Large seeds like beans, squash and sweet corn can be sown by making a single hole for each seed with a dibble and covering them as you go along. When sowing slow-to-germinate seeds such as onion, parsnip and parsley, it is worth mixing a little fast germinating seed such as radish or lettuce in with it. These will grow quickly and indicate where the other crops will follow. It also allows you to hoe between the rows to control weeds without disturbing the emerging vegetable seedling. Radish and lettuce, used in this way, are known as indicator crops.

Once the seedlings are through you must thin them out to the spacings recommended for each crop. All seedlings that are left to grow too thickly and too many together – from radish to cauliflower, carrot to lettuce – will be too small to be of use. It is generally a wise precaution to thin out twice, the first time to one half the required distance and then subsequently to the final distance. If slugs, birds and other pests damage a few seedlings, with the two-stage thinning there is a fifty-fifty chance they will take unwanted seedlings. Some vegetables, like carrots, will in fact provide small but harvestable roots at the second thinning.

Sparrows can play havoc with young seedlings, not only lettuce, which is possibly the worst affected, but also peas, beets and many others. If you cannot protect the emerging seedlings with cloches, place a stick every 3–4 ft (90–120 cm) down the row and twine a few strands of black cotton 2–3 in (5–8 cm) above the seedlings to

Planting broad bean seeds.

Figure 31: Protect young seedlings with lines of thread.

discourage birds.

Quite apart from protection from birds, Hotkaps or polyethylene tunnels are most valuable for seed raising. Placed over the soil a week or two before sowing, they will dry and warm the soil which helps germination. They also protect fine tilth from damage caused by heavy rain.

SEED GERMINATION CHART

There are often too many seeds in one packet to sow in a small plot, so every now and then you will find you have seed left over from previous years. This chart will show whether it is worth sowing left-over seeds in subsequent years. However, if in doubt it is better to use fresh seed than risk the chance of a crop failure.

The figures given in the chart can only be a guide because seed life depends very much on harvesting and storage conditions. Sun, warmth and dry harvesting conditions invariably give top quality seed which has a longer storage life. Cool, damp harvesting conditions are likely to give poorer quality seed with a correspondingly shorter storage life.

Dry conditions and an even temperature are the best storage conditions for long seed germination life. They can be produced most easily by using an airtight container, such as a biscuit tin or screw top jar with a small sachet of silica gel placed inside to keep the atmosphere dry. The back of a damp shed or shelf in the greenhouse where temperatures may rise rapidly and then fall just as quickly are *not* good storage places.

SEED GERMINATION CHART

	1	2	3	4	5	6	7	8	9	10	Years
Asparagus											
Bean, Broad											
Bean, Snap											
Bean, Runner											
Beets											
Broccoli											
Brussels Sprouts											
Cabbage											
Carrot											
Cauliflower											
Celery, Celeriac											
Chicory											
Cucumber											
Kale Kohl Rabi											
Leek											
Lettuce											
Melon											
Onion and Okra											
Parsley and Parsnip											
Peas											
Peppers											
Radish											
Salsify, Scorzonera, Sea Kale											
Spinach											
Rutabaga											
Sweet Corn											
Tomato											
Turnip											

Worth sowing this year

80% or more success rate

50% or more success rate

The 10ft x 12ft (3m x 4m) Vegetable Plot

Gardening on a small scale is the easy way to have all the benefits and satisfaction from growing plants with the minimum of work. Growing your own vegetables also gives garden-fresh food of better quality and flavor as well as saving you money.

Both the newcomer to gardening and the skilled gardener who is used to very large plots need have no fears about operating on what may appear to be a miniature scale. Although the choice of the rectangular dimension at the outset was no more than a convenient size and shape for a television screen and could be accommodated in the studio situation, in practice, the 10 ft × 12 ft (3 m × 4 m) rectangle has proved ideal.

Dividing the plot up into three sections for rotation purposes is easy and the 10 ft (3 m) long rows are sufficient to provide a reasonable gathering at any one time of all the crops grown. Surrounding the plot by grassed, paved or concreted paths gives easy access, even in wet conditions, and makes it possible to do a good part of the cultural and harvesting operations from the side paths. This keeps your feet clean and avoids treading down the soil or trekking soil indoors with you. If you stand alternately on either side of the plot, you will find it is possible to hoe from the middle to the side without putting a foot on the soil. Most of the vegetables can be harvested from the side, so it is really only when you are digging, sowing and doing some planting that it is necessary to actually tread over the plot.

As gardening is still in the province

Vegetables in the plot: from l. to r. sweet corn, pole beans, beets, lettuce as an indicator crop, carrots, onions and peas.

Figure 32: The vegetable plot in late summer. Note cabbage planted to mature in succession.

22

of the 'artist' as well as the 'scientist', there are no unbreakable rules! While the 10 ft × 12 ft (3 m × 4 m) plans are particularly suited to many requirements, there is nothing to stop you reducing the size even further should you so wish.

Our plans are designed to provide at least sufficient of any one vegetable at a gathering to provide a serving for four people. If you need bigger servings and more vegetables then you could cultivate two or more plots simultaneously. Beware of attempting to produce great quantities, however, as you are likely to achieve the maximum returns when you cultivate one 10 ft × 12 ft (3 m × 4 m) plot really well and intensively rather than two less efficiently. Once you have the one

under control and you really know what you are doing, extension is easy and more likely to be successful.

The practical demonstrations of small plot vegetable growing on television have also proved that it is possible to cultivate our basic crop plan spending no more than one hour per week and, in the extreme case, also strictly limiting the money spent both on seeds and other sundry gardening items. Choice of vegetables has been geared to providing a year-round supply, rather than a glut of crops at one time of the year. It also proved that one need not worry too much about soil, as it was necessary to use the soil within reach of the television cameras. After

the first spade or two of digging the site looked almost undiggable, being more grassed-over rubbish than soil! Persevering with the digging, however, proved it was more than possible to grow good vegetables. The criterion would seem to be, if you can dig it – that appears to be good enough! A small area can also be quickly improved by adding well-rotted compost and other organic matter.

BASIC PLAN

This plan is very simple to carry out but achieves all the objectives, so far discussed – that is, rows which are long enough to give yields at one gathering to serve four people, less than one hour per week spent on cultivating the plot and the provision of freshly grown vegetables to eat any week of the year.

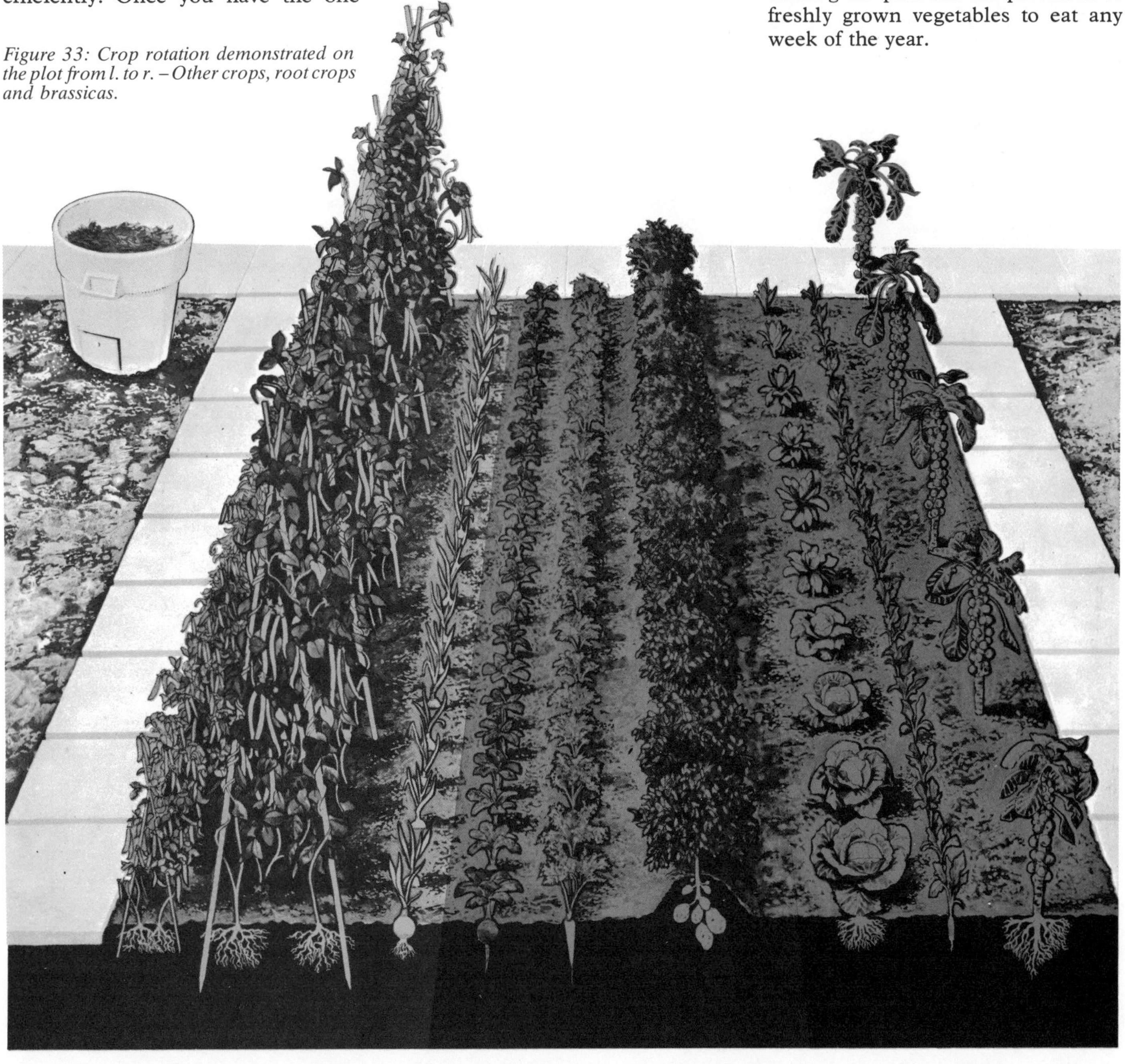

Figure 33: Crop rotation demonstrated on the plot from l. to r. – Other crops, root crops and brassicas.

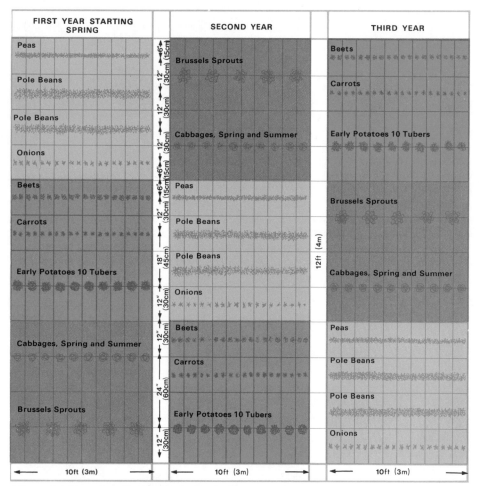

FIRST YEAR STARTING SPRING	SECOND YEAR	THIRD YEAR

First Year Starting Spring:
Peas
Pole Beans
Pole Beans
Onions
Beets
Carrots
Early Potatoes 10 Tubers
Cabbages, Spring and Summer
Brussels Sprouts

Spacings: 6" (15cm), 12" (30cm), 12" (30cm), 12" (30cm), 6" 6" 15cm (15cm), 12" (30cm), 18" (45cm), 12" (30cm), 12" (30cm), 24" (60cm), 12" (30cm)

Second Year:
Brussels Sprouts
Cabbages, Spring and Summer
Peas
Pole Beans
Pole Beans
Onions
Beets
Carrots
Early Potatoes 10 Tubers

Third Year:
Beets
Carrots
Early Potatoes 10 Tubers
Brussels Sprouts
Cabbages, Spring and Summer
Peas
Pole Beans
Pole Beans
Onions

12ft (4m)

10ft (3m)   10ft (3m)   10ft (3m)

Figure 34: Rotation Guide for the Basic Plan.

Our aim has been to get everything possible from the vegetable plot, but if, for example, your family does not like or does not want peas, all you need to do is look for the same rotation colored squares in the vegetable section (pages 42–111), to find an alternative crop to peas. You can then adjust the row spacing accordingly.

Working systematically down the crops in plan order (see figure 34) I will give brief notes on the cultural needs and crop timings. Full details for each crop will be found in the vegetable growing section (pages 42–111).

Peas: Sow in early spring, as soon as the ground can be worked. Early sowings are best because the peas can be harvested in June to give more space for Brussels sprouts or squash which can follow immediately.

Pole Beans: Sow as soon as all danger of frost has passed. Choose bush beans if you don't want to erect supports for pole beans. Pole beans are very prolific, however, and are well worth the effort of providing supports, as they will yield well until frost.

Onions: Push the small sets gently into the soil as early as you can work the ground in spring to give good bulbs from midsummer on. These can be stored for winter use. Plant seeds along the row or elsewhere to provide green onions (scallions) for summer salads.

Beets: Sow as soon as the frost is out of the ground and make successive sowings until about two months before the first severe frost in the fall. The roots can be cooked fresh, stored for use from October to May, and/or pickled.

Carrots: Sow in spring to provide fresh pulled roots as well as roots to store for winter and spring use.

Potatoes: This crop takes up quite a lot of room and replacing it with carrots, parsnips, or other root vegetables would possibly give a better return. However, many people are willing to make a sacrifice in order to have freshly dug new potatoes from the garden! Plant seed potatoes in the garden about two weeks before the latest frost date for your area, and dig the potatoes when the foliage has died. Digging the potatoes in good time clears the soil for fall-maturing greens, and perhaps, if you live in the south, a late-summer planting of lettuce.

Cabbage: Set out plants as soon as soil can be worked, or for a fall crop, set out from June to August. You can make a second planting of summer-maturing cabbage once you have cleared the first. Alternatively, if you cut the early cabbage leaving the stump and a few leaves behind, the stump will produce a second crop of small cabbages.

Brussels sprouts: Set out as soon as soil can be worked for early crop or in June or July for fall crop. Radishes can be grown in the soil on each side of the sprouts. (You will find instructions for interplantings and second crops on the Basic Plan in the vegetable growing instructions on pages 42–111).

The harvest chart below is based on crops that can be grown in the 10 ft × 12 ft (3 × 4 m) plot, but the crops chosen and their harvesting times will depend on a family's taste and the local climates. In the warmest parts harvesting of many crops continues all winter.

HARVEST CHART												
Vegetable	Jan	Feb	Mar	Apr	May	Jun	Jul	Aug	Sep	Oct	Nov	Dec
*Peas						●●●●	●●●●		●●●●	●●●●		
Lettuce					●●●●	●●●●	●●●●		●●●●	●●●●		
*Beans							●●	●●●●	●●●●			
*Onions	oooo	oooo	oooo	oooo				●●●●	●●●●	●●●●	oooo	oooo
Onions, salad			●●	●●●●	●●●●	●●●●	●●					
*Beets	oooo	oooo	oooo			●●●●	●●●●	●●●●	oooo	oooo	oooo	oooo
*Carrots	oooo	oooo	oooo			●●	●●●●	●●●●	oooo	oooo	oooo	oooo
*Cabbage						●●	●●●●	●●●●	●●●●	oooo	oooo	oooo
*Broccoli						●●	●●●●	●●●●	●●●●	●●●●		
*Squash, summer						●●	●●●●	●●●●	●●			
*Tomatoes						●●	●●●●	●●●●	●●●●	oooo		

●●●● Harvesting   oooo Storing   * Freeze

THE BASIC PLAN SIMPLIFIED

The basic plan is geared to year-round crops and a reasonable range of vegetables, but it is possible to get bigger returns for your money and efforts if you reduce the range of vegetables you grow and if you don't necessarily want to achieve maximum year-round harvesting. It could be, for example, that you would like to grow as many beans or peas as possible to put in the freezer for winter use.

If you intend to use your plot this way you will still need to rotate the crops, so as to avoid growing one crop in the same soil year after year. Taking the simplest system, which would be to grow just one kind of vegetable in the 10 ft × 12 ft (3 m × 4 m) plot in any one year, you could actually grow about 210–250 lettuces in two crops! (The greater number would be achieved by growing compact varieties such as 'Tom Thumb'.) Intensive growing of lettuce alone is not really practical for most families, however, because the whole crop will tend to mature at once and there will be far too much to cope with at one time. If you have planted the whole plot with peas or beans, then a large freezer would accommodate the yield, providing you have time to pick and prepare all the crop for freezing, remembering it will all be ready at one time.

Dividing the plot into three sections and planting each section with a vegetable from a different crop rotation group is an easier and more acceptable choice for the average home gardener. Take, for example, lettuce, beans and cabbages: all are easy to grow, all are popular, and all yield well under a

FIRST YEAR STARTING SPRING	SECOND YEAR	THIRD YEAR
Lettuce		Spring Cabbages
Lettuce	Pole Beans Double Row Caned	
Lettuce	Peas	Spring Cabbages
Lettuce	Runner Beans, Pinched	Spring Cabbages
	Chicory	Lettuce
Pole Beans Double Row Caned	Chicory	Lettuce
Peas	Chicory	Lettuce
Pole Beans, Pinched	Chicory	Lettuce
Cabbages Summer	Lettuce	
Cabbages Summer	Lettuce	Pole Beans Double Row Caned
Cabbages Summer	Lettuce	Peas
Cabbages Summer	Lettuce	Pole Beans, Pinched

10ft (3m) — 10ft (3m) — 10ft (3m)

Figure 35: Rotation Guide for the Basic Plan Simplified.

wide range of soil and climatic conditions.

Where fewer, varieties are grown, thus providing greater yields, some form of storage is usually necessary. To take again the example of beans grown as the major crop, for freezing, then spinach and sweet corn are two satisfactory complementary crops.

Sweet corn must be grown in blocks or triple rows and a 10 ft × 4 ft (3 m × 1·2 m) plot will take four rows

Figure 36: Crops as they appear in the second year of the above chart.

of the dwarf varieties, which could provide as many as 40 ears.

It is not practical for most gardeners to grow lettuce to harvest in the middle of winter because heated greenhouse conditions are needed. Where a root crop is needed to help with the rotation, however, then endive can be sown in one third of the plot alongside lettuce – the lettuce will provide salads all summer and the endive roots (harvested in October, stored and a few brought from storage every 10–14 days to force (see page 67)) provide salad leaves in the winter. In this way you can have year-round endive. Interplanting can also be introduced without complicating the three main crops plan too much. For example, you can sow rows of radishes between cabbage and lettuce, or spinach before and between rows of sweet corn. If you are a complete newcomer to gardening, begin with the three simple crops plan, one in each third of the plot, and once these are growing well, introduce one or two crops among them. After that you can move on to the eight to ten crops in the basic plan.

25

ADDITIONS TO THE BASIC PLAN

To get the maximum yield from the small vegetable plot, all the ground space should be covered with foliage, but when you start vegetable growing, you will soon discover that even main crops like potatoes and brussels sprouts do not fully cover the ground with their foliage all the year round. All plants need just enough space to keep their natural leaf spread exposed to sunlight. With this in mind, you can get the maximum from your plot by even more careful planning, and fitting in extra crops wherever and whenever space allows.

There are many ways of intensifying the basic cropping plan and the following suggestions should give you some ideas. Firstly it is possible to plant lettuce raised indoors on each side of a row of peas. Quick maturing lettuce (varieties like 'Tom Thumb') will be cut before peas need the space. Also, if you water the row of peas very well just before the pods are ready to pick, it not only helps to swell the pods and increase the yield but softens the ground to allow another crop, say, beans or squash, to be pushed in beside the old row. The new seedlings develop as the old crop dies down.

You can have an overwintered crop of spring salad onions growing between beets and carrots. Lifting the beets and carrots as early as possible allows time for a second sowing of these crops too. Another choice would be to mix parsnip and early carrot, and then pull all the carrots at the second

An intercrop of lettuce grown between rows of peas, sown in succession.

thinning, leaving only the parsnips to develop. You can lift potatoes in July and clear the ground to allow sowings of three more rows of carrot, beets or spinach. Where the weather is warm and damp it may even be possible to snatch a quick intercrop of spinach from between beets and carrots, or carrots and potatoes.

You can grow a number of rows of radish in the 'greens' (brassica) rotation area as an intercrop. In addition to this, you could also crop two rows of turnips on each side of the row of brussels sprouts. Alternatively you could follow the spring cabbage with two

rows of turnips instead of following summer cabbage with spring cabbage.

If cropping is intensified to the maximum you must make full use of pot raised plants. Sweet corn raised indoors in pots, for example, can be kept growing in the pots while spring cabbages mature and are cut. You will then need to hoe the ground immediately and plant out your very well established sweet corn plants. It is this sort of intensification that allows you to get the maximum output for your labors – one good digging of the plot, say for peas, and you can get two pea crops plus a lettuce crop.

Figure 37: Rotation Guide for Additions to the Basic Plan.

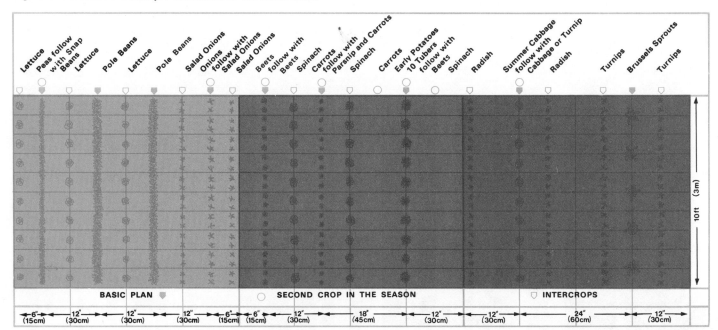

Protection from the Elements

CLIMATE

A number of fairly popular vegetable crops that can be grown in the average garden are nevertheless not hardy and will die if subjected to a degree or two of frost. Temperatures often differ so much between localities not many miles apart that the best planting dates for some one vegetable may differ by several days or possibly as much as two weeks.

Vegetable crops may be roughly grouped and sown according to their hardiness and their temperature requirements. The frost-free date in spring is usually two to three weeks later than the average date of the last freeze in a locality and is approximately the date that oak trees leaf out.

The gardener naturally wants to make the first planting of each vegetable as early as he can without too much danger of its being damaged by cold. Many vegetables are so hardy to cold that they can be planted a month or more before the average date of the last freeze, or about six weeks before the frost-free date.

With a crop such as potatoes, the gamble of early planting is not as great as it would be with an early sowing of snap beans. The potatoes will take several weeks after planting to develop roots and for the shoots to grow above the surface, whereupon any frost would only damage the shoot growth above the ground. Although growth would be checked and the yield of tubers both reduced and delayed as a result, new shoots would still be produced from below ground to carry a crop. On the other hand, if emerging bean seedlings are damaged by frost there would be virtually no chance of recovery and you would have to sow again to get any crop.

The earlier you sow or plant, the earlier the crop will be ready, comparatively speaking, but if you make your moves too early – when heavy frosts are still likely – then the chance of total failure and the need to start again can occur.

In contrast, most, if not all, cold-tolerant crops actually thrive better in cool weather than in hot weather and should not be planted late in the spring in the southern two-thirds of the country where summers are hot. Thus, the gardener must time his planting not only to escape cold but with certain crops also to escape heat. Some vegetables that will not thrive when planted in late spring in areas having rather hot summers may be sown in late summer, however, so that they will make most of their growth in cooler weather.

Throughout this book, I have given instructions to plant out after the chance of frost has passed. A gardener anywhere in the United States can determine his own safe planting dates for different crops by using the maps on the following pages, together with the accompanying plant charts. The maps show the average dates of the last killing frosts in spring and the average dates of the first killing frosts in fall. They are the dates from which planting times can be determined, and such determinations have been so worked out in the charts that any gardener can use them, with only a little trouble, to find out the planting dates for his locality.

Figure 38: Cover tender foliage with newspaper to protect it on frosty nights.

The first chart for use with the map of spring frost dates (on pages 28–29), shows planting dates between January 1 and June 30, covering chiefly spring and early-summer crops. It shows *how early it is safe to plant*; it also shows the spring and early-summer dates *beyond which planting usually gives poor results*.

Opposite each vegetable, the first date in any column is the *earliest generally safe* date that the crop can be sown or transplanted by the gardener using that column. (No gardener needs to use more than one of the columns.) The second date is the latest date that is likely to prove satisfactory for the planting. All times in between these two dates may not, however, give equally good results. Most of the crops listed do better when planted not too far from the earlier date shown.

To determine the best time to plant any vegetable in the spring in your locality:

1. Find your location on the map and then, the solid line on the map that comes nearest to it.

2. Find the date shown on the solid line. This is the average date of the last killing frost. Once you know the date you are through with the map.

3. Turn to the appropriate chart; find the column that has your date over it; and draw a heavy line around this entire column. It is the only date column in the table that you will need.

4. Find the dates in the column that are on a line with the name of the crop you want to plant. These dates show the period during which the crop can safely be planted. The best time is on, or soon after, the first of the two dates. A time halfway between them is very good; the second date is not so good.

For areas in the Plains region that warm up quickly in the spring and are subject to dry weather, very early planting is essential to escape heat and drought. In fact, most of the cool-season crops do not thrive when spring-planted in the southern part of the Great Plains and southern Texas.

The second set of charts is used with the map of fall frost dates in the same way to find the dates for late plantings. The recommendations for late plantings and for those in the South for overwintered crops are less exact and less dependable than those for early planting. Factors other than direct temperature effects—summer rainfall, for example, and the severity of diseases and insects—often make success difficult, especially in the Southeast, although some other areas having the same frost dates are more favorable. A date about halfway between the two shown in the chart will generally be best, although in most areas fair success can be expected within the entire range of dates shown.

Along the northern half of the Pacific coast, warm-weather crops should not be planted quite so late as the frost date and table would indicate. Although frost comes late, very cool weather prevails for some time before frost, retarding late growth of crops like sweet corn, lima beans and tomatoes.

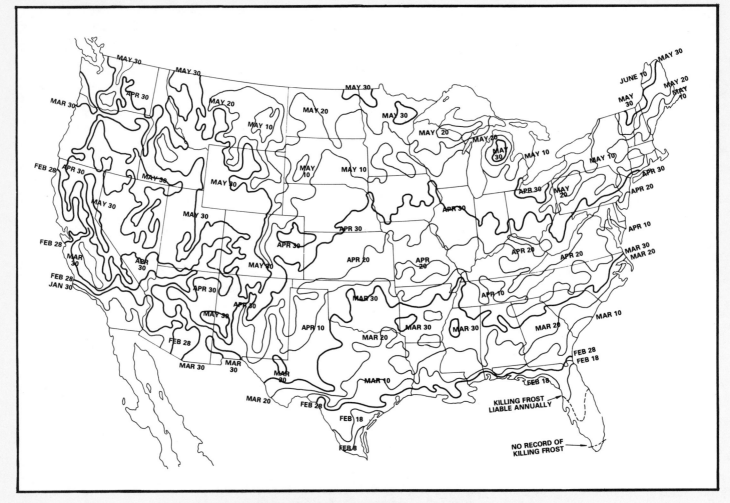

Figure 39 Map to show average dates of last killing frost in spring.

EARLIEST DATES, AND RANGE OF DATES, FOR SAFE SPRING PLANTING OF VEGETABLES IN THE OPEN

Crop	Planting dates for localities in which average date of last freeze is—						
	Jan 30	**Feb 8**	**Feb 18**	**Feb 28**	**Mar 10**	**Mar 20**	**Mar 30**
Asparagus[1]					Jan 1–Mar 1	Feb 1–Mar 10	Feb 15–Mar 20
Beans, lima	Feb 1–Apr 15	Feb 10–May 1	Mar 1–May 1	Mar 15–June 1	Mar 20–June 1	Apr 1–June 15	Apr 15–June 20
Beans, snap	Feb 1–Apr 1	Feb 1–May 1	Mar 1–May 1	Mar 10–May 15	Mar 15–May 15	Mar 15–May 25	Apr 1–June 1
Beet	Jan 1–Mar 15	Jan 10–Mar 15	Jan 20–Apr 1	Feb 1–Apr 15	Feb 15–June 1	Feb 15–May 15	Mar 1–June 1
Broccoli,[1]	Jan 1–30	Jan 1–30	Jan 15–Feb 15	Feb 1–Mar 1	Feb 15–Mar 15	Feb 15–Mar 15	Mar 1–20
Brussels sprouts[1]	Jan 1–30	Jan 1–30	Jan 15–Feb 15	Feb 1–Mar 1	Feb 15–Mar 15	Feb 15–Mar 15	Mar 1–20
Cabbage[1]	Jan 1–15	Jan 1–Feb 10	Jan 1–Feb 25	Jan 15–Feb 25	Jan 25–Mar 1	Feb 1–Mar 1	Feb 15–Mar 10
Cabbage, Chinese	([2])	([2])	([2])	([2])	([2])	([2])	([2])
Carrot	Jan 1–Mar 1	Jan 1–Mar 1	Jan 15–Mar 1	Feb 1–Mar 1	Feb 10–Mar 15	Feb 15–Mar 20	Mar 1–Apr 10
Cauliflower[1]	Jan 1–Feb 1	Jan 1–Feb 1	Jan 10–Feb 10	Jan 20–Feb 20	Feb 1–Mar 1	Feb 10–Mar 10	Feb 20–Mar 20
Celery and celeriac	Jan 1–Feb 1	Jan 10–Feb 10	Jan 20–Feb 20	Feb 1–Mar 1	Feb 20–Mar 20	Mar 1–Apr 1	Mar 15–Apr 15
Chard	Jan 1–Apr 1	Jan 10–Apr 1	Jan 20–Apr 15	Feb 1–May 1	Feb 15–May 15	Feb 20–May 15	Mar 1–May 25
Chervil and chives	Jan 1–Feb 1	Jan 1–Feb 1	Jan 1–Feb 1	Jan 15–Feb 15	Feb 1–Mar 1	Feb 10–Mar 10	Feb 15–Mar 15
Chicory, witloof					June 1–July 1	June 1–July 1	June 1–July 1
Corn salad	Jan 1–Feb 15	Jan 1–Feb 15	Jan 1–Mar 15	Jan 1–Mar 1	Jan 1–Mar 15	Jan 1–Mar 15	Jan 15–Mar 15
Corn, sweet	Feb 1–Mar 15	Feb 10–Apr 1	Feb 20–Apr 15	Mar 1–Apr 15	Mar 10–Apr 15	Mar 15–May 1	Mar 25–May 15
Cress, upland	Jan 1–Feb 1	Jan 1–Feb 15	Jan 15–Feb 15	Feb 1–Mar 1	Feb 10–Mar 15	Feb 20–Mar 15	Mar 1–Apr 1
Cucumber	Feb 15–Mar 15	Feb 15–Apr 1	Feb 15–Apr 15	Mar 1–Apr 15	Mar 15–Apr 15	Apr 1–May 1	Apr 10–May 15
Eggplant[1]	Feb 1–Mar 1	Feb 10–Mar 15	Feb 20–Apr 1	Mar 10–Apr 15	Mar 15–Apr 15	Apr 1–May 1	Apr 15–May 15
Endive	Jan 1–Mar 1	Jan 1–Mar 1	Jan 15–Mar 1	Feb 1–Mar 1	Feb 15–Mar 15	Mar 1–Apr 1	Mar 10–Apr 10
Fennel, Florence	Jan 1–Mar 1	Jan 1–Mar 1	Jan 15–Mar 1	Feb 1–Mar 1	Feb 15–Mar 15	Mar 1–Apr 1	Mar 10–Apr 10
Garlic	([2])	([2])	([2])	([2])	([2])	Feb 1–Mar 1	Feb 10–Mar 10
Horseradish[1]							Mar 1–Apr 1
Kale	Jan 1–Feb 1	Jan 10–Feb 1	Jan 20–Feb 10	Feb 1–20	Feb 10–Mar 1	Feb 20–Mar 10	Mar 1–20
Kohlrabi	Jan 1–Feb 1	Jan 10–Feb 1	Jan 20–Feb 10	Feb 1–20	Feb 10–Mar 1	Feb 25–Mar 1	Mar 1–Apr 1
Leek	Jan 1–Feb 1	Jan 1–Feb 1	Jan 1–Feb 1	Jan 15–Feb 15	Jan 25–Mar 1	Feb 1–Mar 1	Feb 15–Mar 15
Lettuce, head[1]	Jan 1–Feb 1	Jan 1–Feb 1	Jan 1–Feb 1	Jan 15–Feb 15	Feb 1–20	Feb 15–Mar 10	Mar 1–20
Lettuce, leaf	Jan 1–Feb 1	Jan 1–Feb 1	Jan 1–Mar 15	Jan 1–Mar 15	Jan 15–Apr 1	Feb 1–Apr 1	Feb 15–Apr 15
Muskmelon	Feb 15–Mar 15	Feb 15–Apr 1	Feb 15–Apr 15	Mar 1–Apr 15	Mar 15–Apr 15	Apr 1–May 1	Apr 10–May 15
Mustard	Jan 1–Mar 1	Jan 1–Mar 1	Feb 15–Apr 15	Feb 1–Mar 1	Feb 10–Mar 15	Feb 20–Apr 1	Mar 1–Apr 15
Okra	Feb 15–Apr 1	Feb 15–Apr 15	Mar 1–June 1	Mar 10–June 1	Mar 20–June 1	Apr 1–June 15	Apr 10–June 15

Crop	Planting dates for localities in which average date of last freeze is—						
	Jan 30	Feb 8	Feb 18	Feb 28	Mar 10	Mar 20	Mar 30
Onion[1]	Jan 1–15	Jan 1–15	Jan 1–15	Jan 1–Feb 1	Jan 15–Feb 15	Feb 10–Mar 10	Feb 15–Mar 15
Onion, seed	Jan 1–15	Jan 1–15	Jan 1–15	Jan 1–Feb 15	Feb 1–Mar 1	Feb 10–Mar 10	Feb 20–Mar 15
Onion, sets	Jan 1–15	Jan 1–15	Jan 1–15	Jan 1–Mar 1	Jan 15–Mar 10	Feb 1–Mar 20	Feb 15–Mar 20
Parsley	Jan 1–30	Jan 1–30	Jan 1–30	Jan 15–Mar 1	Feb 1–Mar 10	Feb 15–Mar 15	Mar 1–Apr 1
Parsnip			Jan 1–Feb 1	Jan 15–Feb 15	Jan 15–Mar 1	Feb 15–Mar 15	Mar 1–Apr 1
Peas, garden	Jan 1–Feb 15	Jan 1–Feb 15	Jan 1–Mar 1	Jan 15–Mar 1	Jan 15–Mar 15	Feb 1–Mar 15	Feb 10–Mar 20
Pepper[1]	Feb 1–Apr 1	Feb 15–Apr 15	Mar 1–May 1	Mar 15–May 1	Apr 1–June 1	Apr 10–June 1	Apr 15–June 1
Potato	Jan 1–Feb 15	Jan 1–Feb 15	Jan 15–Mar 1	Jan 15–Mar 1	Feb 1–June 1	Feb 10–Mar 15	Feb 20–Mar 20
Radish	Jan 1–Apr 1	Jan 1–Apr 1	Jan 1–Apr 1	Jan 1–Apr 1	Jan 1–Apr 15	Jan 20–May 1	Feb 15–May 1
Rhubarb[1]							
Rutabaga				Jan 1–Feb 1	Jan 15–Feb 15	Jan 15–Mar 1	Feb 1–Mar 1
Salsify	Jan 1–Feb 1	Jan 10–Feb 10	Jan 15–Feb 20	Jan 15–Mar 1	Feb 1–Mar 1	Feb 15–Mar 1	Mar 1–15
Shallot	Jan 1–Feb 1	Jan 1–Feb 10	Jan 1–Feb 20	Jan 1–Mar 1	Jan 15–Mar 1	Feb 1–Mar 10	Feb 15–Mar 15
Sorrel	Jan 1–Mar 1	Jan 1–Mar 1	Jan 15–Mar 1	Feb 1–Mar 10	Feb 10–Mar 15	Feb 10–Mar 20	Feb 20–Apr 1
Spinach	Jan 1–Feb 15	Jan 1–Feb 15	Jan 1–Mar 1	Jan 1–Mar 1	Jan 15–Mar 1	Jan 15–Mar 15	Feb 1–Mar 20
Spinach, New Zealand	Feb 1–Apr 15	Feb 15–Apr 15	Mar 1–Apr 15	Mar 15–May 15	Mar 20–May 15	Apr 1–May 15	Apr 10–June 1
Squash, summer	Feb 1–Apr 15	Feb 15–Apr 15	Mar 1–Apr 15	Mar 15–May 15	Mar 15–May 1	Apr 1–May 15	Apr 10–June 1
Tomato	Feb 1–Apr 1	Feb 20–Apr 10	Mar 1–Apr 20	Mar 10–May 1	Mar 20–May 10	Apr 1–May 20	Apr 10–June 1
Turnip	Jan 1–Mar 1	Jan 1–Mar 1	Jan 10–Mar 1	Jan 20–Mar 1	Feb 1–Mar 1	Feb 10–Mar 10	Feb 20–Mar 20
Watermelon	Feb 15–Mar 15	Feb 15–Apr 1	Feb 15–Apr 15	Mar 1–Apr 15	Mar 15–Apr 15	Apr 1–May 1	Apr 10–May 15

Crop	Planting dates for localities in which average date of last freeze is—						
	Apr 10	Apr 20	Apr 30	May 10	May 20	May 30	June 10
Asparagus[1]	Mar 10–Apr 10	Mar 15–Apr 15	Mar 20–Apr 15	Mar 10–Apr 30	Apr 20–May 15	May 1–June 1	May 15–June 1
Beans, lima	Apr 1–June 30	May 1–June 20	May 15–June 15	May 25–June 15			
Beans, snap	Apr 10–June 30	Apr 25–June 30	May 10–June 30	May 10–June 30	May 15–June 30	May 25–June 15	
Beet	Mar 10–June 1	Mar 20–June 1	Apr 1–June 15	Apr 15–June 15	Apr 25–June 15	May 1–June 15	May 15–June 15
Broccoli[1]	Mar 15–Apr 15	Mar 25–Apr 20	Apr 1–May 1	Apr 15–June 1	May 1–June 15	May 10–June 10	May 20–June 10
Brussels sprouts[1]	Mar 15–Apr 15	Mar 25–Apr 20	Apr 1–May 1	Apr 15–June 1	May 1–June 15	May 10–June 10	May 20–June 10
Cabbage[1]	Mar 1–Apr 1	Mar 10–Apr 1	Mar 15–Apr 10	Apr 1–May 15	May 1–June 15	May 10–June 15	May 20–June 1
Cabbage, Chinese	(2)	(2)	(2)	Apr 1–May 15	May 1–June 15	May 10–June 15	May 20–June 1
Carrot	Mar 10–Apr 20	Apr 1–May 15	Apr 10–June 1	Apr 20–June 15	May 1–June 1	May 10–June 1	May 20–June 1
Cauliflower[1]	Mar 1–Mar 20	Mar 15–Apr 20	Apr 10–May 10	Apr 15–May 15	May 10–June 15	May 20–June 1	June 1–June 15
Celery and celeriac	Apr 1–Apr 20	Apr 10–May 1	Apr 15–May 1	Apr 20–June 15	May 10–June 15	May 20–June 1	June 1–June 15
Chard	Mar 15–June 15	Apr 1–June 15	Apr 15–June 15	Apr 20–June 15	May 10–June 15	May 20–June 1	June 1–June 15
Chervil and chives	Mar 1–Apr 1	Mar 10–Apr 10	Mar 20–Apr 20	Apr 1–May 1	Apr 15–May 15	May 1–June 1	May 15–June 1
Chicory, witloof	June 10–July 1	June 15–July 1	June 15–July 1	June 1–20	June 1–15	June 1–15	June 1–15
Corn salad	Feb 1–Apr 1	Feb 15–Apr 15	Mar 1–May 1	Apr 1–June 1	Apr 15–June 1	May 1–June 15	May 15–June 15
Corn, sweet	Apr 10–June 1	Apr 25–June 15	May 10–June 15	May 10–June 1	May 15–June 1	May 20–June 1	
Cress, upland	Mar 10–Apr 15	Mar 20–May 1	Apr 10–May 10	Apr 20–May 20	May 1–June 1	May 15–June 1	May 15–June 15
Cucumber	Apr 20–June 1	May 1–June 15	May 15–June 15	May 20–June 15	June 1–15		
Eggplant[1]	May 1–June 1	May 10–June 1	May 15–June 10	May 20–June 15	June 1–15		
Endive	Mar 15–Apr 15	Mar 25–Apr 15	Apr 1–May 1	Apr 15–May 15	May 1–30	May 1–30	May 15–June 1
Fennel, Florence	Mar 15–Apr 15	Mar 25–Apr 15	Apr 1–May 1	Apr 15–May 15	May 1–30	May 1–30	May 15–June 1
Garlic	Feb 20–Mar 20	Mar 10–Apr 1	Mar 15–Apr 15	Apr 1–May 1	Apr 15–May 15	May 1–30	May 15–June 1
Horseradish[1]	Mar 10–Apr 10	Mar 20–Apr 20	Apr 1–30	Apr 15–May 15	Apr 20–May 20	May 1–30	May 15–June 1
Kale	Mar 10–Apr 1	Mar 20–Apr 10	Apr 1–20	Apr 10–May 1	Apr 20–May 10	May 1–30	May 15–June 1
Kohlrabi	Mar 10–Apr 10	Mar 20–May 1	Apr 1–May 10	Apr 10–May 15	Apr 20–May 20	May 1–30	May 15–June 1
Leek	Mar 1–Apr 1	Mar 15–Apr 15	Apr 1–May 1	Apr 15–May 15	May 1–May 20	May 1–15	May 1–15
Lettuce, head[1]	Mar 10–Apr 1	Mar 20–Apr 15	Apr 1–May 1	Apr 15–June 15	May 1–June 30	May 10–June 30	May 20–June 30
Lettuce, leaf	Mar 15–May 15	Mar 20–May 15	Apr 1–June 1	Apr 15–June 15	May 1–June 30	May 10–June 30	May 20–June 30
Muskmelon	Apr 20–June 1	May 1–June 15	May 15–June 15	June 1–June 15			
Mustard	Mar 10–Apr 20	Mar 20–May 1	Apr 1–May 10	Apr 15–June 1	May 1–June 30	May 10–June 30	May 20–June 30
Okra	Apr 20–June 15	May 1–June 1	May 10–June 1	May 20–June 10	June 1–20		
Onion[1]	Mar 1–Apr 1	Mar 15–Apr 10	Apr 1–May 1	Apr 10–May 1	Apr 20–May 15	May 1–30	May 10–June 10
Onion, seed	Mar 1–Apr 1	Mar 15–Apr 1	Mar 15–Apr 15	Apr 1–May 1	Apr 20–May 15	May 1–30	May 10–June 10
Onion, sets	Mar 1–Apr 1	Mar 10–Apr 1	Mar 10–Apr 10	Apr 10–May 1	Apr 20–May 15	May 1–30	May 10–June 10
Parsley	Mar 10–Apr 10	Mar 20–Apr 20	Apr 1–May 1	Apr 15–May 15	May 1–20	May 10–June 1	May 20–June 10
Parsnip	Mar 10–Apr 10	Mar 20–Apr 20	Apr 1–May 1	Apr 15–May 15	May 1–20	May 10–June 1	May 20–June 1
Peas, garden	Feb 20–Mar 20	Mar 10–Apr 10	Mar 20–May 1	Apr 1–May 15	Apr 15–June 1	May 1–June 15	May 15–June 15
Peas, black-eye	May 1–July 1	May 10–June 15	May 15–June 1				
Pepper[1]	May 1–June 1	May 10–June 1	May 15–June 10	May 20–June 10	May 25–June 15	June 1–15	
Potato	Mar 10–Apr 1	Mar 15–Apr 10	Mar 20–May 10	Apr 1–June 1	Apr 15–June 15	May 1–June 15	May 15–June 1
Radish	Mar 1–May 1	Mar 10–May 10	Mar 20–May 10	Apr 1–June 1	Apr 15–June 15	May 1–June 15	May 15–June 1
Rhubarb[1]	Mar 1–Apr 1	Mar 10–Apr 10	Mar 20–Apr 15	Apr 1–May 1	Apr 15–May 10	May 1–20	May 15–June 1
Rutabaga			May 1–June 1	May 1–June 1	May 1–20	May 10–20	May 20–June 1
Salsify	Mar 10–Apr 15	Mar 20–May 1	Apr 1–May 15	Apr 15–June 1	May 1–June 1	May 10–June 1	May 20–June 1
Shallot	Mar 1–Apr 1	Mar 15–Apr 15	Apr 1–May 1	Apr 10–May 1	Apr 20–May 10	May 1–June 1	May 10–June 1
Sorrel	Mar 1–Apr 15	Mar 15–May 1	Apr 1–May 15	Apr 15–June 1	May 1–June 1	May 10–June 10	May 20–June 10
Soybean	May 1–June 30	May 10–June 20	May 15–June 15	May 25–June 10			
Spinach	Feb 15–Apr 1	Mar 1–Apr 15	Mar 20–Apr 20	Apr 1–June 15	Apr 15–June 15		May 1–June 15
Spinach, New Zealand	Apr 20–June 1	May 1–June 15	May 1–June 15	May 10–June 15	May 20–June 15	June 1–15	
Squash, summer	Apr 20–June 1	May 1–June 15	May 1–30	May 10–June 10	May 20–June 15	June 1–20	June 10–20
Sweetpotato	May 1–June 1	May 10–June 10	May 20–June 10				
Tomato	Apr 20–June 1	May 5–June 10	May 10–June 15	May 15–June 10	May 25–June 15	June 5–20	June 15–30
Turnip	Mar 1–Apr 1	Mar 10–Apr 1	Mar 20–May 1	Apr 1–June 1	Apr 15–June 1	May 1–June 1	
Watermelon	Apr 20–June 1	May 1–June 15	May 15–June 15	June 1–June 15	June 15–July 1		May 15–June 15

[1] Plants.
[2] Generally fall-planted

29

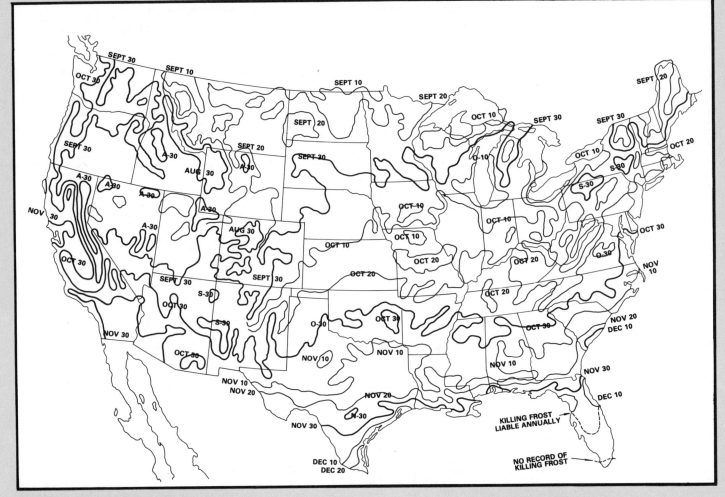

Figure 40: Map to show average dates of first killing frost in fall.

LATEST DATES, AND RANGE OF DATES, FOR SAFE FALL PLANTING OF VEGETABLES IN THE OPEN

Crop	Planting dates for localities in which average dates of first freeze is—					
	Aug 30	Sept 10	Sept 20	Sept 30	Oct 10	Oct 20
Asparagus[1]					Oct 20–Nov 15	Nov 1–Dec 15
Beans, lima				June 1–15	June 1–15	June 15–30
Beans, snap		May 15–June 15	June 1–July 1	June 1–July 10	June 15–July 20	July 1–Aug 1
Beet	May 15–June 15	May 15–June 15	June 1–July 1	June 1–July 10	June 15–July 25	July 1–Aug 5
Broccoli	May 1–June 1	May 1–June 1	May 1–June 15	June 1–30	June 15–July 15	July 1–Aug 1
Brussels sprouts	May 1–June 1	May 1–June 1	May 1–June 15	June 1–30	June 15–July 15	July 1–Aug 1
Cabbage[1]	May 1–June 1	May 1–June 1	May 1–June 15	June 1–July 10	June 1–July 15	July 1–20
Cabbage, Chinese	May 15–June 15	May 15–June 15	June 1–July 1	June 1–July 15	June 15–Aug 1	July 15–Aug 15
Carrot	May 15–June 15	May 15–June 15	June 1–July 1	June 1–July 10	June 1–July 20	June 15–Aug 1
Cauliflower[1]	May 1–June 1	May 1–July 1	May 1–July 1	May 10–July 15	June 1–July 25	July 1–Aug 5
Celery[1] and celeriac	May 1–June 1	May 15–June 15	May 15–July 1	June 1–July 5	June 1–July 15	June 1–Aug. 1
Chard, Swiss	May 15–June 15	May 15–July 1	June 1–July 1	June 1–July 5	June 1–July 20	June 1–Aug 1
Chervil and chives	May 10–June 10	May 1–June 15	May 15–June 15	(2)	(2)	(2)
Chicory, Witloof	May 15–June 15	May 15–June 15	May 15–June 15	June 1–July 1	June 1–July 1	June 15–July 15
Corn salad	May 15–June 15	May 15–July 1	June 15–Aug 1	July 15–Sept 1	Aug 15–Sept 15	Sept 1–Oct 15
Corn, sweet			June 1–July 1	June 1–July 1	June 1–July 10	June 1–July 20
Cress, upland	May 15–June 15	May 15–July 1	June 15–Aug 1	July 15–Sept 1	Aug 15–Sept 15	Sept 1–Oct 15
Cucumber			June 1–15	June 1–July 1	June 1–July 1	June 1–July 15
Eggplant[1]				May 20–June 10	May 15–June 15	June 1–July 1
Endive	June 1–July 1	June 1–July 1	June 15–July 15	June 15–Aug 1	July 1–Aug 15	July 15–Sept 1
Fennel, Florence	May 15–June 15	May 15–July 15	June 1–July 1	June 1–July 1	June 15–July 15	June 15–Aug 1
Garlic	(2)	(2)	(2)	(2)	(2)	(2)
Horseradish[1]	(2)	(2)	(2)	(2)	(2)	(2)
Kale	May 15–June 15	May 15–June 15	June 1–July 1	June 15–July 15	July 1–Aug 1	July 15–Aug 15
Kohlrabi	May 15–June 15	June 1–July 1	June 1–July 15	June 15–July 15	July 1–Aug 1	July 15–Aug 15
Leek	May 1–June 1	May 1–June 1	(2)	(2)	(2)	(2)
Lettuce, head[1]	May 15–July 1	May 15–July 1	June 1–July 15	June 15–Aug 1	July 15–Aug 15	Aug 1–30
Lettuce, leaf	May 15–July 15	May 15–July 15	June 1–Aug 1	June 1–Aug 1	July 15–Sept 1	July 15–Sept 1
Muskmelon			May 1–June 15	May 15–June 1	June 1–June 15	June 15–July 20
Mustard	May 15–July 15	May 15–July 15	June 1–Aug 1	June 15–Aug 1	July 15–Aug 15	Aug 1–Sept 1

Crop	Aug 30	Sept 10	Sept 20	Sept 30	Oct 10	Oct 20
Okra			June 1–20	June 1–July 1	June 1–July 15	June 1–Aug 1
Onion[1]	May 1–June 10	May 1–June 10	(²)	(²)	(²)	(²)
Onion, seed	May 1–June 1	May 1–June 10	(²)	(²)	(²)	(²)
Onion, sets	May 1–June 10	May 1–June 10	(²)	(²)	(²)	(²)
Parsley	May 15–June 15	May 1–June 15	June 1–July 1	June 1–July 15	June 15–Aug 1	July 15–Aug 15
Parsnip	May 15–June 1	May 1–June 15	May 15–June 15	June 1–July 1	June 1–July 10	(²)
Peas, garden	May 10–June 15	May 1–July 1	June 1–July 15	June 1–Aug 1	(²)	(²)
Pepper[1]			June 1–June 20	June 1–July 1	June 1–July 1	June 1–July 10
Potato	May 15–June 1	May 1–June 15	May 1–June 15	May 1–June 15	May 15–June 15	June 15–July 15
Radish	May 1–July 15	May 1–Aug 1	June 1–Aug 15	July 1–Sept 1	July 15–Sept 15	Aug 1–Oct 1
Rhubarb[1]	Sept 1–Oct 1	Sept 15–Oct 15	Sept 15–Nov 1	Oct 1–Nov 1	Oct 15–Nov 15	Oct 15–Dec. 1
Rutabaga	May 15–June 15	May 1–June 15	June 1–July 1	June 1–July 1	June 15–July 15	July 10–20
Salsify	May 15–June 1	May 10–June 10	May 20–June 20	June 1–20	June 1–July 1	June 1–July 1
Shallot	(²)	(²)	(²)	(²)	(²)	(²)
Sorrel	May 15–June 15	May 1–June 15	June 1–July 1	June 1–July 15	July 1–Aug 1	July 15–Aug 15
Spinach	May 15–July 1	June 1–July 15	June 1–Aug 1	July 1–Aug 15	Aug 1–Sept 1	Aug 20–Sept 10
Spinach, New Zealand				May 15–July 1	June 1–July 15	June 1–Aug 1
Squash, summer	June 10–20	June 1–20	May 15–July 1	June 1–July 1	June 1–July 15	June 1–July 20
Squash, winter			May 20–June 10	June 1–15	June 1–July 1	June 1–July 1
Tomato	June 20–30	June 10–20	June 1–20	June 1–20	June 1–20	June 1–July 1
Turnip	May 15–June 15	June 1–July 1	June 1–July 15	June 1–Aug 1	July 1–Aug 1	July 15–Aug 15
Watermelon			May 1–June 15	May 15–June 1	June 1–June 15	June 15–July 20

Crop	Oct 30	Nov 10	Nov 20	Nov 30	Dec 10	Dec 20
Asparagus[1]	Nov 15–Jan 1	Dec 1–Jan 1				
Beans, lima	July 1–Aug 1	July 1–Aug 15	July 15–Sept 1	Aug 1–Sept 15	Sept 1–30	Sept 1–Oct 1
Beans, snap	July 1–Aug 15	July 1–Sept 1	July 1–Sept 10	Aug 15–Sept 20	Sept 1–30	Sept 1–Nov 1
Beet	Aug 1–Sept 1	Aug 1–Oct 1	Sept 1–Dec 1	Sept 1–Dec 15	Sept 1–Dec 31	Sept 1–Dec 31
Broccoli	July 1–Aug 15	Aug 1–Sept 1	Aug 1–Sept 15	Aug 1–Oct 1	Aug 1–Nov 1	Sept 1–Dec 31
Brussels sprouts	July 1–Aug 15	Aug 1–Sept 1	Aug 1–Sept 15	Aug 1–Oct 1	Aug 1–Nov 1	Sept 1–Dec 31
Cabbage[1]	Aug 1–Sept 1	Sept 1–15	Sept 1–Dec 1	Sept 1–Dec 31	Sept 1–Dec 31	Sept 1–Dec 31
Cabbage, Chinese	Aug 1–Sept 15	Aug 15–Oct 1	Sept 1–Oct 15	Sept 1–Nov 1	Sept 15–Nov 15	Sept 1–Dec 1
Carrot	July 1–Aug 15	Aug 1–Sept 1	Sept 1–Nov 1	Sept 15–Dec 1	Sept 15–Dec 1	Sept 15–Dec 1
Cauliflower[1]	July 15–Aug 15	Aug 1–Sept 1	Aug 1–Sept 15	Aug 1–Oct 10	Sept 1–Oct 20	Sept 15–Nov 1
Celery[1] and celeriac	June 15–Aug 15	July 1–Aug 15	July 15–Sept 1	Aug 1–Dec 1	Sept 1–Dec 31	Oct 1–Dec 31
Chard, Swiss	June 1–Sept 10	June 1–Sept 15	June 1–Oct 1	June 1–Nov 1	June 1–Dec 1	June 1–Dec 31
Chervil and chives	(²)	(²)	Nov 1–Dec 31	Nov 1–Dec 31	Nov 1–Dec 31	Nov 1–Dec 31
Chicory, Witloof	July 1–Aug 10	July 10–Aug 20	July 20–Sept 1	Aug 15–Sept 30	Aug 15–Oct 15	Aug 15–Oct 15
Corn salad	Sept 15–Nov 1	Oct 1–Dec 1	Oct 1–Dec 1	Oct 1–Dec 31	Oct 1–Dec 31	Oct 1–Dec 31
Corn, sweet	June 1–Aug 1	June 1–Aug 15	June 1–Sept 1			
Cress, upland	Sept 15–Nov 1	Oct 1–Dec 1	Oct 1–Dec 1	Oct 1–Dec 31	Oct 1–Dec 31	Oct 1–Dec 31
Cucumber	June 1–Aug 1	June 1–Aug 15	June 1–Aug 15	July 15–Sept 15	Aug 15–Oct 1	Aug 15–Oct 1
Eggplant[1]	June 1–July 1	June 1–July 15	June 1–Aug 1	July 1–Sept 1	Aug 1–Sept 30	Aug 1–Sept 30
Endive	July 15–Aug 15	Aug 1–Sept 1	Sept 1–Oct 1	Sept 1–Nov 15	Sept 1–Dec 31	Sept 1–Dec 31
Fennel, Florence	July 1–Aug 1	July 15–Aug 15	Aug 15–Sept 15	Sept 1–Nov 15	Sept 1–Dec 1	Sept 1–Dec 1
Garlic	(²)	Aug 1–Oct 1	Aug 15–Oct 1	Sept 1–Nov 15	Sept 15–Nov 15	Sept 15–Nov 15
Horseradish[1]	(²)	(²)	(²)	(²)	(²)	(²)
Kale	July 15–Sept 1	Aug 1–Sept 15	Aug 15–Oct 15	Sept 1–Dec 1	Sept 1–Dec 31	Sept 1–Dec 31
Kohlrabi	Aug 1–Sept 1	Aug 15–Sept 15	Sept 1–Oct 15	Sept 1–Dec 1	Sept 15–Dec 31	Sept 1–Dec 1
Leek	(²)	(²)	Sept 1–Nov 1	Sept 1–Nov 1	Sept 1–Nov 1	Sept 15–Nov 1
Lettuce, head[1]	Aug 1–Sept 15	Aug 15–Oct 15	Sept 1–Nov 1	Sept 1–Dec 1	Sept 15–Dec 31	Sept 15–Dec 31
Lettuce, leaf	Aug 15–Oct 1	Aug 25–Oct 1	Sept 1–Nov 1	Sept 1–Dec 1	Sept 15–Dec 31	Sept 15–Dec 31
Muskmelon	July 1–July 15	July 15–July 30				
Mustard	Aug 15–Oct 15	Aug 15–Nov 1	Sept 1–Dec 1	Sept 1–Dec 1	Sept 1–Dec 1	Sept 15–Dec 1
Okra	June 1–Aug 10	June 1–Aug 20	June 1–Sept 10	June 1–Sept 20	Aug 1–Oct 1	Aug 1–Oct 1
Onion[1]		Sept 1–Oct 15	Oct 1–Dec 31	Oct 1–Dec 31	Oct 1–Dec 31	Oct 1–Dec 31
Onion, seed			Sept 1–Nov 1	Sept 1–Nov 1	Sept 1–Nov 1	Sept 15–Dec 1
Onion, sets		Oct 1–Dec 1	Nov 1–Dec 31	Nov 1–Dec 31	Nov 1–Dec 31	Nov 1–Dec 31
Parsley	Aug 1–Sept 15	Sept 1–Nov 15	Sept 1–Dec 31	Sept 1–Dec 31	Sept 1–Dec 31	Sept 1–Dec 31
Parsnip	(²)	(²)	Aug 1–Sept 1	Sept 1–Nov 15	Sept 1–Dec 1	Sept 1–Dec 1
Peas, garden	Aug 1–Sept 15	Sept 1–Nov 1	Oct 1–Dec 1	Oct 1–Dec 31	Oct 1–Dec 31	Oct 1–Dec 31
Pepper[1]	June 1–July 20	June 1–Aug 1	June 1–Aug 15	June 15–Sept 1	Aug 15–Oct 1	Aug 15–Oct 1
Potato	July 20–Aug 10	July 25–Aug 20	Aug 10–Sept 15	Aug 1–Sept 15	Aug 1–Sept 15	Aug 1–Sept 15
Radish	Aug 15–Oct 15	Sept 1–Nov 15	Sept 1–Dec 1	Sept 1–Dec 31	Aug 1–Sept 15	Oct 1–Dec 31
Rhubarb[1]	Nov 1–Dec 1					
Rutabaga	July 15–Aug 1	July 15–Aug 15	Aug 1–Sept 1	Sept 1–Nov 15	Oct 1–Nov 15	Oct 15–Nov 15
Salsify	June 1–July 10	June 15–July 20	July 15–Aug 15	Aug 15–Sept 30	Aug 15–Oct 15	Sept 1–Oct 31
Shallot	(²)	Aug 1–Oct 1	Aug 15–Oct 1	Aug 15–Oct 15	Sept 15–Nov 1	Sept 15–Nov 1
Sorrel	Aug 1–Sept 15	Aug 15–Oct 1	Aug 15–Oct 15	Sept 1–Nov 15	Sept 1–Dec 15	Sept 1–Dec 31
Spinach	Sept 1–Oct 1	Sept 15–Nov 1	Oct 1–Dec 1	Oct 1–Dec 31	Oct 1–Dec 31	Oct 1–Dec 31
Spinach, New Zealand	June 1–Aug 1	June 1–Aug 15	June 1–Aug 15			
Squash, summer	June 1–Aug 1	June 1–Aug 10	June 1–Aug 20	June 1–Sept 1	June 1–Sept 15	June 1–Oct 1
Squash, winter	June 10–July 10	June 20–July 20	July 1–Aug 1	July 15–Aug 15	Aug 1–Sept 1	Aug 1–Sept 1
Tomato	June 1–July 1	June 1–July 15	June 1–Aug 1	Aug 1–Sept 1	Aug 1–Sept 1	Sept 1–Nov 1
Turnip	Aug 1–Sept 15	Sept 1–Oct 15	Sept 1–Nov 15	Sept 1–Nov 15	Oct 1–Dec 1	Oct 1–Dec 31
Watermelon	July 1–July 15	July 15–July 30				

[1] Plants.
[2] Generally spring-planted.

If wind blows continually through plants it will cool the leaves and slow down the speed of plant growth and development. The full effects of this are well illustrated by the stunted trees and shrubs that grow on exposed hillsides and dunes. Hedges, fences and screens positioned in and around suburban gardens naturally 'break' the wind and the term 'sheltered' usually refers to adequate wind protection.

Almost any kind of material can be used to equal effect as a windbreak, although the wind-filtering effect of trees, shrubs and hedges is much better than a nearly impenetrable fence. The important thing to remember when erecting or planning a windbreak is that something which offers a 50 per cent obstruction to wind will be the most effective. If you build a solid wall, the wind will hit it hard, rising up the structure only to plunge over it into the vacuum formed behind. A general guide is that a shelter one unit high will give seven units length of wind protection beyond.

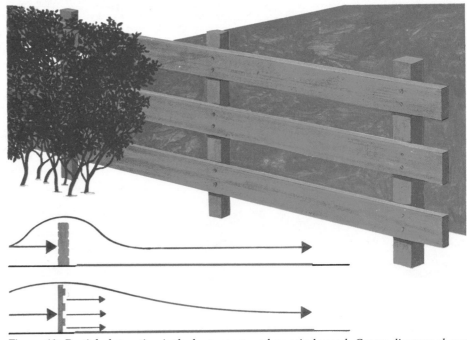

Figure 41: Partial obstruction is the best way to reduce wind speed. Center diagram shows how an impenetrable screen can increase wind force in the lee.

Windbreak Structures

Placing twiggy sticks around early crops such as peas will give some wind protection, as will wire netting seedling guards. If you add a covering to the windbreak which lets in light and retains heat, the speed of plant growth will be increased even further. This leads on to a wide range of structures which can be used for crop protection – from low cloches such as Hotkaps to somewhat larger frames, to – largest of all – walk-in greenhouses.

Covering Material

There are three main choices of covering material for protected cropping. Glass is at present the cheapest permanent material which will retain the maximum amount of heat and give the best light penetration. Semi-rigid, clear plastics are rapidly coming to the fore and although they are more expensive, they have obvious advantages in domestic situations, in avoiding the possibility of broken glass.

Thin polyethylene sheet is the cheapest material and is very useful for both suburban and commercial crop protection. Its only drawback is that its heat retention quality is not as good as that of the other materials. If you are going to use it for garden crop protection make sure you buy ultra-violet light-inhibited polyethylene sheet. This is usually sold as UVI polyethylene, and even the thinnest

gauges will give enough use for one full summer and two winters. If you roll up the polyethylene and put it away in summer, so it is not exposed to strong ultraviolet summer sunlight, its useful life will be extended considerably. Thicker sheets used for covering greenhouse structures will have proportionally longer life, for example, the 500 gauge (125 micron) thickness will be cheaper but not as long lasting in sunlight as the more expensive 600 gauge material.

Light Reflection

Another point worth consideration is that white, silver and light colors reflect light, while black and dark colors absorb heat. Thus the wall of a lean-to greenhouse painted white will reflect light needed by plants and a mulch of black peat around crops under cloches will help the soil to absorb more heat. Maximum light transmission and heat retention during cold periods will give the fastest and strongest plant growth.

Materials for polyethylene tunnel cloche.

Hoops pushed into soil in position.

Figure 42: Cross-section across tunnel showing plants in situ.

Figure 43: Push up sheet to obtain access to plants in tunnel, for watering, cultural treatment or harvesting. Some mail-order garden firms offer baits for polyethylene tunnels.

POLYETHYLENE TUNNELS

Catching on in the USA from England is the polyethylene, or plastic tunnel, best described as a long greenhouse over a row of plants flexible in length, width and height (the wider any hoop is spaced the lower will be the coverage), easy to handle and perfectly safe. It protects crops from birds; it will bring harvesting times forward by a week or two; it keeps crops such as lettuce clean from soil splashed by rain and it is easily taken up, rolled and packed away. Irrigation presents no problems as rain running over the sides goes straight into the soil and will spread sufficiently for plant roots to take it up in all but the hottest, driest weather. When these conditions prevail, it is easy enough to raise one side of the plastic, giving easy access for watering the plants.

There is a knack to erecting these tunnels and you are well advised to try to perfect it. The first requirements are a wire hoop with two loops, about 4 in (10 cm) from each end of the wire and a sheet of plastic. Push hoops into the soil 3–4 ft (90–120 cm) apart. Secure one end by burying it in the soil (see right, 1 and 2). Unroll plastic over hoops and secure other end (see 3 and 4). Tension plastic by fixing a wire or rotproof string to the loop on one side, taking it over the plastic and securing it to the loop on the other side (see 5).

When you want to get at the crop for hoeing, watering and harvesting just lift one side of the sheet like a curtain, between the hoop and the tensioning wire (see right, 6). Replace it when you have finished your work.

1. Secure end either by tying or 2. by burying in soil. 3. Unroll plastic over the wires. 4. Secure other end. 5. Tension plastic with string or wire. 6. Lift sheet for access.

CLOCHES AND FRAMES

On a very small scale and for virtually no cost, small 'cloches' can be made from salvaged clear plastic containers. Just cut away the base and cover single or small groups of plants, such as radish, making sure you 'screw' the cut edge into the soil for ½ in (1 cm) or so to prevent the wind blowing the container away. Remove the cap on the top to ventilate in very hot weather and to apply water. Lettuce grows par-

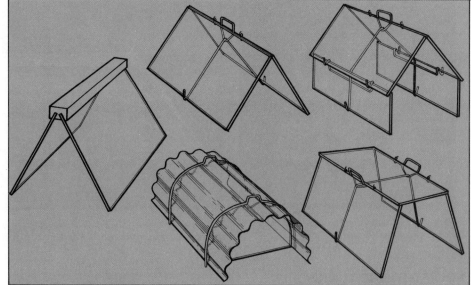

Figure 46: Various types of cloche; from l. to r. top: home-made, tent, barn, plastic sheet, flat-topped cloche.

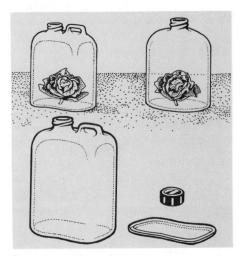

Figure 44: Clear plastic containers can be turned into 'cloches'.

ticularly well under these containers.

On a similar principle, old glass jars placed over such seedlings as squash and cucumber during the early raising stages will provide favorable conditions for germination and growth of these vegetables.

There is a variety of glass and plas-

tic cloches which can be used singly or placed end to end to construct a continuous row. Rainfall on all these cloches will run down the sides and into the soil to the crop, so special watering arrangements are not necessary. In the USA, the most popular cloche is the Hotkap, waxed paper cones or tents that are placed over seeds or seedlings in early spring. They are readily obtained at all garden centers.

'Do-it-Yourself' Covers

Another simple glass cover can be constructed using a wooden box, merely by removing the base and placing a sheet of glass on top of it (see figure 45). Step up the dimensions of

this and you have a cold frame, for the basis of a frame is just four side walls with a sloping glass or clear plastic covered roof. A single frame has one taller side at the back and a double frame is just higher at the centre (see figure 45).

The clear roof of these frames comprises several wooden or metal framed units to hold the glass or plastic, known as 'frames' or 'sashes'. In hot weather you should raise the lights fractionally to provide ventilation, but keep them closed at night and in cold weather. You can use these frames to raise seeds and propagate cuttings, as well as for growing crops such as lettuce and cress to maturity.

Very keen gardeners may also heat their frame. There are three methods of heating: electrical soil-warming cables (probably the best way to heat frames); an electric tube heater fitted to one frame wall; or the cheapest method of all, placing the frame on top of a bed of fresh manure (known as a 'hot bed') covered with soil. Heat is generated from the decomposing manure and speeds plant growth accordingly. Hot beds can be used effectively for such crops as early carrots, but they are especially good for starting seedlings.

GREENHOUSES

Greenhouses may have a basic structure of wood or metal; wood, especially red cedar, will last well, but aluminium structures are undoubtedly the best. They require no maintenance and offer the very least obstruction to light. Modern units can be pur-

Figure 45: Various types of frame: from l. to r. single span frame, double span frame and a home-made frame using a box and a sheet of glass.

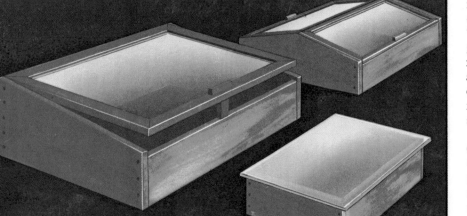

chased packed in cases to be taken home and erected easily over a weekend or so.

If the greenhouse is artificially heated the range of crops you can grow, especially in the fall, winter and spring, is increased yet again. The cost of heating may however be the deciding factor, and in cold, exposed conditions more heat – incurring greater cost – will be needed. Hedges and screens around the greenhouse will break the wind and, as long as they are far enough away to avoid casting shadows across the house, will also save heat. Bear in mind that the cost of heating is likely to be twice as much on a windy day as on a calm one.

There are a few other factors to remember about heating and heat loss. One is that the greater the surface area of the structure, the greater the heat loss will be. Long narrow houses have a greater surface area than an almost square one. If you raise the side walls of a greenhouse, for example, on the traditionally shaped house 6 ft × 4 ft (180 × 120 cm) from 4 ft (120 cm) to 6 ft (180 cm), you increase the surface area through which heat can be lost by 40 sq ft (3·7 sq m). Compare this kind of house with the total surface area of the 10 ft × 12 ft (3 m × 4 m) plastic tunnel house (see overleaf) which has some 300 sq ft (27 sq m). The plastic house will have about 2½ sq ft (0·2 sq m) of outer structure for every 1 sq ft (900 sq cm) of covered soil, while the tall 6 ft × 4 ft (180 × 120 cm) house will have 7½ sq ft (0·7 sq m) to

Figure 47: Three examples of greenhouse; from l. to r. lean-to, traditionally shaped brick-based and greenhouse made of Dutch Light.

1 sq ft (900 sq cm) covered. Houses less than 8 ft × 8 ft (240 × 240 cm) are really too small in practice to heat easily and ventilate adequately.

Heat Loss

Heat is lost more rapidly through plastic than glass but the plastic structure is virtually air tight, while heat will be lost through the gaps between panes with glass.

Finally, the greater the temperature difference between inside and outside, the greater will be the heat loss. It is

much cheaper to keep a house just frost free through the winter than it is to hold a near tropical temperature inside when conditions are near arctic outside. You can reduce heat loss in such conditions by erecting a sheet of plastic on the north side of the house to give the effect of double glazing. If you line the whole house you will have a 35 per cent loss of light which is too great; lining the north side only gives an acceptable 18 per cent loss of light.

The rule-of-thumb method of calculating the amount of heat needed is to begin by measuring the surface area of the house. To keep the house at a chosen temperature evenly each square foot of surface area needs 1·4 BTUs (British Thermal Units) per hour for every degree Fahrenheit of difference between the outside temperature and your chosen heat level. If, for example, you wish to hold an 8 × 8 ft (2·4 × 2·4 m) greenhouse, which will have 64 square feet (5·76 sq m) of surface area, at 40°F (4·4°C) through the winter and the temperature outdoors might drop to 20°F (−5·4°C) your heater would need to be able to produce 7000 to 8000 BTUs an hour.

It should be obvious now that heating a home greenhouse, in these times of high energy costs, is no frivolous matter. Talk to heating engineers and when possible owners of established greenhouses. Whatever you do, don't put up the greenhouse, then worry about heating!

Figure 48: A sheet of polyethylene or plastic lining against the north side of a greenhouse, and nearby hedges forming screens, reduce heat loss in winter.

N

35

POLYETHYLENE TUNNEL GREENHOUSE

By stepping up the size of cloches and frames even further, you can progress to the walk-in structures, more commonly known as greenhouses. These again can be of glass or polyethylene – a polyethylene-clad house being cheaper than a greenhouse as it is a lighter structure and cheaper materials can be used in its construction.

The tunnel house shown here is based on a design from England's Lee Valley Experimental Horticulture Station but gardeners elsewhere will find it an inexpensive substitute for a more permanent greenhouse. It is especially useful in mild climates where winter temperatures do not drop drastically, but can also be very useful in colder regions in the spring. In most regions, some sort of space heater will be necessary. (The United States Department of Agriculture has designed a similar plastic-covered house. Write your state agricultural experiment station or call your local extension agent, requesting Plan No. 5946.)

The following instructions are for the construction of a plastic covered house, which would completely cover a 10 ft × 12 ft (3 m × 4 m) plot. If, however, you reduced the height – the width and the area of soil covered would be correspondingly increased.

You will need:

3 × 21 ft (6·4 m) lengths ½ in (1 cm) bore galvanized water pipe (hoops)

2 × 5 ft (1·5 m) lengths ½ in (1 cm) bore galvanized pipe (ridge pieces)

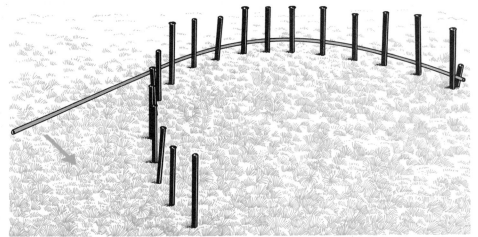

Figure 50: End posts must be secure before bending the pipe.

A metal sheet around the posts helps achieve a circular bend.

One person can easily construct the framework of the house alone.

6 × 2 ft (60 cm) lengths 1 in (2·5 m) bore galvanized pipe (foundation stakes)

1 × 20 ft (6 m) length of 10 gauge galvanized fencing wire

4 × 8 ft (2·4 m) lengths of 2 in × 2 in (5 × 5 cm) timber (lintels for doors)

2 × 4 ft (1·2 m) lengths of 2 in × 2 in (5 × 5 cm) timber (lintels for doors)

4 × 6 ft (1·8 m) lengths of 2 in × 1 in (5 × 2·5 m) timber*

2 × 4 ft (1·2 m) lengths of 2 in × 1 in (5 × 2·5 cm) timber*

Quantity of laths for roller blind door

Quantity of nails

1 sheet polyethylene film 24 ft × 24 ft (7·3 × 7·3 m) 500 gauge (125 micron) (be sure it is *Ultraviolet Inhibited* (sold as UVI) film)

*Any thin lath wood; alternatively staples and wire will do for this.

Construction

Drive a series of short posts into the ground and bend the three 21 ft lengths (6·4 m) of pipe round them to form a semi-circular hoop 12 ft (4 m) in diameter. Then measure the site to mark out a 10 ft × 12 ft (3 m × 4 m) area. Take out a trench 10 in (25 cm) wide and 12 in (30 cm) deep around the outside, 2 in (5 cm) out from the marked plot. Throw the soil out of the area, *not* into it. Drive the 2 ft (60 cm) long foundation stakes firmly into the

Figure 49: Framework erected ready for construction of door and polyethylene.

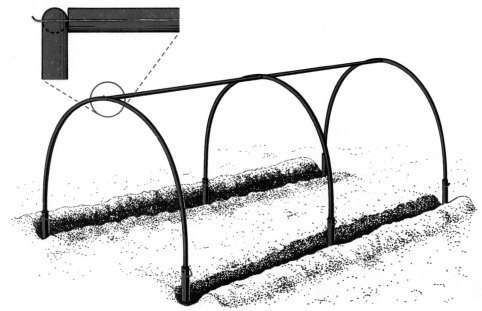

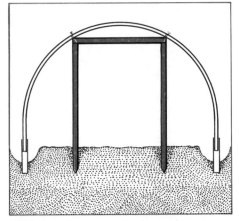

Figure 51: Door frame in position.

Long nails are used to hold door blind.

ground, one at each corner and one in the center of each side. Leave 6–9 in (15–23 cm) protruding above ground.

Drill a hole through the foundation stakes and the end of each hoop and place the hoops in the foundation stakes to erect the main structure. Secure by putting a short piece of wire or bolt through both holes you have drilled. If the plastic cover becomes slack at any future time, you can lift up the hoop a fraction, drill another hole and secure in the same way to take up the slack.

Drill a hole horizontally through the top of each hoop, making sure it is in the top and center. Thread wire through the hole in an end hoop, through the length of one ridge piece, through the center hoop, through the next ridge pipe and through the other end hoop. Secure both ends of the wire to form a rigid structure.

Bury the base of the 8 ft (2·4 m) long 2 × 2 in (5 × 5 cm) wooden uprights 4 ft (1·2 m) apart into the soil to construct the door lintels. Hold the 4 ft (1·2 m) cross timbers in place by driv-

ing nails through holes in the hoops, through the cross pieces and into the uprights. (Alternatively use thick strips of rubber over the pipes and nail them to the cross pieces and uprights.)

Cover all rough or sharp edges with insulating tape or strips of poly-ethylene, and then cover the whole structure with the polyethylene sheet.

Covering

This must fit firmly to give the whole structure strength and wind resis-tance. If it is allowed to flap it will quickly wear through. Fit the cover in warm weather because as the film cools it will shrink and tighten further.

Cover the frame with the sheet, making sure the 'skirt' around the base is the same length all the way round. Fill in trenches with soil – firming it so as to tighten the film over the frame.

Cut out the polyethylene inside the lintels, fold the polyethylene edge around the lintels and nail it securely with timber laths and nails. Make the doors either as lift-up blinds or as polyethylene-covered frames secured as sliding doors. (Both doors must be open to allow adequate ventilation of the structure.)

Figure 52: The polyethylene house completed. Note that it has doors at either end for through ventilation.

Irrigation Principles

The evaporation of moisture from a plant's leaves gives it energy to suck in more water and plant foods through its roots. While this may be an over-simplification of the complete process, for simple vegetable growing it is a sufficient interpretation. The strength and amount of sunlight, the temperature, the humidity of the surrounding atmosphere and the effect of drying winds all control the speed of plant growth. If the drying effects are greater than the moisture available to be taken up by the roots, leaves will begin to wilt. Wilting prevents too great a loss of moisture in plants.

Although initial wilting provides protection for the plant, it also slows down growth. This means less rapidly produced succulent tissue, while any growth that does occur is likely to be unpalatable, tough, stringy and fibrous. If you want succulent vegetables, therefore, it is worth ensuring that most of your plants do not lack water. I say most because there are some exceptions to this general rule – turnips that grow rapidly will be succulent and possess the desired mild flavor, but if, for example, tomatoes have too much lush growth, the fruits are likely to be watery, pale colored and have a poor flavor.

Moderation applies as much to watering as any other garden practice and you should aim to avoid both waterlogged and desert-dry soils. As I have stressed before, the addition of plenty of well-rotted organic matter, manure, compost and similar materials is a great help in controlling the amount of water in soil. It improves drainage in waterlogged soils, and helps light, sandy and chalky soils to retain as much water as possible.

When supplies are short, use water already used for washing up, bathing

'Lay flat' polyethylene tubing being used to irrigate seedlings.

or washing clothes, unless bleach or bath salts have been added.

Drainage

Digging ditches and constructing pipe and clinker drains to drain water-logged soil is not very practical for most gardens. Where, for example, do you drain off water, if you have neighbors on three sides? If your garden tends to be waterlogged (usually a problem in winter and spring) the most efficient way to drain it is probably to build up the level of your small vegetable plot. The water will then drain from the plot into the gulleys, paths, lawns and other surrounding areas. You will actually raise the plot automatically by adding organic matter and repeatedly digging the soil. If the drainage is really poor, the area must be raised 12 in (13·5 cm). Raised

beds can be convenient to work and attractive. Contain the soil with concrete blocks, boards or brickwork.

Waterlogged plots can be improved, then, by raising the level, which you can do by digging in plenty of organic matter and also by adding coarse sand and well-weathered ashes in moderation. Light, sandy soils, however, have an opposing problem: they dry out too quickly. Here the solution lies in adding organic matter to hold water, thereby stopping it from just draining away. If you 'mulch' the surface of the soil which means covering it with well-rotted compost and leaves, the speed at which water evaporates from the surface will also be reduced.

Evaporation

Water evaporates from wet soil at much the same rate as it does from soil

Figure 53: 'Lay flat' type of hose is one of the simplest and most efficient forms of irrigation.

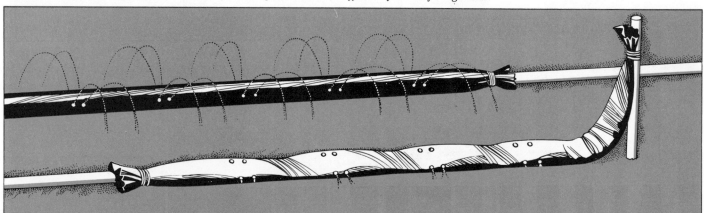

which is maintaining a crop of vegetables. On a bright summer's day something like 2–3 mm of water will be lost and 20–30 mm of rain (25 mm = 1 in) would be needed after eight to ten bright days to make up the evaporation. Strong-growing weeds will drain the soil of water to the same extent as vegetables, which is one of the reasons why it is important to control weeds. If the surface of the soil is dry and especially if it is hoed to maintain a shallow layer of fine dry soil or 'tilth', it will lose very little water.

Once soil gets really dry it is virtually impossible to *partially* moisten it throughout. The immediate remedy is to saturate the surface, after which the more water you add the greater will be the depth of saturation. This is why it is better to water really well occasionally than give repeated light waterings which will do little more than just dampen the surface. The surface, after all, is actually the place where it is important to retain a dry tilth which will then preserve moisture at a lower level.

Water Equipment

There is an amazing range of automatic and semi-automatic watering or irrigating equipment on the market – from static spray nozzles to automatically oscillating sprinklers. Most of these, in my opinion, are rather expensive luxuries and there are really only three pieces of equipment that you need. In order of priority these are a good watering can, a hose long enough to reach the vegetable plot and a perforated flat-lying hose.

Bear in mind that watering from the spout of a can or the end of a hose produces very heavy water droplets and applications of this kind, unless carefully applied, can batter down the soil surface, destroying the tilth you are trying to retain. The closer the spout is to the soil and therefore the more gentle the delivery, the better. As long as it is delivered carefully, however, water directed to one area does penetrate better than if you spread a small amount of water over a larger surface. This is just quickly lost in evaporation.

If you need to repeatedly water single plants such as tomatoes, a good tip is to sink a flower pot into the soil close to the plant. Keep this repeatedly filled with water, which will then trickle slowly through the base of the pot getting moisture down to the area of roots where it is required. It also

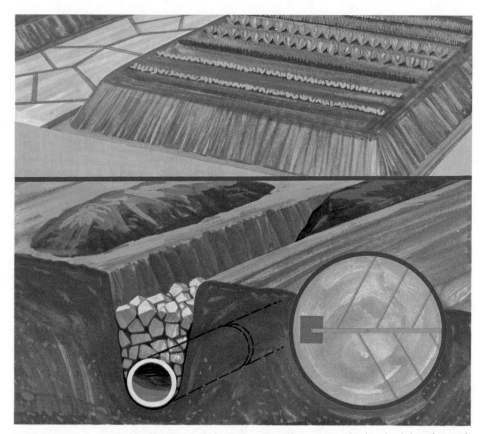

Figure 54: Two ways of effecting soil drainage. Top, by raising the level of the plot with repeated digging and adding organic matter. Bottom, in extreme cases, by constructing pipe and clinker drains. The inset shows the pattern for laying drains, the small square being a 'sump' made from a bin punctured at the bottom and filled with rubble, sunk below ground level.

prevents pressure of water applied in other ways from destroying the soil structure.

It is difficult to find out just how much water is required by plants without getting a spade or trowel and actually digging to see the dampness of the soil 6–8 in (15–20 cm) down. As a guide, if the soil looks and feels damp when you dig down all will be

Figure 55: A good way to water plants that need constant irrigation.

well, but if it does not, a really good watering will be necessary to get the required penetration. Whatever you do, avoid deep digging during drying and drought conditions as this will speed evaporation considerably.

By far the best method of watering vegetables and many other plants is through a flat-lying soaker hose which has tiny holes punctured in it at intervals. To use it unroll the hose along the rows and place it close to the stems of plants. Then use any pressure source (from the mains or a syphon from a rainwater tank) to feed water into the tube. It will slowly drip through the holes into the soil and, if left running for long enough, the steady, gentle flow will give deep penetration. If you increase the water pressure or reduce the length of tube, the water will spurt from the holes in small jets rather than drip so increasing the watered area. Low water pressure and steady dripping gives the most efficient water distribution.

Fertilizers can be added at the same time as watering – liquid kinds when watering with a can, and powdered fertilizers under the trickle tube connected to a hose.

Growing Your Own Vegetables

It is difficult to over-emphasize just how easy it is to grow almost all kinds of vegetable. Yet, understandably, when faced with yields perhaps not quite as good as hoped for, or when starting out with a new plot, many gardeners may feel that the brief instructions available on seed packets are not sufficiently informative to ensure really first-class produce. For this reason, we have given here complete cultural and harvesting details for each individual vegetable, covering the whole cycle from siting, sowing and growing to harvesting.

The wide range of different varieties of vegetable now available to home-growers has added a great deal to the experimental interest and fun of vegetable-growing, so as much coverage as space permits has been included for some of the less familiar types. Send for the catalogs of a few mail-order seed houses and study them carefully before ordering seeds. The catalogs will contain up-to-the-minute information on new varieties for which there are often claims of earlier and heavier yields, better quality and higher resistance to pests and diseases. But grow new varieties alongside old faithfuls rather than always going for novelty, so that you can gradually assess what best suits your garden conditions, as well as your palate.

Of course, no one has perfect site and soil conditions for growing every kind of vegetable, although repeated cultivation and the addition of organic matter will do much to improve them. Crops such as carrots and peas will also help in breaking-in soil not previously or recently used for vegetables. Our information in the section that follows should help you to select crops that are likely to give satisfactory yields in the conditions provided by your own plot.

When sowing seed, try to avoid the temptation to sow it too thickly and deeply. Most seeds need no more than a light covering of soil, particularly if the soil is good and moist. In dry conditions, it is worth running some water along the base of the drill before sowing, especially if you are using pelleted seed. Germination depends to some extent on weather conditions and the vegetable in question, but in some cases, it takes two or three weeks – longer in cold weather.

It is hard to give hard and fast rulings on how many vegetables a packet of seed or a certain length of row will produce. Again, this can be subject to the vagaries of soil and weather. Wherever possible, we have attempted to give an indication of average yields, but remember that a heavier crop of such vegetables as tomato and sweet corn can be expected after a warm, sunny summer than after a cool, damp one. For root and leafy crops, such as carrots and cabbages, the reverse is true.

Pests and other problems affecting vegetables are discussed briefly in each case, but further information on dealing with them, should you need it, is given on pages 112 to 115. The 'tips' are snippets of useful information gained from my personal experience of vegetable-growing.

Artichokes

Apart from sharing a name and the fact that they are both perennial vegetables the globe and Jerusalem artichokes have little in common and are really best considered separately.

GLOBE ARTICHOKE

The large globe-shaped flower buds produced by these plants *(Cynara scolymus)* should be cut green to provide a delectable vegetable. They are cooked by boiling in salted water for a half hour and may be eaten hot or served cold with a vinaigrette sauce. One globe is served per person. The plant produces very attractively cut silvery-gray leaves.

Site and Soil

Choose a sheltered sunny site in a fenced or hedged-round garden. Dig the soil well and improve it by adding well-rotted compost and/or manure. This gives strong growth and increases the number of 'globes'. Avoid planting in heavy wet soils.

Special Siting

In the USA, globe artichokes are grown commercially in the cool, coastal areas of California – around San Francisco. The plants rarely survive winter in cold climates – even with careful protection. For those in mild climates, three or four plants should be sufficient for a small garden. (See 'Useful Tip' on facing page.)

Propagating and Planting

Either buy young suckers (the side shoots growing around the main stem) or cut from established plants in April (see figure 56). Plant out suckers in the growing area 2–2½ ft (60–75 cm) apart (see figure 56). If the soil is very fertile, go for the wider spacing. Firm the suckers well. The cut root stem will soon produce roots and grow away to

Globe Artichokes.

Figure 56:
Propagating globe artichokes from suckers.

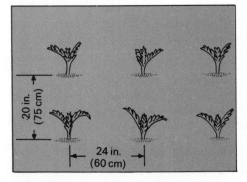

20 in. (75 cm)

24 in. (60 cm)

provide flower buds which you can cut in August and September. The best crops occur in the second and third year – after this, plant out more suckers to replace three-year-old plants. Old plants yield smaller and fewer buds.

Give the newly planted offsets plenty of water in dry weather until they are well established. Hoe occasionally to eliminate weeds. In early winter, when the leaves start to die down, cut away the old flower stems and tie the younger leaves up together before drawing soil up round the stems. This soil will help protect the tender crowns from frost damage.

Harvesting

You can start harvesting established plants in July, when the flower buds are plump and fully swollen and before the scales have hard brown tips. Cut them with a sharp knife or pruners, taking the large central, or 'king' globe, first and subsequently harvesting the smaller side-shoot globes. Once the scales turn purplish and the flowers begin to show, the buds are inedible.

Possible Problems

Lack of moisture and poor soil give small, hard and woody globes. Try watering the plants with foliar fertilizer to give a quick improvement. Subsequently add general fertilizer in spring at the rate of 2–3 oz per sq yd (60–85 gms per sq m) and mulch with well-rotted manure or compost to improve plant growth.

Jerusalem artichokes.

Figure 57: Jerusalem artichokes form an attractive screen.

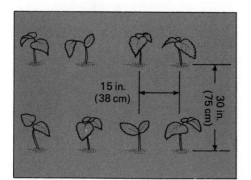

15 in. (38 cm)

30 in. (75 cm)

USEFUL TIP
A single plant or group of two or three look very attractive in a herbaceous border and to the front of a shrub border. Remember they grow 3–4 ft (90–120 cm) high.

JERUSALEM ARTICHOKE

This plant (*Helianthus tuberosus*) is grown for the tubers which are like knobbly potatoes. The stems grow 6–8 ft (1·8–2·5 m) high and are perfect for a quick summer screen, perhaps to hide an ugly shed or form a temporary hedge in a new garden (see figure 57). The soft green sunflower leaves are also useful as a background foil to flower arrangements but remember, however, that cutting the foliage will inevitably reduce the size of your vegetable crop.

Site and Soil
Full sun or sun and partial shade provide suitable sites. Any soil, even the worst possible, will provide some tubers, although better soils produce heavier crops.

Propagating and Planting
Save a few small tubers from your previous crop or purchase a few to start your cropping from scratch. Plant the tubers in spring. 4–6 in (10–15 cm) deep, 15 in (38 cm) apart.

How to Grow
Hoe to eliminate weeds, cut down foliage in the fall and pinch out tips to prevent flower buds developing.

Harvesting
The tubers will be ready for harvesting in late fall. Either leave them in the soil and dig them up as you want them, or lift and store in damp sand in a cool but frost-free shed or cellar.

Possible Problems
The plants can become invasive and a nuisance in the small vegetable plot.

Asparagus

Commercial asparagus (*Asparagus officinalis*) except at the height of the local season, is almost prohibitively expensive. Once established in your garden, however, asparagus will produce year after year with very little trouble and at virtually no cost. The feathery green foliage, sometimes called asparagus fern, is also used in floral decorations, but cut it sparingly if you want a good crop of spears the following year.

Site and Soil

Select an open sunny site and well-drained soil. Light soils tending to the sandy are ideal; add sand to very heavy soils to improve drainage. Dig the soil very thoroughly in the fall to remove all perennial weed roots, and add as much well-rotted garden compost and manure as you can get. If you suspect your soil is very acid, test the pH and add limestone accordingly. The pH should be no lower than 6·5. Once planted, the bed can produce for twenty years or more, so it is wise to see it has a good foundation and is free of perennial weeds.

Sowing and Propagating

Asparagus can be started from seed or roots. Seed should be sown 2 in (5 cm) in the open soil in spring to raise new plants, and the seedlings thinned to stand 6 in (15 cm) apart when they are big enough to handle. Always use fresh seed – if it is more than one year old it quickly loses its germination properties.

A more common way of starting asparagus is to buy one- or two-year-old roots ('crowns') in spring. This saves a full year's growing time. Don't let the roots get dry – if you have to

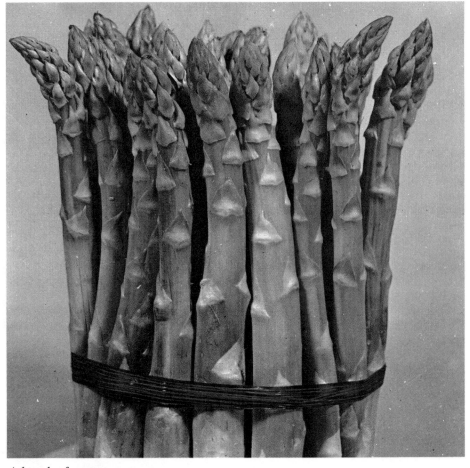

A bunch of asparagus spears.

delay planting them for a few days store in damp peat moss in a cool place.

How to Grow

Dig out a trench 8–10 in (20–25 cm) deep and 12 in (30 cm) wide. Then form a shallow ridge 3 in (7·5 cm) high at the base (see figure 58). Space the crowns 12–18 in (38–45 cm) apart with the string-like small roots spread over both sides of the ridge. Then cover the crowns with 2–3 in (5–7·5 cm) of soil and subsequently, when hoeing to control weeds, slowly fill up the trench with soil. Space the rows 3–5 ft (120–150 cm) apart if you are growing more than one row. When the foliage is fully grown you may have to erect a few stakes and run a string of wire down each side of the row to support the stems and prevent them from blowing over. Cut the foliage down to

Figure 58: Planting a single row of asparagus crowns.

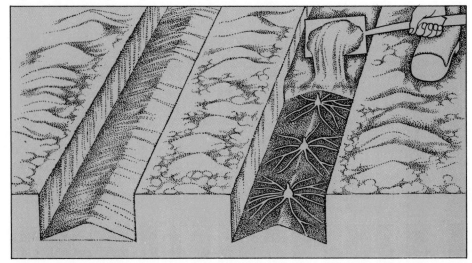

Asparagus spears at harvest time.

within 2 in (5 cm) of the soil in the fall. In fact, the time to do this is usually just after the first frost when the foliage turns yellow and before the berries on female plants fall to the ground. If the berries are allowed to fall they will produce scattered seedlings which will be difficult to remove from the established plants. Cutting the foliage too early reduces the build-up of vigor in the plants for the next season's crop.

Sprinkle a general fertilizer along the row in spring at the rate of 2–3 oz per sq yd (60–85 g per sq m). Mulch with well-rotted compost after mid-June to smother seedling weeds, retain moisture and improve both the soil and asparagus growth in future years.

Harvesting

A year after the roots are planted one spear can be cut from each plant. The

Figure 60: Support growing foliage with stakes and wires to keep tidy rather than cutting it back which reduces the ensuing crop.

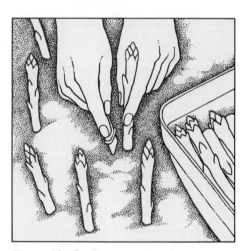

Figure 59: Cutting asparagus spears.

following year all the spears can be cut over a four-week period, and in the third year (when plants are four or five years old) spears can be cut for six weeks. Then stop *all* cutting to allow the plants to build up strength for the next season's crop.

Cut the spears (the emerging shoots) when they are 4–6 in (10–15 cm) above the soil. Always cut them before the tip starts to open into foliage-producing shoots. This means cutting spears every three days or so in cooler weather and almost daily in hot weather. An old kitchen knife with a broken tip is the perfect cutting tool. Sharpen the squared-off end, run this gently down the side of the spear, and cut approximately 2–4 in (5–10 cm) below the soil surface. After practice it is also possible to bend the shoots toward you and snap the spears from the roots by hand.

Possible Problems

If you see the foliage and young growth being eaten by grayish grubs and their parent asparagus beetles, dust or spray with rotenone.

Note

Asparagus is a perennial and not a rotational crop, which makes its inclusion in the 10×12 ft (3×4 m) vegetable plot rather extravagant on space. You could have a row of plants at one end of the plot, but it is better to find space to grow it elsewhere if possible.

Asparagus foliage in summer.

USEFUL TIP

Be sure to cut regularly, ideally every day to get the most palatable spears. If you are not going to cook the spears at once, either freeze them or stand the cut ends in cool water. If you leave the spears too long, they will go stale, limp, and slightly bitter.

Eggplant

Eggplant (*Solanum melongena ovigerum*), called aubergine in Europe, is an extremely versatile vegetable and may be grilled, fried, stuffed, or stewed. Eggplants need growing conditions similar to those for tomatoes but in the North are more difficult to grow than the tomato or the third *Solanum*, the potato. While all three plants have the typical *Solanum* flowers, the purple and yellow of the eggplant are the largest and most attractive. These and the large purple fruit make it an attractive plant to grow in pots on a patio. (There are white- and green-fruited varieties and some Japanese hybrids that bear smaller fruits, excellent in Northern areas with short growing seasons and in tubs or pots.)

Site and Soil

Choose the warmest, sunniest and most sheltered site, such as a south-facing fence or wall. On heavy soils, which are low and tend to stay wet, raise small hills of soil to give better drainage to the planting position. Best results will be achieved either in light soils containing plenty of well-rotted organic matter or in pots filled with a commercial synthetic soil mixture.

Sowing Instructions

Sow seed indoors in a temperature of 55°–60°F (13°–15°C). The earlier in spring this can be done the longer the bearing period and the heavier the crop. Plan on sowing the seeds 6–8 weeks before you can set the plants safely outside. Grow in a sunny window or under fluorescent lights. Or buy seedling plants to put directly into the garden after the soil is warm, about the time you plant tomato seedlings.

Figure 61: Eggplants grow well in fertilized peat bags (used in England) and other containers.

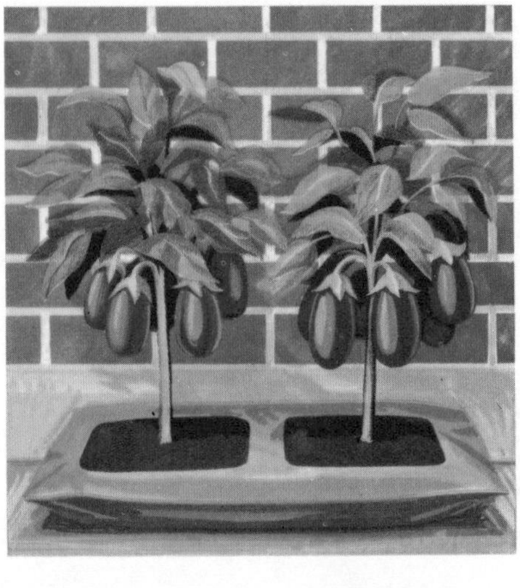

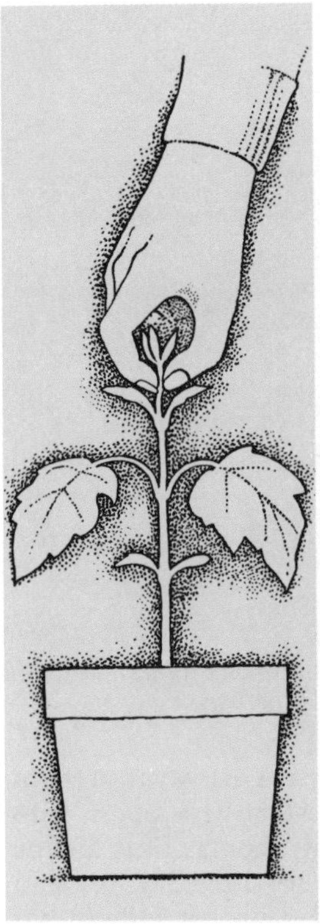

Figure 62: Pinch out growing tips.

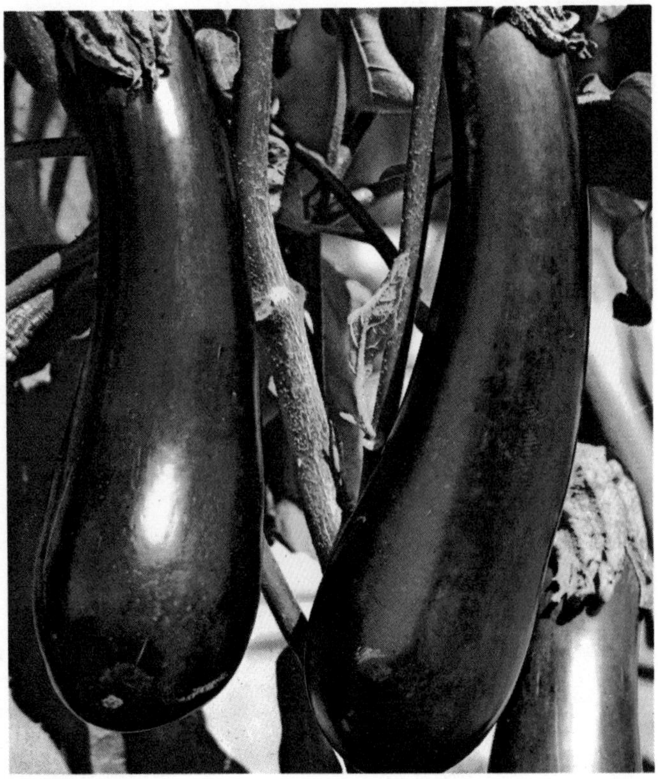

Eggplants growing on the plant.

A warm climate and a long growing period will give you crops of ten to twelve fruits, each one weighing up to 1 lb (0·45 kg), depending on variety. A shorter growing season gives four to six fruits per plant.

How to Grow

Set out the plants after the soil is thoroughly warm. If there is still danger of frost or the weather remains cool, setting under Hotkaps is suggested. When the plants are 6 in (15 cm) high, pinch out the growing tip to encourage several branches to form (see figure 62). Reduce the number of young branches once the required number of fruits start to swell. This will avoid the production of too many very small fruits although these are preferred by some cooks. Give plenty of water in dry weather and a liquid plant food (tomato food is ideal) every 10–14 days once the fruits start to swell. This will make them larger.

Harvesting

When the fruits have a rich purple shine (in late summer/early fall) they are ready to gather. Cut then with a sharp knife to avoid bruising. Once the fruits lose their shine they also lose their flavor and the seeds turn brown and bitter.

Possible Problems

Few pests bother the eggplant. Flea beetles can make small holes in the foliage in early summer. Spray or dust with Sevin or methorychlor. White flies sometimes are troublesome. Spray with diazinon.

USEFUL TIPS

1. Eggplants grow well in plastic bags filled with fertilized peat moss or synthetic soil mix, sometimes aptly described as 'pillow growing' (see figure 61).
2. Try to obtain varieties which have F_1 hybrid after their name. You are likely to get bigger and better crops from these.

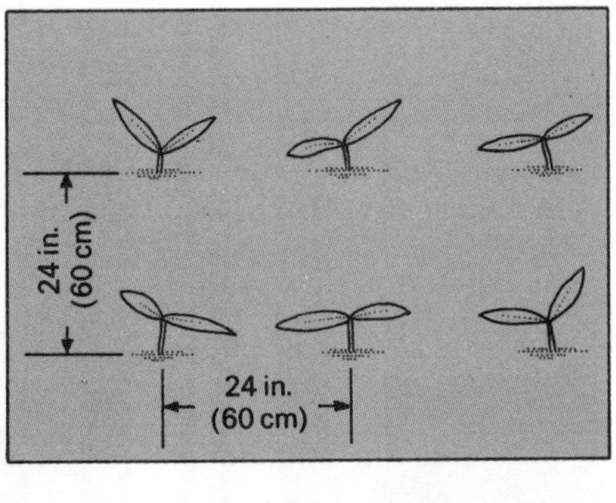

Beans

BROAD BEANS

Although broad beans (*Vicia faba*) also called Windsor and fava bean, are more commonly grown in Europe than in the USA, they are sufficiently planted to be listed in every American seed catalogue. More Americans might grow these beans if they realized that their cultural requirements are more akin to those of the pea than the more popular snap bean. In common with the pea, broad beans must be planted in very early spring in order to make most of their growth while the weather is cool. Harvesting of the pods is in early summer in most Northern regions. They are therefore a good crop for Northern gardeners who like to start their gardening activities in very early spring. When they have finished bearing, there is

Broad Beans.

Figure 63: If black aphids appear on broad beans pinch out growing tips.

still plenty of time to sow other crops in their place. In mild winter regions, broad beans can be sown in the fall for spring harvest. The pods are shelled, as with peas and lima beans, each pod yielding 5 to 7 large beans.

Varieties

Not much choice, 'Long Pod' (85 days) being the usual offering in catalogs.

Site and Soil

All garden sites and soil will give reasonable results, but in mild climates, where broad beans are grown in winter, try to choose a site sheltered from cold winds. Well cultivated soils will give the heaviest yields – over 6 lb (2·7 kg) to a 10 ft (3 m) row.

Sowing Instructions

Sow beans 2 in (5 cm) deep in the open garden in late October/early November in mild climates and from February to April in Northern regions. Space 9–12 in (23–30 cm) apart in double rows with 18 in–2 ft (45–60 cm) between them. Early sowings not only give earlier crops but often the heaviest yields as well. Try sowing some seeds indoors in pots in early February, and plant them out under Hotkaps as soon as soil conditions allow. These will yield the earliest beans of all.

USEFUL TIP

Once early sown crops are gathered, cut the stems almost to the ground and water well with liquid fertilizer to get a second flush of growth and a small late crop. However, this technique will work only in high altitude regions and elsewhere where summers are cool and moist.

How to Grow

The strong growing plants may need to be supported as they grow. Push a few canes into the soil, either side of

the beans and run a string around the row to hold up the plants.

Harvesting

Start to gather the lower pods as soon as the beans are large enough to shell out (the pods will be about ½ in (1 cm) wide). If you leave the beans to get very large and the scar, where the bean seed joins the pod, has turned brown or black, they will be too old to eat.

Possible Problems

Black aphids are often a nuisance on the growing tips of broad beans. You can control the pest by pinching out the growing tips as the aphids arrive (see figure 63).

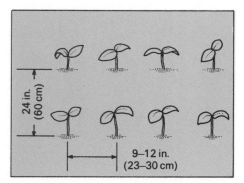

Snap beans.

SNAP BEANS and LIMA BEANS

For the small garden that needs a heavy-producing summer vegetable, there isn't a better choice than the snap bean *(Phaseolus vulgaris)*, also called green bean or French bean – or simply 'bean'. The old name of string bean is no longer used since pods of modern varieties are mostly stringless. Snap beans are among the easiest, quickest (about 48 to 55 days) and most prolific garden vegetables and are ideal for freezing. There are many varieties as well as two types: bush, which, as the name indicates, are low, bushy plants 12–18 in (30–45 cm) high; and pole or climbing, the vines of which require support. Both have rounded, slim pods 4–6 in (10–15 cm) long. The whole pod should be picked when young. At this stage, the pods snap easily when being prepared for cooking, which is doubtless why they are now called snap beans. Varieties with yellow pods are called wax beans. As well as the round-podded varieties there are flat-podded ones (Italian types) that require the same cultural treatment.

Lima beans *(Phaseolus lunatus)* can also be grown in bush or climbing

Wax snap beans – yellow-podded variety.

forms. They require a longer growing season (from 65 to 90 days, according to variety) than snap beans and need warmer conditions to develop the beans fully. Unlike snap beans, their pods must be shelled. The lima bean is a popular dried bean. The pods are allowed to fully mature and dry on the vines, then are shelled and the beans stored for winter use. Dried beans must be soaked before cooking. The fresh lima bean is also excellent for freezing.

Site and Soil

An open sunny site will give the best crops and any well cultivated garden soil is suitable. Like peas, bean roots use bacteria to fix nitrogen from the air and convert it to nitrogenous plant food. As a result they leave the soil richer in nitrogen and after harvesting their roots should be allowed to decay in place.

Special Siting

Bush snap beans are the perfect window-box vegetable. Try growing them also in plant tubs, patio containers and pots (see figure 66) on patios, balconies and on roof gardens.

Figure 64: Snap beans will break cleanly when they are ripe.

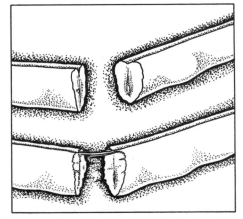

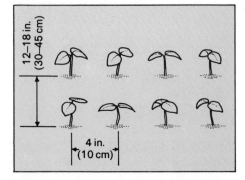

Sowing Instructions

All bean seeds, including snap and lima beans, are easy to sow in their permanent rows in the garden because of their size. Make the furrows 1–2 in (2·5–5 cm) deep and sow the seeds about 3–4 in (7·5–10 cm) apart, finally thinning to stand 4–6 in (7·5–15 cm) apart. Don't attempt to sow the seeds until the soil and weather have warmed and frost danger is passed. Both snap and lima beans revel in warmth and the seeds will simply rot

Figure 65: Two strings support a thick row of snap beans.

in cold, wet soil. All seedlings of legumes (beans, peas) are difficult to transplant, but sowing the seeds in Jiffy 7 peat pots or standard peat pots in which pot and plant are both set in the ground, thereby avoiding root disturbance, makes it possible to get an early start by sowing seeds indoors. A second sowing of snap beans can be made in midsummer in almost all Northern gardens.

How to Grow

Hoe occasionally to keep down weeds and in hot dry weather water the plants well and also spray them from above. In hot dry atmospheres the flowers will just drop off and fail to set pods. Support pole beans with tall poles, nets or strings (see figure 68).

Harvesting

Gather when young. Test snap beans for ripeness by snapping the pod in

Figure 66: Snap beans growing in a pot.

half – if it breaks in half with a succulent crack, it is ready for picking. A 10 ft (3 m) row is likely to yield 2–3 lb (1–1·25 kg) of fresh pods. Harvest lima beans when the beans are prominent in the pods.

Possible Problems

If beans are grown in greenhouses and in hot, dry atmospheres, red spider mite may turn the leaves a dull, rusty, yellowish green. Syringe repeatedly with water to deter attack. When beans are grown out of doors few

problems are likely. The Mexican bean beetle can be controlled by Sevin or malathion.

SCARLET RUNNER BEANS

Scarlet runner beans (*Phaseolus coccineus syn Phaseolus multiflorus*) are usually only grown in the USA as an ornamental, although they are widely grown in Britain for culinary purposes. They are grown in parts of California, where the growing season is long, as a vegetable, and occasionally elsewhere. The pods are eaten, but they can also be shelled for green beans, or the beans from mature pods can be dried.

Site and Soil

Scarlet runner beans grow best in an open sunny site. They will also bear in all good garden soils, but the more organic matter in the form of peat moss, well-rotted compost and manure dug into the soil to retain moisture, the heavier will be the crop.

Figure 67: Climbing beans grown in peat-filled bags, and (below) to form a 'wig-wam'.

49

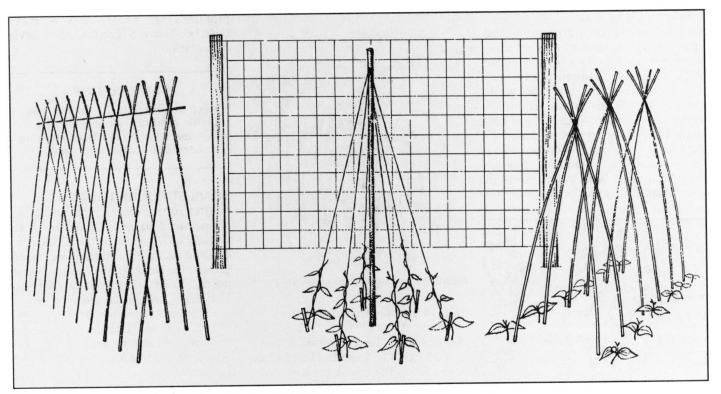

Figure 68: Various ways of supporting all kinds of climbing beans as they grow.

Sowing Instructions

Sow the large seeds 1–2 in (2–5 cm) deep, directly where they are to grow, a week or so before the likely date of your last frost in spring. Sow enough seeds to give four plants per 3 ft (90 cm) of row, up to eight plants per sq yd (0·8 sq m) for maximum yield. In most regions, the seeds must be started indoors in peat pots about five weeks before the soil warms outdoors, since it takes from 115 to 120 days from seed to harvesting.

How to Grow

It is possible to grow runner beans unsupported like dwarf beans if you pinch out the growing tips every time they exceed 12–18 in (30–45 cm). For this method sow two seeds per 12 in

NB: Spacing for double rows: 9 in (23 cm) between plants, 18 in (45 cm) between lines, 42 in (106 cm) between double rows.

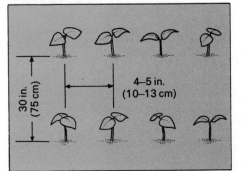

(30 cm) of single row, spacing rows 2 ft 6 in (75–80 cm) apart. However, beans grown this way trail in the soil and are often curled and splashed with earth when gathered, so where possible it is better to grow them up some form of support (see figure 68). Give added strengthening to cane and bean poles used to support a double row of runner beans by tying the tops of a few together, like wigwams (see figure 68). This will prevent the whole row blowing over on exposed sites should one pole break.

See that these plants never lack moisture. When the first flowers appear water regularly with diluted liquid fertilizer and mulch with well-rotted compost to retain moisture. This will increase the yield. Syringing the leaves and flowers during hot weather will also help the flowers to set, thus increasing the crop.

USEFUL TIPS

1. Growing runner or pole snap or lima beans up poles and netting forms excellent temporary screens in summer, particularly if, for example, you are waiting for a hedge to grow.
2. Pinched-out plants will crop slightly earlier and more heavily for the first few weeks and then supported plants outyield them.

Harvesting

Pick regularly, at least twice a week when the beans are 10 in (25 cm) or more long. The more you pick the more beans the plants produce. You will have greater chances of cropping well into the fall by regular feeding and picking rather than making a second and later sowing.

Figure 69: Pinch out tips, and runner beans will grow without cane support.

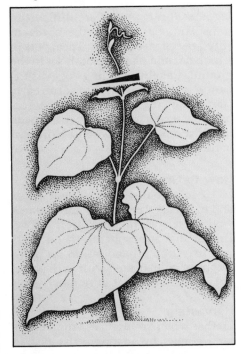

Beets and Swiss Chard

Whether boiled and preserved in vinegar to eat with salad, or boiled with or without their green tops the best (*Beta vulgaris*) is a most valuable vegetable which the home gardener can grow all summer. Recent times have seen the introduction of the golden beet, Burpees 'Golden' which has orange skin and bright yellow flesh. It also has the added advantage of providing a dual-purpose vegetable in that the leaves can be cooked and served like spinach.

Varieties

'Detroit Dark Red' (60 days) is a standard variety with a globe shape and is available as Medium Top or Short Top. Medium Top is best for greens. 'Cylindra' (60 days) is a long beet recommended for slicing. 'Lutz Green Leaf Winter Keeper' (80 days) is the best bet for storage.

Site and Soil

Any sunny site and most well-dug garden soils are suitable. Add humus-forming materials such as compost

Young beets are the sweetest.

Golden beet.

and peat moss to very light sandy soils to help retain moisture.

Sowing Instructions

Each knobbly piece from the seed packet is in fact a cluster of seeds and not just one seed. Space these clusters 2–3 in (5–7 cm) apart down the row, 1 in (2·5 cm) deep with 9–15 in (23–38 cm) between the rows. If you intend to pull the roots as soon as they are golfball size the closer row spacing

is suitable. Make the first sowing as soon as the frost is out of the ground, and sow every two or three weeks until about two months before the first heavy frost is due in your area.

How to Grow

Thin out the seedlings if more than one grows at each station. Don't let the plants suffer from drought which will make the roots tough and woody. Hoe occasionally to keep down weeds.

USEFUL TIP

A very light sprinkling of common salt, no more than ½ oz (14 g) down 2 yds (1·8 m) of row, watered in, will improve growth and color of the roots. You should be aiming to grow tender roots with no sign of woody white rings when the beet is cut in half. Plenty of moisture and the sprinkling of salt help achieve this; shortage of moisture and slow growth makes the roots a bit on the woody and tough side.

Harvesting

The tender young roots are the most delicious, so pull out every other plant as soon as the root is large enough. This spaces the remaining plants 6 in (15 cm) apart and leaves ample room for full development of the later har-

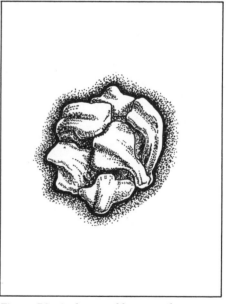

Figure 70: A cluster of beets seeds.

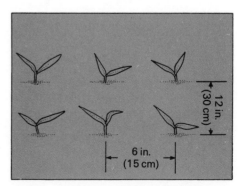

12 in. (30 cm)

6 in. (15 cm)

An example of long beet.

Swiss chard.

vested roots. When pulling beets always twist the leaves neatly from the root by hand rather than cutting with a knife – unless you wish to cook the leaves as greens. This leaves the roots ready for cooking once any soil has been washed off.

Possible Problems

Beets need steady, uncrowded growth for high-quality, sweet roots.

SWISS CHARD

This is a beet (*Beta vulgaris cicla*) which is grown for its leaves; the roots are not edible. The plants are very attractive, especially in late summer and early fall. The common variety has dark green leaves and white stalks; the variety sometimes called 'Rhubarb Chard', which has bright red stalks and reddish leaves, is particularly beautiful and looks equally at home in flower beds and in vegetable patches. The leaves and stalks are cooked like spinach; the leaf stems may need longer cooking.

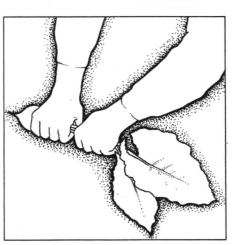

Figure: 71 Twist off the leaves of beets.

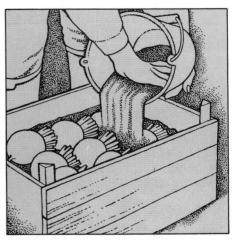

Figure 72: Store beets in peat or sand.

Sowing Instructions

Sow from early spring as soon as the soil can be worked to late spring, in rows 18 in (45 cm) apart. As the seedlings grow, thin them to stand finally at 8 in (20 cm) apart.

Harvesting

Pull off the outer leaves as you require them for eating. The inner younger leaves will then develop to provide a succession. The leaves continue well into the winter in all but the coldest regions.

Possible Problems

There are none.

USEFUL TIP

Grow a group of the red and white stemmed varieties in a circular patch in an herbaceous border, for example in front of phlox; or plant close to contrasting silver and purple foliage in the front of shrub borders for a striking effect. Swiss chard provides attractive foliage for flower arrangers.

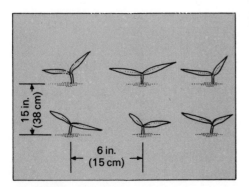

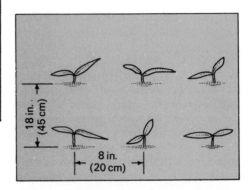

How to Grow

Hoe occasionally to control weeds.

52

Broccoli, Cauliflower and Kale

Broccoli (*Brassica oleracea cymosa*) is a member of the cabbage family which might be described as a branching cauliflower.

Kale (*Brassica oleracea acephala*) has been linked with broccoli because the more recent types are similar in both growing habit and culinary use. They also complete a year-round cycle of fresh green vegetable production.

While broccoli and kale require similar cultural treatment, broccoli (sold in frozen form as broccoli spears), is ready for harvesting first. Kale follows and survives even in fairly cold climates to provide fresh greens through the winter. In warm climates broccoli can be planted in the fall and will be available for picking from early spring to early summer.

Figure 73: Broccoli seeds can be grown in Jiffy 7 peat pellets.

Site and Soil
Kale will stand very exposed conditions but choose a more sheltered site for broccoli, and remember that it forms very large plants. Good, well-cultivated soils that have been improved by the addition of compost, well-rotted manures and other humus-forming materials are best. Set

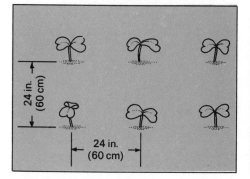

out between rows of early peas and beans for ideally suitable soil conditions, or set out plants after peas have been fully harvested.

Sowing Instructions
For summer harvests, sow broccoli seed indoors five to seven weeks before setting out. Two seeds can be sown in a Jiffy 7 peat pellet or peat pot and the weaker of the two seedlings pinched out. As soon as the soil can be worked, transplant the resulting seedlings when they are big enough to handle (4–6 in (10–15 cm) high) or buy started plants to set out into the growing site, 20–30 in (50–75 cm) apart. Rows should also be spaced 20–30 in (50–75 cm) apart. You can plant out broccoli more closely, down to 12 × 9 in (30 × 23 cm) if you want to produce an abundance of small heads for freezing. For late summer to fall harvesting, sow broccoli seeds in the garden in late spring to early summer. Kale can be sown directly into the garden as soon as the soil can be worked, or it can be sown in late summer for a fall and winter crop.

Varieties
The variety 'Calabrese' gives the home gardener a long and heavy harvest because after the main center head is cut, many smaller heads are borne by the side branches. 'Green Comet Hybrid' needs only 55 days

White sprouting cauliflower

from seed to full maturity and it is resistant to heat.

How to Grow
Water broccoli well before transplanting into the garden. When transplanting put the plant stems well down in the soil – this will improve the plant's anchorage and help it to withstand strong winds. Of course, if the seedlings are in peat pots, pot and plant both go into the soil, but it is important to water well after planting. The only other cultural treatment necessary is occasional hoeing to control weeds (but a mulch is better) and to water well in dry weather.

Purple cauliflowers.

Broccoli 'calabrese'.

Harvesting

As the broccoli plants produce the main head and smaller side heads large enough to pick, start cutting regularly. The more you pick, the more new shoots will be produced. If you leave the first shoots to flower, the whole plant will turn woody and inedible. Pick the larger center heads first and don't discard the young leaves around them as these are quite as succulent as the flower buds. The stems are also edible but may have to be peeled before cooking.

Possible Problems

If these and other plants of the cabbage family are grown on the same soil without rotation, build up of the disease club root and cabbage worms is a possibility. You can control club root by pouring one cup of Terrachlor mixed according to directions on the container in the planting hole. ·

Pick off by hand the green caterpillars of the cabbage white butterfly or spray or dust plants with rotenone or Sevin according to directions on the container.

CAULIFLOWER

Seed catalogs list several varieties of cauliflower (*Brassica oleracea* variety *botrytis*) but success with this vegetable depends on working backward from the date of maturity (for more details see CABBAGE, page 58) so the plants begin to mature in cool weather. In most regions this means fall. Unless you live in a cool moist climate and have really fertile soil, cauliflower will probably present more problems than broccoli, kale or cabbage. The quicker growing varieties can be set out as soon as the danger of frost is

Figure 74: Use a narrow trowel or dibble to set out young plants.

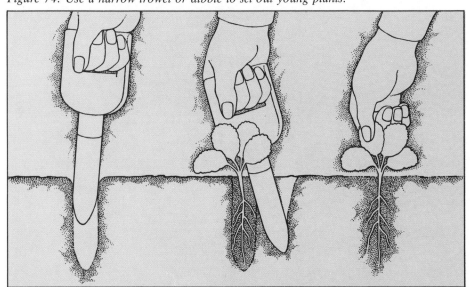

Kale.

54

past to secure rapid growth before hot weather. However, it is best grown as a late fall crop, setting out plants in mid-summer.

Cauliflower has the reputation of being difficult to grow, but in practice success depends on the quality of the soil. In good soils, rich in organic matter, they are easy; in poor soils the gardener's skills are fully tested and in this situation the fall-maturing varieties will often be the most successful.

Site and Soil
Select an open sunny site. Cauliflower grows best in well-cultivated soils which you can further improve by adding plenty of very well-rotted organic matter. This gives rapid growth and good-sized curds (the name given to the white cauliflower heads). If the soil is acid, give it a dusting of lime. This is a help to all the cabbage family.

EARLY VARIETIES
Summer Maturing Cauliflowers

Sowing Instructions
Sow indoors in peat pots eight to ten weeks before average date of last frost. After the third leaf (two round seed leaves will be followed by the third,

Cauliflower. Below: Figure 75: Control root fly by using cardboard disks.

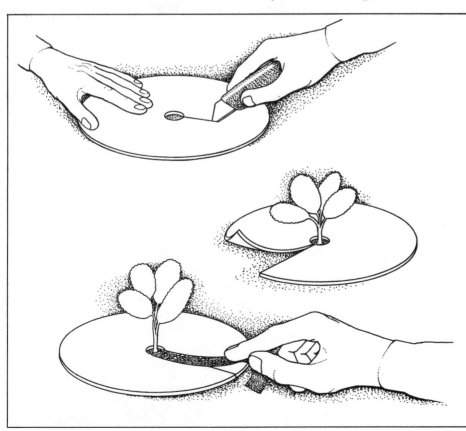

which is rough-edged and the first true leaf) appears, the potted seedlings need cold frame or Hotkap protection to produce sturdy plants.

How to Grow
Plant out in the growing site 18 in (45 cm) apart after danger of frost is past. Hoe occasionally to control weeds or mulch the plants. If cold wet conditions cause a check to growth,

---

USEFUL TIPS
1. Occasionally a shortage of boron occurs in soils and this causes the leaves to grow narrow and turn brown. The cauliflower will be bitter. Correct this by hoeing a dusting of borax into the soil at 1 oz to 60 sq yd (30 g to 50 sq m).
2. For something less common, with excellent flavor, try purple cauliflower, such as 'Purple Head' or the green 'Chartreuse'. Treat culturally as for other fall-maturing kinds, but do not blanch.

Figure 76: Fold outer leaves over to protect developing curds as cauliflower grows.

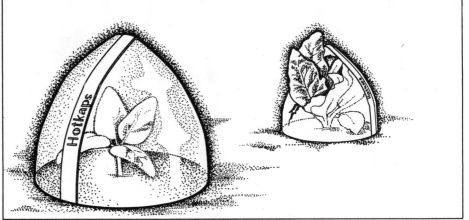

Figure: 77 Hotkaps, waxed paper 'tents' are placed over seedlings in early to mid-spring for temporary protection. A slit should be made in the top for ventilation.

turning the plants bluish green, apply liquid fertilizer or scratch in a nitrogen-high fertilizer such as nitrate of soda or sulphate of ammonia into the soil around plants at the rate of 1 oz per sq yd (30 gm per sq m).

FALL
Late Cauliflowers

Sowing Instructions
Sow outdoors in a seed bed in early summer, the seed just covered, in rows 9 in (23 cm) apart.

How to Grow
Water the plants well before transplanting into the growing site. Leave 20–24 in (50–60 cm) between plants and between rows. As the curds (heads) begin to develop break the midrib of a few large leaves and fold these outer leaves over the cauliflower head. This keeps the head beautifully white. The purple and green varieties do not require blanching.

Harvesting
Rows of cauliflower have the habit of all maturing ready for harvest at the same time. When you have a surplus

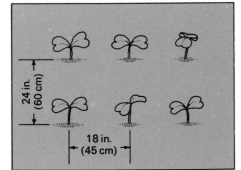

you can store some temporarily by lifting mature plants and hanging them by the stalk in a cool shed. Syringe these lifted plants with water occasionally to keep them fresh for the longest possible period. Cauliflower

An attractive variety of cauliflower.

surplus can be frozen and retains its quality very well.

Possible Problems
The problems are the same as those under CABBAGE.

Brussels Sprouts

The key to producing quality crops of this cold-hardy vegetable (*Brassica oleacea gemmifera*) is to select hybrid varieties from which you pick the sprouts while they are small and firm. Cook them for a few minutes only in fiercely boiling water, so they remain whole and keep a rich green color. Cook them for long and they turn into an unappetizing, yellow, soggy mess!

Site and Soil
Brussels sprouts are very winter-hardy requiring only a sunny site and well cultivated soils. The most recently introduced heavy-yielding and firm-buttoned F_1 hybrid varieties need good soil and ample moisture.

> ### USEFUL TIP
> Don't be in a hurry to pull up the stalks after harvesting. Instead pinch out the tops and pick any young shoots that develop during mild weather. These cook as well as spring greens such as turnip greens.

Sowing Instructions
If you live where summers are cool, sow indoors four to six weeks before outdoor planting date and set out as soon as soil can be worked in spring. This will give a harvest in summer. In most regions where summers are hot, it is better to sow seeds in late spring to early summer so sprouts mature during cool days of the fall and early winter.

How to Grow
Water the seedlings well before transplanting into the growing site. Transplant as described for broccoli. Apply an organic mulch – compost, leafmold, rotted manures – to help keep the soil cool and to suppress weed growth. During very dry weather help growth by watering well and giving liquid fertilizer. This will be essential for some of the new F_1 hybrids.

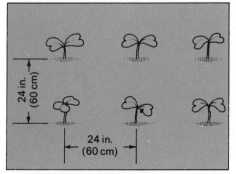

Brussels sprouts.

Harvesting
Start cutting off the largest and lower sprouts as soon as they are big enough, about 1 in (3 cm) in diameter.

The varieties that are especially bred to provide sprouts for freezing tend to mature all at once, and you can usually pull up the plant to pick off all the sprouts. For general purposes, late varieties are preferable as they can be harvested over a much longer period.

Possible Problems
Plants subjected to dry conditions from late summer onward are liable to be attacked by white flies. These are very easily controlled by spraying plants with the pesticides based on resmethrin, a chemical close to the natural pyrethrum. Sprouts can be eaten within a day or so of spraying. Pick off the green caterpillars of cabbage white butterflies.

Figure 78: Cardboard tubes pushed into the soil protect young plants from cutworms.

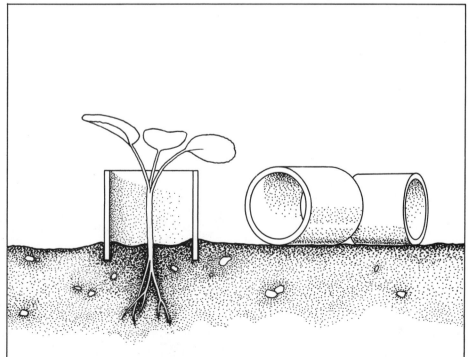

Cabbages

Cabbages (*Brassica oleracea capitata*) including the Savoy types (*Brassica oleracea bullata*) cut fresh while still young and tender are quite unrecognizable in flavor from the tough old cabbages which have been cut and stored for months before even reaching the market. They are a very easy crop to grow, and whether you sow seeds to produce plants for transplanting, buy seedlings or sow direct into the garden, the attention they need is minimal.

It is very important to select varieties from the right group for any one time of year, much more so than to select an actual cultivar from the group. This is simple, as long as you make your selection by working back from the cabbages' maturity period and settle whether you wish to harvest your cabbages in summer or late fall – or both. And of course mild climate gardeners can harvest cabbages all winter as needed. This can all add up to a lot of cabbage – especially for the small garden, where space is generally limited.

Winter cabbages, especially the tight headed white cabbages and varieties like Celtic Cross F₁, are useful not only as a cooked vegetable but also chopped for use in salads.

Summer maturing cabbage.

Site and Soil

Most sites and just about all garden soils are suitable. In the very poorest soils and partially shady locations, cabbages may not produce very good hearts, but these conditions can be improved by adding compost, well-

Figure 79: Small cabbages will form on the stump of a cut cabbage.

rotted manure if available and a complete fertilizer, such as 5–10–5, or 5–10–10. Watering with liquid fertilizers several times will also help.

SUMMER MATURING CABBAGE
Sowing Instructions

Sow seeds indoors (in March in the North, from mid-January to February in mild climates) and grow in a greenhouse, on a window sill or under fluorescent lights. Put the resulting plants outdoors from four to six weeks later. Don't leave the early seedlings in too warm conditions for too long, however, or they will become pale

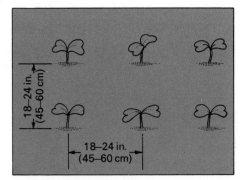

green, thin and sickly. Once they are up and well established with two or three leaves, it is best to put them in a cold frame, if available. These sowings, or transplants purchased later in the spring, provide the earliest cabbage. Sow outdoors in the open garden at regular intervals from April to May to provide a succession of cabbage through the summer.

How to Grow

The tender early plants raised indoors will be soft and will require a hardening-off process – gradual exposure to outdoor conditions for about a week or so – before they can be set in the open ground. Space plants 18–24 in (38–60 cm) apart with the same distance between rows. The larger you want the cabbage, the wider apart you should space the plants and rows.

Harvesting

Start to cut the cabbage as soon as the hearts begin to firm. If you wait until the hearts are fully developed the whole row will need cutting at once so it is better to start cutting early. In any

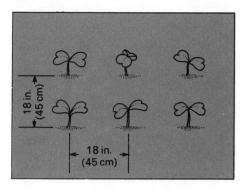

event the young cabbage hearts are the most tasty.

SPRING CABBAGE
Sowing Instructions
Sow in shallow drills ½–1 in (1–2·5 cm) deep, the rows 6 in (15 cm) or so apart in spring in open ground or cold frame. Water the resulting seedlings well before lifting and setting in the garden where they are to grow. If seedlings are not to be transplanted, thin rows when seedlings are big enough to handle.

How to Grow
Spacing 6 in (15 cm) apart in the row allows you to cut every second and/or third plant while still immature as

'greens'. Space the rows 15–25 in (40–60 cm) apart. Once again the wider the spacing, the larger the cabbage will be, but the younger, smaller ones are still the best to eat.

WINTER CABBAGE AND SAVOYS
You can recognize the Savoys easily by their large, thick, dark green leaves which have a bubbly-shaped surface. They are very easy to grow and a useful late or winter vegetable. Winter cabbage varieties, which can be left in the vegetable plot all winter in mild climates, elsewhere are harvested in late fall and stored for winter use as needed.

Sowing Instructions
Sow in drills ½–1 in (1–2·5 cm) deep, 6–9 in (15–23 cm) apart in April/May. An earlier sowing gives a slightly earlier start to harvesting.

How to Grow
Water the seedlings well before transplanting into soil which has been well cultivated for a previous crop, such as peas. Space the plants 15–24 in (40–60 cm) apart in the row and the rows 18–24 in (45–60 cm) apart. Firm planting is advisable for these winter cabbages.

RED CABBAGE
The very attractive deep reddish-green cabbage is sown April/May and treated culturally like other early to mid-season cabbage. It is most often grown for pickling, which turns the cabbage heart bright red, but is also delicious cooked fresh or used raw in salads.

Possible Problems
The following problems are common to all cabbage types. Although they occur quite often, they seldom prevent the harvesting of a crop, so they need not cause too much worry.

Winter maturing cabbage.

Caterpillars of cabbage white butterflies will eat holes into any cabbages from midsummer to late fall and may be controlled either by crushing the eggs and picking off the caterpillars by hand or spraying or dusting with rotenone, Sevin or Thuricide.

Swollen knobbly roots are caused by the disease club root. Attack can be reduced or even prevented by Terraclor, diluted according to directions, one cupful to a planting hole. Don't grow brassica crops repeatedly on the same site or else diseases like club root will build up in the soil.

An example of a point-headed cabbage.

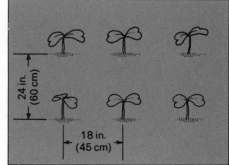

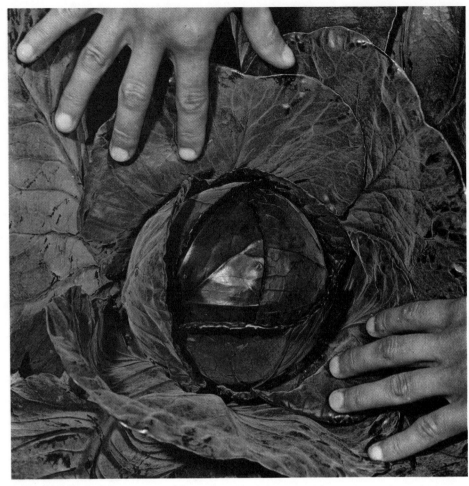

Red cabbage.

Figure 81: Cabbage root fly maggots.

The holes are eaten out by flea beetles which are easily controlled either by watering well each evening or dusting the seedlings with Sevin. For maximum effect dust in early morning while the leaves still have the dew on them, so the insecticide sticks to the dew and thus to the leaves.

Small white maggots which are the offspring of cabbage root fly may eat the roots. Pull up plants that wilt in hot weather, and if you find these white maggots, destroy the plants, ideally by burning so as to eliminate this pest. If you know this pest occurs in your garden treat the roots with diazinon, diluted according to directions, when planting and again seven days later.

You may notice neat round holes in the first two seedling leaves during periods of hot, dry weather; this may be particularly the case if you are growing the seedlings under cloches.

USEFUL TIPS

1. Growth can be speeded up by the application of nitrogen fertilizers. For example nitrate of soda or sulphate of ammonia applied in early spring around early maturing cabbage at up to 2 oz per square yard (75 gms per 1 sq m) will bring forward the harvesting period. Any of the common liquid fertilizers will also do this. For the fastest growth try watering or spraying with foliar fertilizer (i.e. fertilizers which are absorbed through the leaves).
2. Foliar feeding in midsummer in dry weather helps winter maturing brassicas develop.
3. Leave the stumps after cutting maturing cabbage if green vegetables are in short supply because they will produce another crop of small cabbages.
4. To prevent cabbage root fly laying its eggs in the soil against the plant stem, make center holes in discs of rubber carpet underlay 6–8 in (15–20 cm) across, slit radius and fit round plant stems.

Damage from birds may occur in some regions in winter and can only be controlled by erecting a temporary net. The other common problem is white aphid and white fly, which if allowed to, will work into the centers

Figure 80: Young cabbage seedlings and plants are particularly vulnerable to attack from birds, which, given the opportunity, will completely decimate a new crop. Protection can be given in various ways – (left) by enclosing seedlings with netting on all sides to form a pen. Birds will not fly down into this. Alternatively (right) they can be protected by erecting temporary netting to completely cover them.

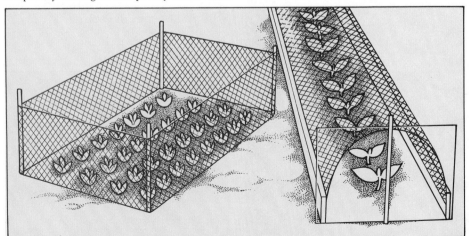

and hearts of your crop. Control as soon as you see them by spraying with malathion or diazinon, always taking great care to follow the directions for dilution and use on the container.

CABBAGE – CHINESE

Chinese cabbage is a brassica but quite different in appearance to the other kinds. It is sometimes called by its common name 'Pe-Tsai', and looks more like a cos lettuce than cabbage. It has several culinary uses – it may be boiled in the same way as cabbage, but does not generate the typical cabbage smell when cooking and has a much milder flavour. Alternatively, the leaf ribs of outer leaves may be cooked like asparagus or Swiss chard and the hearts may be shredded and used raw for salads.

Site and Soil

Chinese cabbage flourishes in similar sites to other cabbage crops. A soil improved by the addition of well-rotted organic matter is essential to retain moisture.

Sowing Instructions

Sow direct in the growing site in early July. It is better to sow and then thin out, as transplanting sometimes causes the plant to shoot up and form unwanted seed heads. Just cover the seed with soil and thin out the seedlings to stand 9–12 in (23–30 cm) apart, in rows spaced 12–15 in (30–38 cm) apart.

How to Grow

Make sure the plants do not lack moisture at the roots during hot weather. Otherwise just hoe occasionally to control weeds.

Possible Problems

There are none as long as you keep the plants growing strongly. F₁ hybrid varieties will grow quite large for fall harvesting.

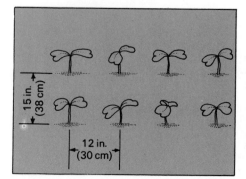

CABBAGE CHART		
Variety	Days to Maturity	Remarks
Copenhagen Market (early)	72	Well-rounded heads, 6½ in (16·5 cm) across.
Dwarf Morden (very early)	55	Miniature Canadian variety especially suited to small gardens. Round, split-proof heads, 4 in (10 cm) across.
Early Dark Green Savoy (early)	72	Small for Savoy type, with heads 5½–6 in (14–15 cm) across. Recommended for home plots.
Early Jersy Wakefield (early)	63	Yellows resistant. Small pointed heads, 7 in (18·5 cm) deep. Mild flavor.
Emerald Cross Hybrid (early)	63	Round compact heads, 6–9 in (15·5–23 cm) across. Resistant to splitting.
Penn State Ballhead (late-winter)	110	Improved Danish Ballhead variety. Recommended for storing. Heads 7–8 in (17·5–20·5 cm) across.
Red Acre (midseason)	86	Deep red, compact variety resistant to splitting.
Savoy King (midseason-late)	90	Large heads. Heat-resistant. Can be harvested at early as well as mature stage, making it desirable for home gardeners who don't want to eat cabbage every day.
Stonehead Hybrid (early)	70	Yellows resistant. Compact 6 in (15 cm) spread. Recommended especially for home vegetable plots.

Chinese cabbage.

Carrots

Carrots (*Daucus carota*) may all be bright orangy-red in colour, but owing to the modern varieties, you can now grow any number of different shapes! In fact the purist vegetable grower dedicated to producing the super long exhibition specimens is being left behind as more tender roots in shapes more suited to chopping, shredding and serving whole appear in seed form each year.

Breeding new varieties over recent years has been directed towards removing the woody yellow cores from carrot roots and this explains the terms 'red cored' and 'red cored improved' attached to some varietal names.

Figure 82: Different types of carrot: from l. to r. top row: Round, Slender Nantes, Amsterdam types, Autumn King, Intermediate, Long type. Bottom row: Larger Nantes, Early Nantes, Royal Chantenay.

A variety of Nantes type.

Varieties

Be adventuresome in the selection of carrot varieties, for they are all equally easy to grow. The small round carrots (see figure 82) are lovely cooked whole as are the young slender finger-long Amsterdam and Nantes types. The various maincrop varieties will all produce larger roots which may be left to grow and then lifted in the fall to store through the winter. All varieties can, however, be lifted young for the best and most tasty roots and all can be left to grow to full size, before lifting and storing. The best way to grow carrots therefore is to sow them sufficiently thickly to allow you to pull some young while leaving others to get larger to provide the maincrop for storing.

Site and Soil

Only very heavily shaded sites cause difficulties in growing carrots and all garden soils will yield reasonable crops although ideally the soil should be of a lighter, sandy nature for the straightest, well shaped roots.

Sowing Instructions

Sow the earliest crops under glass and polyethylene in February, and follow with outdoor sowings as soon as soil conditions are suitable (i.e. not too wet or hard). It is better to delay sowing than to sow when the soil is cold, wet and too sticky under foot. Sow the seed in shallow drills ½–1 in (1–2·5 cm) deep and just cover it with soil. Space the rows 9–12 in (23–30 cm) apart: employ the wider spacing if you have plenty of room and want really big carrots.

Make several regular sowings from April to July (perhaps one a month), to give a succession of tender young carrots to pull throughout the season

A variety of Chantenay carrot.

while still leaving sufficient to store for use in the winter.

How to Grow

Thin the seedlings to stand 1 in (2·5 cm) or so apart. When they are large enough to handle, this will allow you to pull either every other carrot, or every two in three, from the stage when they reach finger thickness. Leave the remaining carrots to reach maincrop size. Hoe regularly between plants and rows to remove weeds, but be careful to keep the hoe blade away from the roots and so avoid cutting into the carrot. If your carrots do not grow as quickly as you would like, water the foliage with a foliar feed from time to time.

If you are growing carrots as a maincrop, with the intention of lifting the roots for use through the winter, make sure the 'shoulder' – that is the top of the root – does not grow out of the soil. This turns it green and inedible. Prevent this by pulling a little soil up around the base of the leaf stalks.

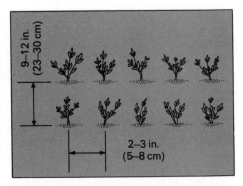

An early carrot type.

Harvesting

Once again, I can't stress enough the merit of pulling your carrots young for the best flavor. The earliest crops, pulled and shredded, are delicious in salads or boiled and served with butter. Lift maincrops carefully, easing them out of the soil with a fork or spade. Trim off the tops with a knife, then cover with sand, peat or loose soil and store in a shed or similar cool, dry storage place. Alternatively, leave in the soil and lift as you require them.

Possible Problems

Pest problems with carrots are virtually unknown. Roots, however, will split when very dry weather is followed by heavy rain, so water the soil in dry periods to reduce the chance of this happening.

The seeds are slow to germinate and when the seedlings finally break through the soil, beginning gardeners

A round rooted variety ideal for heavy or rocky soils.

may hardly be able to detect them from the weeds, especially if the weather has been moist and encouraged weed seed germination. This is the time to put 'an indicator' crop, mentioned earlier in this book, to practical application. Quick-germinating radish seeds are the traditional ones to sow with the carrot seeds and will mark the rows as well as help to space out the carrots.

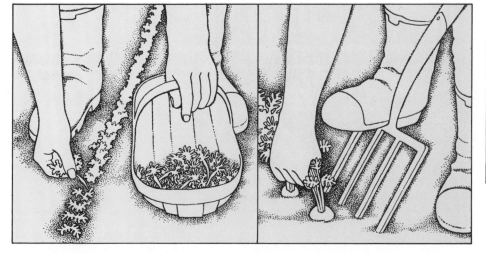

USEFUL TIP

If your gardening space is very limited, or you must grow vegetables in boxes and planters on a terrace, search the seed catalogs for miniature varieties. A few you might find are 'Tiny Sweet', 'Short 'n Sweet' and 'Little Fingers'.

Figure 83: Thin seedlings when they are large enough to handle. Be careful not to spike the carrot when lifting.

63

Celery and Celeriac

Both of these vegetables provide the distinctive flavor so familiar to gardeners and non-gardeners alike. Celeriac (*Apium graveolens rapaceum*) is perhaps more subtle in flavor and is less well known. The old method for growing celery (*A. graveolens dulce*), a method still followed by some home and market gardeners, was to blanch the stems pure white by drawing up around the leaf stalks.

Much less work to grow and with recently introduced varieties of improved quality, are the self-blanching kinds which have white stems and yellowish-green leaves. There is also the green self-blanching celery which has green stems, rich green leaves and is very crisp and easy to grow. Both the self-blanching kinds are less hardy than the blanched types and need to be harvested before severe frost occurs and ruins the crops.

Then there is celeriac, commonly and very descriptively called turnip-rooted or knob celery. This plant produces a swollen root which may be cooked as a flavoring for soups and stews or shredded raw for salads.

Site and Soil

A sunny situation and a deeply dug, humus-rich soil are required for the best results by both celery and celeriac. Celery, especially, needs a constant supply of moisture in the soil and this can mean daily watering in sandy soils. The constant moisture is less critical with celeriac but it too needs a rich soil that does not become bone dry.

Sowing Instructions

In most localities, seedling celery plants are available from local outlets at the correct time for setting them outside, but this is rarely true with the less popular celeriac. Seeds should be sown indoors about 10 weeks before planting outdoors – when temperatures range between 50°F–60°F (10°C–15°C). Sow seeds in a flat or tray, barely covering the seeds. Keep in a polyethylene bag until after germination which can be slow. Grow in a sunny window or under lights. Then transplant seedlings into peat pots. Harden off seedlings and plant outside when night temperatures have warmed; if in doubt plant under Hotkaps.

How to Grow

Celeriac: make a deep drill and plant seedlings in it 9–12 in (23–30 cm)

Celeriac.

apart. The drill makes subsequent watering easier as growth and succulence is dependent on ample moisture. Space the rows 15–18 in (38–45 cm) apart. Hoe to control weeds, and remove side shoots which may distort root shape. Also remove old yellow leaves as the plants develop.

Figure 84: Surround plants with cardboard before earthing up.

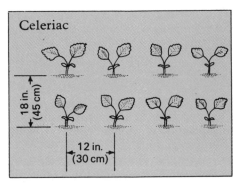

Self-blanching celery.

Figure 85: Young plants established in the trench, ready for earthing up.

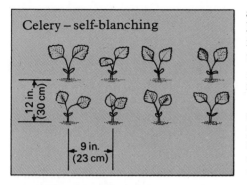
Celery – self-blanching

12 in (30 cm)

9 in. (23 cm)

Celery – all self-blanching kinds: plant in a square block of several rows. The inner plants will become more blanched and better to eat than those growing in the outside and in single rows. Set out plants 9–12 in (23–30 cm) apart in both directions, using the wider spacing on the best soils where you can expect to grow very large plants. Once established, hoe in a general fertilizer at 1 oz per sq yd (33 gms per sq m) and water well in dry weather.

Tuck in some protective material such as straw around the outside rows to help blanch the outer stems and bring them up to the quality of plants in the center of the block. Such material will also give a little protection against frost if you wish to extend the harvest period.

Self-blanching celery is a very good summer crop for cold frames. Remove glass sash when the plants are well established in the base soil. The side walls will help blanch the plants in the outer rows.

Celery – which needs blanching: the traditional way to grow these cultivars is to dig trenches in spring which are one spade deep, 12–15 in (30–38 cm) wide and 3 ft (90 cm) apart. Dig well-rotted manure and/or compost into the base of the trench and leave it to settle before setting out the plants 6 in (15 cm) apart in the base of the trench in midspring.

Celery varieties which need blanching can be grown on the surface of the soil without trenching either by earthing-up like potatoes or by placing a wooden board on each side of the row and filling with peat. It is also a good idea to surround the plants with a collar of corrugated cardboard before you do any form of earthing (see figure 84). This holds the leaves together, preventing soil getting into the celery hearts.

You can begin the earthing up and blanching procedures when the leaves

are 12–15 in (30–38 cm) high. Always leave the green leaves exposed and increase the height of blanching up the stem in stages over several weeks. Six to eight weeks at least will be needed to blanch stems and heart.

Once fully earthed up, the soil gives considerable frost protection to the plants and if you cover the leaves with straw and similar material as well, you can lift late maturing varieties from the soil into early winter in most areas.

USEFUL TIP

Celery tea is said to be a good medicinal aid to help rheumatism. Pour a pint (½ liter) of boiling water over 1 oz (25 gms) of seed to make the tea. *When using celery seed for medicinal and culinary purposes, be sure the seed has not been treated with disease-preventing chemicals.*

Harvesting

Celeriac: plants can be pulled as soon as the roots are large enough. Generally they are lifted in October/November and stored in sand or peat for winter use.

Celery – self-blanching: lift as soon as the plants are large enough, usually from early September or earlier if grown under polyethylene.

Celery – blanched: many people claim the flavor is best after frost but you can begin to harvest this type of celery from September onwards – as soon as the inner heart is developed. When it is ready to lift remove the soil or

A modern celery type.

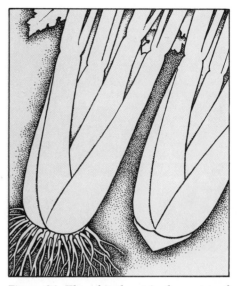

Figure 86: The white heart in the center of the root is very succulent.

blanching material from around the stems as you want to lift the roots. Shake off the soil and cut off the loose fibrous roots with a sharp knife. Try to retain the white heart in the centre of the root however – it is one of the best pieces of blanched celery.

Possible Problems

Brown spots on the leaves, usually spreading in the fall, are caused by celery leaf spot fungus. Protective seed treatment has considerably reduced the chance of infection (the better stocks of seed are already treated with Thiram when purchased) but you can control the disease, should it occur, with sprays of bordeaux mixture or maneb- or zineb-based materials.

Celery fly or leaf miner may cause trouble that you can identify by brown blisters which appear on the leaves from May. Pick off infested leaf parts and pinch to destroy the small larvae which tunnel between the two surfaces of the leaves. Where attacks persist treat with malathion spray.

Slugs can be a problem with earthed up celery. Buy special slug baits and use according to directions.

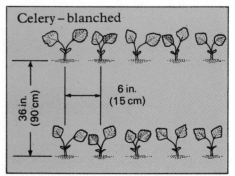
Celery – blanched

36 in. (90 cm)

6 in. (15 cm)

Chicory and Endives

Shredded chicons make good salad ingredients.

Forced roots at harvest time.

The plump, cream and white forced shoots of chicory (*Cichorium intybus*), called 'chicons', provide succulent, crisp salad in winter. The young blanched leaves are superb for mixed salads, to eat with cheese as a light snack, mixed with prawns and french dressing as an appetizer or as an additional sandwich filling. Chicons can also be wrapped in bacon and braised.

Left in the ground a second year, chicory produces attractive sky blue

Chicory growing in mid-summer.

flowers for an herbaceous border.

Site and Soil
Pretty well all garden sites are suitable, but avoid those that are very heavily shaded. All well cultivated soils are suitable, but it is best to grow them in soils which have had manure and well-rotted compost added for previous crops. Raising chicory in freshly manured soils or soils which dry out considerably in summer encourages twisted forked shoots which are not easy to fit into containers.

Sowing Instructions
Sow variety 'Witloof' (French endive) in rows in the garden in late spring, just covering the seed with soil. Single out the seedlings to the correct distance apart, 6 in (15 cm) as soon as they are large enough to separate easily with your fingers. Space the rows 15–18 in (38–45 cm) apart.

How to Grow
Hoe occasionally to kill weeds and in very dry weather give a few heavy waterings to help to swell the roots.

Harvesting
When the leaves start to turn yellow in October/November and before there is a hard frost, lift the roots with a spade or fork. Holding the root in one hand twist off the leaves with the other and cut or snap off the thin root end to give plump roots 8 in (21 cm) long. Store these roots in a box of dry peat or sand in a cool, frost-free place.

From December to March put five or six roots upright in an 8 in (21 cm) diameter flower pot (more roots can be placed in a larger container such as a wooden box), packing damp sand, light soil or peat around and over the

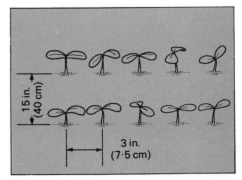

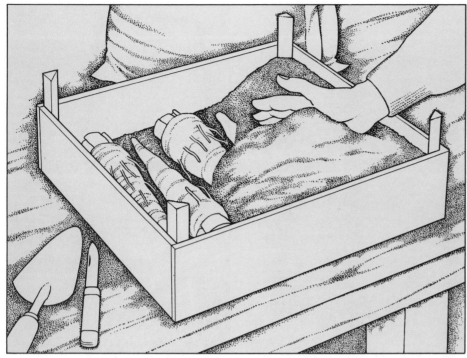

Figure 87: Storing lifted roots for later forcing.

if you re-cover them immediately, it is possible to harvest a second crop of thin leaves. Bring a few roots into the forcing area each week and this will provide you with a succession of chicons.

Possible Problems
There are none.

roots to give them a fairly deep covering. Invert a size larger pot and cover the holes. Keep the soil moist and in a temperature of 50°F (10°C), and every root will form a chicon in approximately three to four weeks. Warmer temperatures will give faster growth but keep the soil damp and the shoots completely dark – if they come into contact with light the leaves will turn green and bitter tasting.

Pick the chicons by just snapping them from the root. After this it is usual practice to discard the roots, but

Figure 88: Potting up roots for forcing.
Figure 89: Pick leaves for salads.

Roots in the foreground are forced to produce the chicons seen on the left.

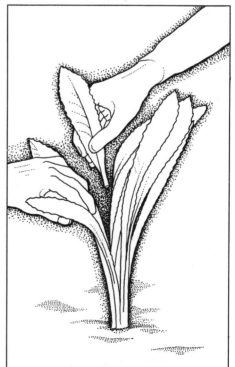

Endive.

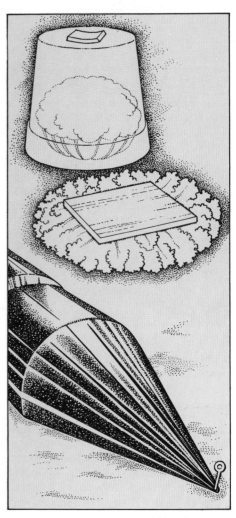
Figure 90: Various ways of blanching.

ENDIVE

Perhaps more popular in France than other places, endive (*Cichorium endivia*) is a useful salad crop, especially in early winter when lettuce crops have ended everywhere, except in heated greenhouses. It is often listed in seed catalogs with lettuce and chicory, but as the Latin name indicates it is really correct to place it with chicory as it is a member of the same genus. There are two main types of endive – the Batavian, which resembles a cos lettuce, and the curled, which has divided and curled leaves.

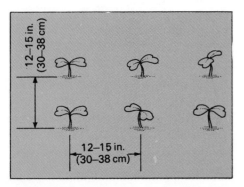

Site and Soil
All garden sites and any well-cultivated garden soil are suitable. Soils which have been improved over several years by adding well-rotted manure and compost will give the best results.

Sowing Instructions
Take a chance on sowing in April to provide a summer crop, but only if your summers are fairly cool and moist. You will, however, obtain more successful crops from sowings of the hardy 'Broad-leaved Batavian', (otherwise known as Batavian), type in late June to early August to mature in the fall. Sow in rows 12–15 in (30–38 cm) apart, where you want the crops to be, as both the check caused by actual transplanting of seedlings and dry weather affecting the early sown crop can cause the plants to form seed heads prematurely.

How to Grow
Thin the seedlings to stand 12–15 in (30–38 cm) apart (the wider spacing

for the main sowing). Hoe occasionally to control weeds and apply a top dressing of nitrogenous fertilizer or liquid feed to encourage the desired rapid growth.

Harvesting
When the plants are well developed either cover with an upturned flower pot or place a square of light board over the center of the plant. This blanches the leaves over a period of three to six weeks according to speed of growth and makes them more succulent and less bitter to taste. If you cover winter crops with polyethylene tunnels, use black polyethylene as this will blanch the plants.

You can extend cropping by lifting the plants carefully, planting them in boxes of soil and storing them in a dark and frost-free shed. The frost protection extends the life of these plants and the darkness does the blanching.

Possible Problems
None so long as you encourage rapid growth in summer (see How to Grow).

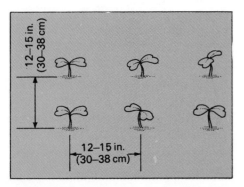

Cucumbers

CUCUMBERS under cover

The long smooth skinned cucumbers (*Cucsumis sativus*) sold in the shops all the year round are varieties suited to growing in greenhouse and frame. They really demand a warm 65°F (18°C), moist atmosphere and protection from pollination by insects.

Site and Soil

It is necessary to have a greenhouse, lean-to sun lounge, cold frame or polyethylene tunnel house to grow these cucumbers. The growing medium needs to contain a considerable amount of organic material. Synthetic soil mixes are useful in the home greenhouse especially since they are sterilized. Growing cucumber vines in containers is a good idea, particularly if you want no more than two or three plants. One strong, well-grown plant will produce more than ten good cucumbers.

If you have access to strawy manure, build a bed of several 4–5 in (10–12·5 cm) layers of manure, and good garden soil or loam up to 2 ft (60cm) capping finally with soil.

Sowing Instructions

Sow single seeds in 3½–4¼ in (9–11 cm) pots half filled with seed compost, any time from January to April. Remember 64°F (18°C) temperature is required for these plants. If sowing in unheated structures, delay sowing until April. The seed germinates very quickly, given sufficient warmth, and once the first two leaves open above the rim, fill up the pot with further compost. The cucumber is stem rooting and more roots will be made into the new compost.

How to Grow

When the stems are about 9–12 in (23–30 cm) long, the plants will be ready to plant out in the cropping site. Provide support for plants grown in greenhouses, either with canes or wires. As the main stem of the cucumber develops, tie it carefully to the cane or string. As it reaches the top of the cane, pinch out the growing tip. Side shoots (laterals) will then develop – pinch the growing tip out, either two leaves past the first fruit or certainly once the stem is 18–24 in (45–60 cm) long. Stop sub-laterals completely after one or two leaves have formed. Leave these side growths to hang or tie them to cross wires or a net-like backing support.

Watch for the two kinds of flower to

Cucumbers in the garden.

form – the male flowers have just a simple stem and should be removed; and the female flowers which have an immature cucumber behind the flower. If you leave the male flowers on the plant and bees cross-pollinate, you will get misshapen bitter cucumbers as a result.

If you are growing the cucumbers in frames, you don't need to provide support but you should pinch them out in a similar way. Stop the first main stem at six to eight leaves or when the plant reaches across the frame. Stop side shoots at two leaves past the first fruit,

Example of slicing cucumbers.

or when they are 18–24 in (45–60 cm) long. Keep the sub-laterals, which develop, very short and remove them altogether when the frame becomes too densely filled with foliage. Lift fruits on frame-grown plants and place them on a piece of wood or tile to keep them clean. Give the plants liquid feed every ten to fourteen days when the first fruits have started to swell.

> ## USEFUL TIPS
> 1. Select F₁ hybrid 'all female' flowering varieties to avoid the problems of cross pollination. These varieties need temperatures of 65–70°F (18–21°C).
> 2. Mulch midsummer with potting compost 3–4 in (7·5–10 cm) deep around the stem to encourage new root growth and more cucumbers.
> 3. Avoid growing cucumbers in the same greenhouse soil one year after another.

Harvesting

Cut as soon as the cucumbers have reached full length and have swollen nicely. Don't leave them until they start to turn yellowish-green.

Possible Problems

Keep the greenhouse regularly sprayed with water to encourage plant

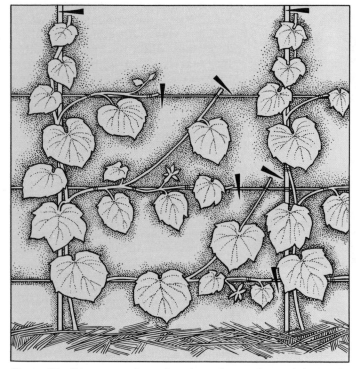

Figure 91: Diagrammatic explanation of cucumber training under glass. Laterals and sub-laterals are tied to cross wires.

Cordon-trained cucumbers in a greenhouse – note how sub-laterals are left to hang.

growth. It will also help to reduce the likelihood of attack by red spider mite as this pest likes a hot, dry atmosphere. Red spider mites turn cucumber leaves yellowish-bronze rather than rich green.

When the temperature is warm enough and growth rapid, problems are few.

CUCUMBERS OUTDOORS

Since many gardeners don't have a greenhouse, this is the way cucumbers are mostly grown – outdoors. In fact, cucumbers are one of the highlights of the summer garden. Pickling cucumbers are grown the same way as those for slicing and salads.

Site and Soil

A sunny position and soil that has been improved by the addition of

Figure 92: Male and female flowers.

plenty of organic matter – rotted manures, compost and/or peat moss, or anything that will retain moisture – are needed.

Sowing Instructions

Either sow indoors in Jiffy 7 or peat pots in April/early May or outside. If raising indoors sow two seeds per pot and thin to one as soon as the seedlings are large enough to handle. Plant out 3–4 ft (90–120 cm) apart in late May/early June and *after* the chance of frost if Hotkap protection is not available. You can sow a group of three seeds outdoors and thin down to the strongest plant once established.

USEFUL TIP

It is not necessary to plant cucumbers, and other cucurbits for that matter, on a 'mound' or 'hill' of soil and compost. In fact, the reverse may be practiced, that is, sowing the seeds in slightly recessed areas is recommended in many sandy soils. Cucumbers need plenty of moisture in the rooting area but *not* waterlogged soil.

How to Grow

Let the plants run and give occasional liquid feeds and plenty of water in dry weather. Although it is not essential, it is best to stop the main stem at six to eight leaves, thus encouraging the side shoots to develop.

Be sure to *retain* the male flowers on *ridge* cucumbers. Cross pollination is essential in these plants and some hand fertilization, (i.e. taking the male flower, and placing the pollen-bearing parts in the mouth of the female flower) will help to set fruit.

In the small garden, space is saved when vines are trained up a trellis or chicken wire fence.

Harvesting

Cut the fruits as soon as they are large enough – the more you cut the more the plant will produce. One well grown plant will yield sufficient cucumbers for one or two people from late July up until frost occurs.

Possible Problems

Watch for slugs at the early stages. If plants are allowed to get dry, mildew (a grayish growth on the leaves) is likely to occur. Use a systemic fungicide to control this.

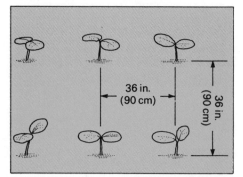

36 in. (90 cm)

36 in. (90 cm)

Herbs

A number of herbs make very attractive plants in their own right. The stately evergreen bay, the powder blue flowers of rosemary and the ground-covering purple and cream variegated sage provide excellent examples. It is their attractive and appealing aromatic flavors which bring them into happy partnership with vegetables, however, and all vegetable gardeners should find some space to grow herbs. They can be grown in between vegetables in the plot or away from it altogether as a small herb border.

The strongest flavors will be produced by plants that are grown in full sunlight and well-drained soils. Don't worry too much if you are unable to provide the ideal conditions, however, because in practice the common herbs will grow easily in all soils although heavy wet soils make for a short life in some herbs (two to three years).

Most people require small quantities of herbs for flavoring – a sprig of mint for new potatoes and a sprinkling of chives for cream cheese, for example. A few plants grown in pots, window boxes or tubs placed near the back door will prove very handy and herbs used fresh will yield up maximum flavor.

Taking the convenience aspect even further, a few selected plants can be grown indoors on the window sill, either in small troughs or in hanging

Figure 94: Formal trained bay trees. (Above) Bay tree growing without root restriction.

Figure 93: Herbs grown in strawberry pots.

plant containers. The perennial kinds like mint, sage and thyme are good for this, and so is parsley, although if it is close to hand you will find yourself using it so often you will soon need to replace it!

Don't be afraid to pinch the shoots of most herbs regularly. Plants such as sage and thyme will grow away again strongly after each pinching and produce more compact and bushy plants.

BASIL
Basil (*Ocimum basilicum*) has fragrant foliage with an almost clovelike flavor. It is most used in tomato dishes but is also good with squash and other vegetables. It is as easy to grow from seed as marigolds or zinnias or buy seedlings. Most basil varieties grow to about 2 ft (60 cm) but there is a small-leaved form only 6 in (15 cm) tall.

BAY
Fresh and dried leaves of this evergreen (*Laurus nobilis*) are used com-bined with other herbs in a bouquet garni and on their own to flavor many dishes. Although it is a hardy evergreen, it will not survive winters outdoors in the North. Plants grown in pots are best taken into a light garage or an outbuilding for protection in the depths of winter.

Over the years bay will grow into a small tree, but it also responds to pot culture, either as a low bushy plant, possibly trimmed to a pyramid, or grown on a stem to form the typical standard round-headed plant seen in tubs outside restaurants. Shaped plants will need trimming with pruners two or three times a year to retain their shape, but don't use shears as these cut the leaves in half.

You can obtain new plants by rooting young tips when stems start to harden in July/August. Once well rooted, grow on in potting compost and then plant in the garden when they are well established (September and March/April are good times to plant in the open garden in mild climates).

Leaves can be dried for future use in several ways, the easiest being to place several in a shallow tray in a very cool oven. Dried leaves are likely to have a stronger flavor than leaves which are gathered for use fresh.

CHIVES

Grassy chives (*Allium schoenoprasum*) chopped foliage gives a delicate onion flavor to salads, egg dishes, cream cheese, soups and sauces.

Sow seeds at any time except during winter in the North. But to get the largest plants in a hurry, buy plants from a specialist or divide the potted plants carried by markets in the fresh produce section.

Chives flourish in a sunny or part shaded border. Once plants are established cut them back to the soil regularly to encourage new growth. Lift and divide established clumps every few years in spring or fall. Cut off flower heads as they appear.

Chives.

The bright green color is lost if the leaves are dried and it is much better either to keep supplies of fresh leaves coming along or deep freeze some.

DANDELION

Dandelion (*Taraxacum officinale*)

can be classed as a herb as its roots may be roasted and ground to make either a coffee substitute or additive. Alternatively it may be grown as a vegetable – to use the leaves raw in salads (the large-leaved varieties available from specialist seedsmen are particularly suitable), cooked like spinach or used as a flavoring for soups, for example, like sorrel. The ubiquitous dandelion is such a weed that it seems strange to buy seeds, but for culinary uses, seed-grown varieties are better.

Sow it in spring (April is a good month) in small groups and thin the plants as they grow to stand 6 in (15 cm) apart. Blanch them the following spring with an upturned pot or box. This will give you a succession of blanched leaves for salads. After blanching and picking the leaves, give the plants a rest to rebuild their vigor before blanching a few more leaves.

If you wish to use the roots of dandelion, you can harvest them at any time after the growth has begun to slow down in the fall.

Dandelion.

Dill.

DILL

This plant (*Anethum graveolens*) is grown for its thin feathery foliage. It is an annual, so must be raised each year from a spring sowing. Give it a fair amount of room, because plants will grow to 3 ft (90 cm) in height. If you are growing several plants space them 9–12 in (23–30 cm) apart.

Both leaves and seeds give a flavor akin to caraway and aniseed, but use them sparingly because the flavor is quite strong. Use chopped leaves to flavor soups, sauces and savoury stews and add seeds to vinegar to produce dill vinegar for pickled gherkins. Try sprinkling a little seed over sliced cucumber in sandwiches.

Florence Fennel.

FENNEL

There are two plants with the common name 'fennel' – the perennial *Foeniculum vulgare*, common fennel, grown only for the foliage to use as a herb and *Foeniculum vulgare dulce*, the Florence fennel or finocchio which has similar feather foliage but is also grown for the swollen leaf bases, which may be eaten raw in salads or cooked to flavor stews.

These fennels are tender perennials so, in most of the USA, they are grown as annuals from seeds each year.

Sow common fennel in March/May in rows 15 in (38 cm) apart. If you want seed heads to develop so as to use the seed for herbal purposes, go for the early sowing. Thin the seedlings to stand 12 in (30 cm) apart. Leaves cannot easily be stored so either deep freeze some or pot up some plants to grow indoors to provide winter flavoring. Cut seed heads in September and October and hang them upside down in paper bags to dry.

Florence fennel grows best in cool, moist weather, so in most regions the seed is sown in summer so the bulbs can mature in the fall. In regions where summers remain cool, the seeds can be sown in spring. Sow in rows 20 in (50 cm) apart and thin the seedlings to 9–12 in (23–30 cm) apart. Put them in rich, well-drained soil in a sunny position. As the leaf bases start to swell, hoe soil up around them to give the blanched white color.

GARLIC

Although garlic (*Allium sativum*) is used as a flavoring it is in fact a form of onion and can be grown in just the

Garlic.

same way as shallots and onion sets. Divide a bought bulb into cloves and plant these 6 in (15 cm) apart in rows 12 in (30 cm) apart. Plant in October for harvestable bulbs in spring/summer in mild climates and in spring for bulbs in the fall in Northern regions. Lift the bulbs when the leaves start to yellow and put them in trays to dry.

Garlic cloves should be crushed, not chopped, for use in cooking.

HORSERADISH

Shredded slivers from the white cylindrical roots of horseradish (*Armoracia rusticana*), used fresh in cream sauces provide the traditional, hot mustardy flavored relish to go with roast beef. The fresh root scrapings can also be used to flavor fish and other dishes to give a pungent flavor.

Any small piece of root will grow, but the top crown-shooting part (which is unusable for culinary purposes) is best. Plant in spring, 18 in (45 cm) apart, but plant sparingly because once established the deep

searching thongy roots soon become very invasive and take some digging out. Leaves will grow 2 ft (60 cm) or so high. Lift the roots from November and store in sand and peat for use when the soil is frozen.

Horseradish roots cut to make planting thongs.

MARJORAM – sweet

Used in mixed herbs with thyme or as an alternative flavoring to thyme, sweet marjoram (*Origanum majorana*) is actually a perennial. However it is best treated as an annual as it will die outdoors in winter in all but the most mild climates.

Sow the seed indoors in March and plant out the seedlings later 9–12 in (23–30 cm) apart in a warm sunny position. Alternatively, sow direct into the growing position in spring. Gather the leaves as they get large enough and before the plant develops flower heads. Chop them for use fresh and dry some for winter supplies.

Marjoram.

For a stronger flavor and to provide fresh leaves in winter grow pot marjoram (*Origanum onites*), of which there are two types, a green-stemmed, white-flowered form and purple stemmed and flowered form.

Although pot marjoram or oregano is a perennial, it is not always winter-hardy in the North. Grow in a warm, protected place in the garden. Sow seeds in spring in drills 12 in (30 cm) apart. Thin the seedlings or transplant them 12 in (30 cm) apart. Or buy plants from specialists.

MINT

The common mint (*Mentha spicata*) or spearmint (as shown in the photograph) is the species most frequently found in gardens and is most recommended for mint sauce, although there are more than six kinds frequently listed in catalogs. Another

Mint. Figure 95: (right) To get early mint, grow indoors in a pot.

type worthy of note is *Mentha rotundifolia* the round-leaved or Apple Mint, a type not affected by the disease rust and claimed by many as the best to use with new potatoes. There is a very attractive white variegated form of apple mint.

The growth of mint usually needs restraining rather than encouraging, and a good tip is to plant the pieces of root, from which new plants are grown, in an old plastic bucket, or similar container with a hole in the base. Bury this in the garden to within 2 in (5 cm) of the rim and fill it with

Parsley.

soil. Mint roots are then contained and do not spread all over the garden.

Lift some roots in the fall and grow in pots indoors to supply young sprigs in winter and early spring.

PARSLEY

Parsley (*Petroselinum crispum*) is one of the most useful of all our herbs – ideal for garnishing, in sauces and stuffings and as a constituent of bouquet garni. It is a biennial plant which will produce leaves for several seasons if the flowering stems are cut out before they fully develop. It is available in several varieties which vary in the degree of curling and cut edges to the leaves.

Sow the seed in rows 9–12 in (23–30 cm) apart in spring for summer and fall use and late July/early August for winter use. Thin the seedlings to stand 6–12 in apart (15–30 cm). Protect the winter crop in a cold frame.

Parsley seed is slow to germinate and the old cottage gardener's tip of pouring boiling water along the drill sometimes speeds germination. Avoid germination failure by not using old seed. Parsley will stand some shade and produces a lot more leaf if it is given the occasional liquid feed. Fresh leaves are by far the best, but you can ensure additional winter supplies by air-drying bunches of foliage in summer and rubbing them down before storing in sealed jars. To retain the

Rosemary. Figure 96: (below) Plant cuttings of rosemary or thyme in sandy soil.

Young plants will yield the most useful flavor foliage in well-drained soil and a warm sunny site.

Plants from all species can be raised easily from seed sown from March to June. Propagate from cuttings rooted in sandy compost in late spring.

Trim off the purple flowers before they open. Cut plants back to get a harvest of shoots and also to encourage more basal growth and foliage. Plants also become rough and untidy-looking if not regularly trimmed back. The rather woody stems and thick leaves gathered for storing take quite a long time to dry. Keep them in a warm, airy place and once dry just rub the leaves in your hands to break them up. Store in an airtight jar. One good bush cut over twice in a season will provide quite enough sage for a year's use.

THYME
Common garden thyme (*Thymus vulgaris*) is a really attractive plant. Used as a low decorative shrub and planted close to the path or near the back door, you will be aware of the delicious thyme fragrance every time you brush by. Young shoots need cutting to dry for herb use, but if left, the 8–12 in (20–30 cm) plants are covered with pretty purple flowers in June. There are very many thyme species, among them a golden-leaved form, *Thymus vulgaris* 'Aureus'. Another particularly attractive type is the lemon thyme, *Thymus x citriodorus* which has silver and golden-leaved forms.

Choose a sunny site and light, sandy soil for these plants. Propagate by cuttings taken with a heel in May/June or raise common thyme by sowing seed any time from March to July. Once established, put out young plants in the garden 9–12 in (23–30 cm) apart or grow in pots and window boxes.

color dip fresh leaves in boiling water for a minute or so, shake dry and then dry quickly in a cooling oven.

ROSEMARY
You can raise the shrubby evergreen rosemary (*Rosmarinus officinalis*) from seed sown in spring and summer or by propagating from cuttings in August, September and October. Lighter soils give best results and although it is a virtually hardy plant, it is not reliably winter-hardy in the North. New growth will often come through again from the base where the plants have been damaged by frost. Rosemary grows well in pots.

Try to find a space towards the front of a small shrub border. Plants will grow quite large and will spread, but to no more than 2–3 ft (60–90 cm) high if trimmed back in spring to keep tidy. There are some very attractive gold and silver variegated forms, but these are not as strong growing as the green types.

SAGE
Sage (*Salvia officinalis*) is another shrubby herb and as well as the true species with its attractive grayish-green leaves, there are purple-green and cream and pink and green variegated forms. All make attractive low shrubs and can be used as ground cover in a purely decorative role.

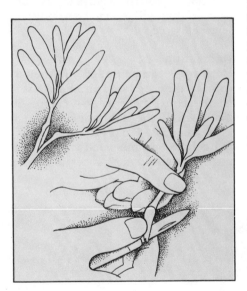

Sage.

Thyme.

Kohlrabi and Rutabaga

The kohlrabi (*Brassica caulorapa*) is an interesting and attractive plant to grow. Its swollen stem, which looks like a 'root', can either be cooked or sliced raw to eat in salads, and it tastes like a mixture of turnip and cabbage. Red- or green-colored varieties are available.

Rutabagas (*Brassica napobrassica*) are sometimes confused with turnips but they are in fact larger and sweeter. The one-time practice of field-growing great big rutabaga roots and selling them as vegetables when they were actually more suited to cattle food has happily largely been replaced by the more enlightened approach of growing smaller roots for home use. Both rutabagas and kohlrabi are very useful root vegetables, but may take too much space in the small garden.

Site and Soil

Pretty well any site, as long as it is not too overshadowed or dry, and any well-cultivated garden soil are suitable for both vegetables.

Sowing Instructions

Sow kohlrabi any time from March to early August, and for a succession of crops, sow two or three batches over this period. Sow rutabaga in May or June. Space seed rows 15 in (38 cm) apart and thin seedlings to stand 6–9 in (15–23 cm) apart in a row. The smaller roots at the closer spacing, lifted while they are young, are the best to eat.

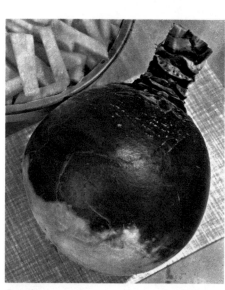

Rutabaga.

How to Grow

Dust acid soils with lime before sowing. Other than this just hoe occasionally to destroy weeds and water well, ideally with some liquid fertilizer, in very dry weather. If plants experience a check in growth because of dry conditions, they will tend to be woody and less palatable.

Harvesting

Both crops can be pulled and used as soon as they are large enough, that is from about 2½–3 in (6–7·5 cm) in diameter. If the kohlrabi gets much more than 3½–4 in (9–10 cm) across it is likely to become woody in the center. Later sowings of kohlrabi can be pulled and stored in sand or peat to use into the winter. Where frost is not too severe the rutabaga could be left in the ground and used as required.

Possible Problems

Pretty well trouble-free although the same pests and diseases that attack all brassicas can occur, including club root and root maggots. See cabbage for controls.

USEFUL TIP

To time the kohlrabi sowing, remember it is ready to pull in twelve weeks, given reasonable seed germination conditions. Sown early and widely spaced, rutabagas will grow to a large size and are super for children to carve out into faces for Hallowe'en. The long columnar stump which carries the leaves forms the neck and the flesh glows pink if lit inside with a candle.

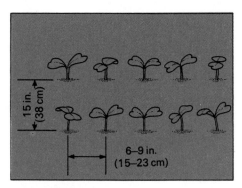

15 in. (38 cm)
6–9 in. (15–23 cm)

Green Kohlrabi.

Red Kohlrabi.

Leeks

Leeks (*Allium porrum*) are really tough, hardy plants which will survive hard frost and are thus a useful winter vegetable. They are members of the onion family and one of the easiest to grow. When plants grow strongly they produce masses of vigorous white root which breaks up heavy soil and, after lifting, leaves soil much more crumbly and friable. If your garden soil is heavy and tends to stay in great lumps, try growing a patch of leeks (as well as adding plenty of well-rotted organic matter) to improve the texture of the soil.

Site and Soil
Most sites, except those which are heavily shaded, and all well-cultivated soils are suitable.

Sowing Instructions
Sow early in the year, in February/March, under cover to get the earliest and largest blanched stems. An outdoor sowing in March/April will provide adequate crops, however. Transplant early seedlings into the growing site in May, and the outdoor raised plants in June and even into July. Space plants 9 in (23 cm) apart in the row, the rows 12–15 in (30–38 cm) apart. Closer spacing produces smaller roots which are easier to handle in the kitchen.

How to Grow
Water the indoor seedlings and those in rows outdoors well before transplanting. Use a dibble to make a good hole 1 in (2·5 cm) or more in diameter, 6–8 in (15–20 cm) deep, drop the young plant into this and water it in. There is no need to fill back any soil, the effect of watering is sufficient to cover the roots with soil and the space allows some room for blanched stem development before hoeing and weathering fill in the hole. When lifting the seedlings from outdoor rows they are easier to handle if you shorten the leaves by a third, cutting them

Figure 97: Use a dibble to plant out. (Above) Leeks being harvested.

back level with a knife. Leave them long enough to just reach the top of the hole as you drop them in.

Control weeds by hoeing between the rows and apply a dilute liquid fertilizer in dry weather. When hoeing, draw soil up round the stem a little at a time to lengthen the blanched stem, but not so high that it goes over the point where the leaf joins the stem because if soil gets into the blanched stem the leeks are gritty.

USEFUL TIP

Reduce the length of big old leaves by half to encourage a greater length of blanched stem.

Harvesting
Dig up the leeks as you need them from September to April. If you want to clear the ground for other crops in spring lift the leeks and just 'heel them in' (covering the roots and stem with soil) using a spare part of the garden. This heeling in also helps extend the period leeks remain fit to eat, as once lifted the plant becomes less quick to

make the second season growth which leads to flowering.

Possible Problems
Should orange dusty spots occur on the leaves, lift plants and destroy leaves (the stem will be edible). Be sure to rotate crops thereafter to avoid future problems.

Figure 98: Young plants must be watered in at transplanting.

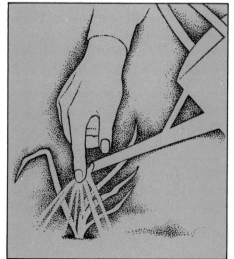

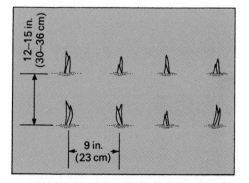

Lettuces

There are four main groups of lettuce (*Lactuca sativa*) varieties – the rounded cabbage types which are further subdivided into soft leaved or butterhead; the curly crisp types; the upright Cos lettuce and finally the open-hearted cut-leaved or oak-leaved types. All require similar cultural conditions although many varieties have specific seasons for sowing and harvesting which are best followed for assured crops.

LETTUCE – BOSTON OR BUTTERHEAD

The Boston or butterhead lettuce types are the most popular lettuces now in the home plot as well as market and there are many varieties. The common name of butterhead aptly refers to the rich green heads, sometimes yellowish in the heart and rather soft-leaved.

Site and Soil

Any well-cultivated soil is suitable and open sunny sites are best – although most lettuces tolerate some shade, especially as hot summer weather arrives.

Varieties

Fast-maturing (about 75 days), small kinds such as 'Buttercrunch', 'Bibb', 'Tom Thumb' are best for spring sowing, maturing well before hot weather arrives. 'Deer Tongue' (also called 'Matchless') is tolerant of heat. 'Dark Green Boston' is a larger variety requiring 80 days to mature.

Sowing Instruction

Sow indoors in late winter and plant out in early spring under cloches or in cold frames for the earliest crops. As soon as soil conditions allow (i.e. the soil is sufficiently dry and free from frost) sow in the open ground in rows 12 in (30 cm) apart.

Sow a few seeds every 14 days

Boston lettuce.

throughout spring so you have a succession of lettuce crops. In regions where summers are very hot and dry, most lettuces languish, but a few varieties, such as 'Deer Tongue', 'Ruby', 'Salad Bowl' and 'Oak Leaf', are heat resistant. In late summer, start sowing lettuces for fall and early winter use. Where cold, freezing weather arrives early, plant lettuce in a cold frame or protect under polyethylene tunnels. Such sheeting is now available from many supply houses.

How to Grow

Prick out your indoor raised seedlings into small pots (peat pots are ideal) before planting out. Thin out the crops sown directly into the ground as soon as they are large enough to handle, spacing them 9–12 in (23–30 cm) apart. Water the plants well in dry weather, giving them an occasional good soaking, rather than repeated light waterings. Give liquid fertilizer in dry weather to speed growth.

Little cultural treatment is needed.

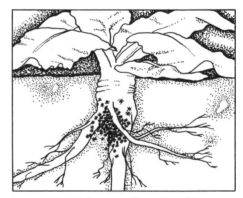

Figure 99: If leaves wilt, root aphis may be attacking the plant.

Harvesting

When the weather is warm, crops will be ready to eat within 70 days of sowing. At cooler times of the year they will take up to 90 days. Before cutting to eat, bear down gently on the heart of the lettuce with the back of your hand to test its firmness. Never be tempted to pinch it as this causes bruising of the heart.

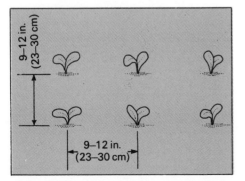

Possible Problems
You can avoid seedling damage in early spring and in wet conditions by using slug bait.

LETTUCE – CRISP
This group includes the large curly crisp lettuces, particularly popular in USA where they are usually known as the 'Great Lakes' and 'Iceberg'. Very crisp leaf ribs and hearts are produced by all varieties which stand well in hot weather and, given ideal growing conditions, will grow to a great size. These are not, however, prized by home gardeners.

Figure 100: Lettuce can be grown under cloches or cold frames through the winter.

Site and Soil
Dig all the organic matter you can obtain into the soil to be sown with lettuce. Well-rotted compost or manure thoroughly mixed with the garden soil retains moisture, and gives the best conditions. As they are shallow-rooted plants it is not necessary to dig the compost deep into the ground. Avoid sites which are heavily shaded by trees overhead and where there is competition from tree roots for moisture. These make it difficult to grow good lettuce.

Sowing Instructions
Sow in the growing site in rows 12–15 in (30–38 cm) apart every four-teen days or so from March to July. If winter conditions allow (i.e. if frost is not too severe) you can also sow hardy and fast-maturing varieties like 'Premier Great Lakes' in October to over-winter under cloches or in frames. Alternatively sow them indoors in January/February and plant out in spring. They will be ready to harvest in May.

How to Grow
It is much better in summer to sow small quantities successively than to transplant seedlings. You can thin out seedlings from the sown row and transplant them for early summer maturing crops. This extends the cropping by two to three weeks from one sowing. Thin the seedlings to stand 12 in (30 cm) apart, or a little wider. A wider spacing ensures that largest plants grow in midsummer.

Harvesting
Once the centers start to curl in you can begin to cut the lettuce. As it grows so rapidly start to cut just before the centers are firm and fully developed so you get the longest possible harvest period. As with butterhead test firmness of the heart with the back of your upturned fingers, being careful not to bruise the heart.

Crisp lettuce.

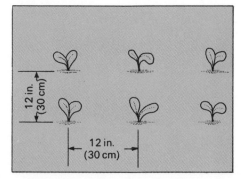

Cos lettuce.

Possible Problems
Sparrows and other small birds can play havoc at an early stage by eating the leaves of lettuce seedlings. Prevent this by covering the seedlings with polyethylene tunnel cloches or, for an alternative practical method of protection, push short sticks into the soil along the row and stretch occasional strands of black cotton between them.

LETTUCE – COS or ROMAINE
Straight upright leaves typify the cos lettuce, which is sometimes called leaf lettuce. The very big-leaved varieties will produce crisp white hearts, and provide an appetizing alternative to celery. In my experience these types

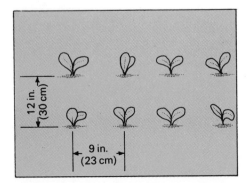

are not quite as easy to grow as the tightly self-hearting butterhead lettuce. However the crisp texture and good flavor makes it well worth persevering at growing this type. Romaine is popular for Caesar Salad.

Site and Soil
Any open site and any well-cultivated soil is suitable.

Sowing Instructions
These are the same as instructions for the butterhead lettuce. That is – sow in late January/early February indoors, transplant the seedlings singly into small pots and plant out early spring. Sow in the growing site at fortnightly intervals from March to June. Make drills ½–1 in (1–2·5 cm) deep and just cover the seeds with soil. Sow again in late summer.

How to Grow
Thin and plant out seedlings so they are 9 in (23 cm) apart and with 12 in (30 cm) between the rows.

Very large-leaved kinds like the 'Parris White' or 'Dark Green Cos' both require about 85 days to reach full maturity, but leaves may be gathered for use before this. They will

form the densest blanched hearts if you tie in the outer leaves with raffia or string.

Harvesting
Start to gather the lettuces as soon as the centers begin to develop. By the time you are harvesting the last plants in the row the hearts will be fully developed. If the cutting of any lettuce for eating is delayed particularly in very hot dry weather, plants burst their hearts as the flower head develops. Such plants are then bitter to taste.

Possible Problems
Aphids can attack lettuce in mid-summer and may overwinter. Maintaining hygienic conditions by keeping the plot clear of weeds and old crop remains, which may carry pests, helps considerably in avoiding overwintered plant attack. The likelihood of this pest can also be reduced in the summer by keeping the lettuce well watered and thus growing fast. Use sprays based on malathion to knock out aphids quickly.

USEFUL TIP

Never plant lettuce seedlings too deep: this can prevent the formation of hearts. The seedlings should flop over when first transplanted: they soon straighten.

LETTUCE – OTHER KINDS
Fringed, curled and cut leaves on open centered plants constitute the majority of varieties under this heading. They include the loose-leaved 'Salad Bowl', which produces an abundance of

Figure 101: Tie loosely round the outer leaves to improve the hearts.

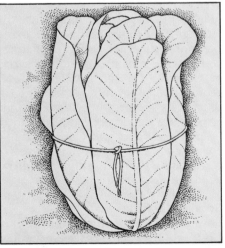

Corn Salad.

Red-leaved lettuces such as 'Salad Trim', 'Prizehead' and 'Ruby' are decorative in the salad bowl.

succulent stem, can be used like celery – either cooked or fresh in salads.

Corn salad (*Valerianella olitoria*) is not a lettuce at all but its leaves are often mixed with lettuce in salads. It is quite hardy and its seeds are usually sown in late summer in the North where, with protection, the leaves are harvested through winter and into spring.

Site and Soil
All garden soils are suitable. Site in similar places to other lettuce types.

Special Siting
While all lettuce may be grown as a crop in its own right or as a quick maturing intercrop between rows of vegetables which take a long time to mature, they are very adaptable plants. Varieties like 'Buttercrunch' and 'Grand Rapids' for example can be grown in window boxes.

The butterhead types grow well indoors and on a patio. Compact bright green types like 'Tom Thumb' do not look strangely out of place among flowers and the bronzed 'Ruby' is attractive as well as tasty.

Sowing Instructions
Sow all varieties, except corn salad, from April to June in 14 days successional sowings. 'Grand Rapids' can

small curled and cut leaves like endive. Another variety – 'Grand Rapids' – is useful to grow under glass to provide winter lettuce leaves for salad, as well as outdoor summer lettuce leaves. The variety 'Prizehead' may also be included in this group.

It is especially resistant to hot weather and the attractive copper bronzing makes it a novelty.

Celtuce (*Lactuca sativa angustana*) is often described as a mixture of celery and lettuce because the outer leaves are used as lettuce and the heart, including a good proportion of

also be sown in the fall for planting in greenhouses or cold frames in winter. Sow corn salad in August and September.

How to Grow
Water well in dry weather and hoe to control weeds. Thin out corn salad plants to 3–4 ins (7·5–10 cm) apart, and protect from severe frost with straw and dried grass.

Harvesting
Gather a few leaves at a time from all varieties and corn salad except celtuce.

Possible Problems
None to worry about.

Figure 102: Cut young cos lettuce leaving a stump. A second lettuce will then grow.

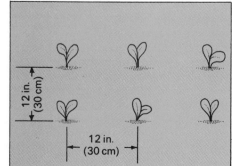

Squashes

One of the earliest and perhaps one of the fastest growing of our garden vegetables is summer squash (*Cucurbita pepo ovifera*). Since all summer squash varieties are borne on bush rather than trailing plants, even the smallest home plant can accommodate a few plants. Less common in small gardens are the fall (Butternut and Acorn) and winter (Hubbard) varieties simply because they are vines that take up space and require a long growing season. Included as summer squash are zucchini varieties (the marrows and courgettes of English and Continental gardens) and patty pan varieties that bear the white disklike fruits with scalloped edges that are almost too pretty to eat.

Site and Soil

Sunny sites are best (if there is too much shade the leaves will become very large and drawn and harvests will be reduced). An open soil containing plenty of well-rotted compost and manure to retain moisture is the ideal, although perfectly adequate crops may be produced in ordinary garden soil.

A type of zucchini.

Figure 103: Sow squash seeds on a compost heap. A jam jar protects the seedlings.

All squashes will also grow very well planted on the top of well decomposed compost heaps or heaps of rotted down leaves, lawn mowings etc. Perching plants up on the compost heap is a good idea as the large rather sprawling leaves can spread over and smother adjacent crops on small plots. Squashes will grow very fast, but to do so they demand plenty of water. This will be retained by rotted down organic matter. Given this and warm conditions the plants will grow fast.

Special Siting

In addition to planting on a compost heap you can also train climbing or trailing varieties along a fence. Alternatively you can train three plants up a wooden framework to form a wigwam shape. In general however the compact bush types are better for the 10 ft × 12 ft (3 m × 4 m) vegetable plot than the trailing kinds.

Golden zucchini.

People who live in flats and homes without gardens can grow bush or summer squash in planters, boxes or tubs placed on a patio, balcony, or outside a back door.

Sowing Instructions

Sow seed in 3½ ins (9 cm) pots – two to a pot – in early May. Single out the seedlings as soon as possible and

Figure 104: Cross pollination by hand.

Large white vegetable marrow bush squash.

transplant the young plants to the growing site in late spring when there is no more likelihood of frost. Remember, these plants are tender – one frost will kill them and you will have to start again.

An alternative method is to sow three seeds direct in each growing site in late spring, so they are timed to emerge immediately after any possibility of frost. If you do this it is a good

Vegetable marrow bush squash and zucchini (above). A fall or winter squash (below).

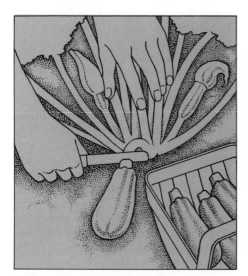
Figure 105: Use an old knife to cut squash to avoid damaging plant.

idea to cover the seeds with cloches or Hotkaps until the seedlings are well established. A simple way to get plants established is to sow two or three seeds under a Hotkap which acts as an effective cloche.

How to Grow
Keep the plants very well watered in dry weather and hoe between them to control weeds until the leaves give sufficient canopy to smother any likely weed growth. These plants produce male and female flowers and if you cross-pollinate them by hand, it will increase bearing. To do this, pick a male flower (male flowers have *no* embryo fruit behind the flowers), carefully tear off the petals and gently push the pollen-bearing anthers into several female flowers.

Harvesting
Cut all summer squash when the fruits are 4–5 ins (10–12·5 cm) long. Nearly all varieties are best harvested while still young. You can continue harvesting from late July until the first frost.

The exception to cutting young is fall and american winter squash which need a long, warm summer to fully mature. When cut, store by hanging in nets in a dry cool place. Remember that winter squash won't keep unless the fruits have fully matured on the vines.

Two or three well grown plants of most varieties will produce sufficient for the average family of four's needs.

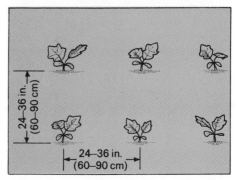

Vegetable Spaghetti.

Patty pan squash.

Perhaps the best all-time zucchini squash is 'Greyzini' but also worth seeking out are 'Clarita', 'Chefini', 'Aristocrat' and 'Ambassador'. All of these zucchini or Italian squashes are hybrids and can be expected to produce bountifully over a long period.

Perhaps the best all-time zucchini squash is 'Greyzini' but also worth seeking out are 'Clarita', 'Chefini', 'Aristocrat' and 'Ambassador'. All of these zucchini or Italian squashes are hybrids and can be expected to produce bountifully over a long period.

Although zucchini varieties are much more popular in American home gardens today than the yellow summer squash, either with or without the 'familiar crooknecks,' most gardeners still like to include a few yellow varieties. Recommended are 'Butterbar' (45 days), 'Goldneck' (50 days) and 'Early Prolific Straightneck' (50 days). As with zucchini and patty pan squash the quality of these squashes declines with age.

Among fall squash, 'Butternut' is the favorite, but its extensive vining habit eliminates it in the small garden. There are acorn winter squash varieties that form a bush, making them possibilities for small gardens. Two are 'Gold Nugget' (95 days) and bush acorn 'Table King' (75 days).

A little more bizarre are the patty pans. There are white and yellow-skinned varieties, and they should be cooked young for the best flavor.

Finally there is the squash 'Vegetable Spaghetti', which is ready for the first harvesting in 70 days from sowing, providing it has had warm growing conditions. The fruits should be cut when they are 8 ins (20 cm) or so long. To cook them place in boiling water for 20-30 minutes. Cut open the squash, remove the spaghetti-like center, season it with salt and pepper before eating. This variety is a vining plant and the runners can go all over the small garden.

USEFUL TIP

With all squashes, cucumbers and pumpkins, push the flat seeds pointed end downwards into the soil rather than sowing the flat seeds on their sides. In warm conditions all these seeds germinate in a very few days so don't leave them too long indoors after sowing without checking them.

Possible Problems

Watch out for slugs as the seedlings develop and put down slug bait if necessary. The squash vine borer is a common, persistent pest of all kinds of squash, both bush and vine types. Spray or dust plants with methoxychlor in late spring and repeat two more times at ten-day intervals. Wait one day before harvesting. Always follow container directions carefully.

Lack of moisture is likely to cause mildew in the form of a grayish mold on their leaves. Providing this is not too severe, it should not affect the crop's growth or flavor.

Varieties

Zucchini. Varieties are now available which have been especially bred to produce masses of small fruits 3–5 in (7·5–12·5 cm) long over an extended period. They include smooth, rich green skinned fruits; mottled cream and green fruits and the rich golden yellow of varieties like 'Golden Zucchini'. If the fruits are left on these plants they will develop further to give fruits 12 ins (30 cm) or so long. These may either be stuffed and baked or cooked separately.

Figure 106: Acorn squash on a tripod.

Melons and Watermelons

Melons (*Cucumis melo*), also called muskmelon or cantaloupe, need a warm dry climate to produce the best fruits. Winter melons (Persian, Honeydew, Casaba and Crenshaw types) require a long growing season (about 120 days) so are only grown in mild climate regions. Watermelon (*Citrullus vulgaris*) also requires a long-growing season and is readily grown in the South. Hybridizers have produced some watermelons for the North that are smaller and earlier-maturing, such as 'New Hampshire Midget' (70 days) and 'Sugar Baby' (75 days). No melon is really suitable for the small home plot, though, because the vines eat up space over a long growing period and then yield a small crop per vine. In the larger vegetable garden, a melon 'patch' of both muskmelons and watermelons can be successful and if, in the North, the seeds are started indoors in peat pots.

Figure 107: Support melons as they grow to keep them free from dirt splashes.

Site and Soil
The soil requires masses of well-rotted manures or compost which encourages extensive root development and retains moisture. Choose your warmest, most sunny positions.

Sowing Instructions
Sow seeds in the North indoors about four weeks before you would sow outside – late spring or whenever frost danger is over. Put seeds singly in peat pots or Jiffy 7 pellets, or use two seeds to a pot, but reduce to one as soon as the seedlings are well along. Grow in a warm, sunny window or under fluorescent lights. Ideal temperatures are 70°F (21°C) for germinating the seeds and 55°–60°F (13°–15°C) for further growing. When the weather outdoors warms, plant the seedlings under Hotkaps, being sure to slit the tops for ventilation.

Cantaloupe melon or muskmelon.

USEFUL TIP

Fresh cut melons can be cubed and kept in the deep freeze to give succulent fruit the whole year round.

How to Grow
A mulch of black plastic is recommended because it retains soil heat.

Put two plants in an area 4 ft × 6 ft (120 × 180 cm) and 'hill' up the soil a little to plant on a mound. Avoid water resting around the stem.

Once the main stem has produced five large leaves, pinch out the growing tip (see cucumber). Pinch out subsequent side-shoots at the growing tip when three leaves have developed or the frame will become filled with leafy growth and the plants will produce few or no fruits.

When the plants are growing strongly keep them well watered, and give them liquid feed as the first young fruits reach the size of a walnut. Reduce feeding and watering when the fruits begin to reach their harvesting size.

Harvesting
Test for ripeness by pressing the end furthest from the stalk with your thumb. If the fruit 'gives' a little it will be ripe. Brown, corky cracking on the fruit and a sweet, delicious smell also indicate that the fruit is ripe.

Melons growing.

Possible Problems
Plants may be subject to attack from red spider mites which can be avoided by keeping the growing atmosphere really damp (spraying the foliage regularly with water helps to achieve this). In hot dry conditions red spiders multiply quickly. They turn the leaves bronzy-brown and check plant growth.

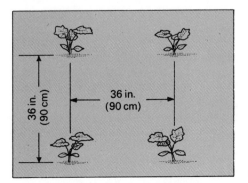

Mustard, Cress and Watercress

Mustard and cress (*Brassica juncea* and *Lepidium sativum*) are the simplest salad ingredients to grow. There are two kinds of cress, the curled – which may give a little more bulk – and the plain-leaved type. There are also several mustard varieties that are grown in the garden like spinach and cooked as 'greens'.

Watercress (*Nasturtium officinale*) can be grown in garden soil, or in a cool greenhouse as long as the soil is kept constantly moist. However, a stream or running water is really needed if it is to bear repeatedly over a number of years from one planting. Alternatively, successive sowings (except in very hot weather) of plain cress makes a good substitute.

MUSTARD AND CRESS
Sowing Instructions

You can sow the seeds at any time of the year. In a temperature of about 50°F (10°C), allow two to three weeks between sowing and harvesting. If you want to grow mustard and cress so they are ready at the same time, sow

Watercress.

the cress four days before the mustard. Sow a small quantity every fourteen days to obtain a succession of harvestable foliage.

How to Grow

All you need is a saucer covered with two or three dampened paper tissues, a piece of kitchen paper towel or blotting paper on which you scatter the seeds. An alternative growing method is to fill a shallow plastic tray ¼–1 in (1–2 cm) deep with peat moss, vermiculite or compost. Sprinkle the

Mustard and Cress.

cress seed over this; keep it damp and in the dark for three days and then sprinkle the mustard seed on top, or grow the two separately if you prefer. Once the seed leaves start to unfold immediately move the tray under fluorescent tubes or to a window sill. Leave it there until you cut the crop for eating. The main advantage of growing cress in peat is that the brown seed cases are more likely to be left behind at the harvesting stage, thus saving you the trouble of washing them off when preparing for eating.

Harvesting

Cut off at the base of the stem when the plants are 2 in (5 cm) or so high. You can slice them off with a sharp knife but the easier method is to take a handful of tops in the fingers of one hand and cut off a bundle of stems using scissors.

Problems

There are none.

Notes

Mustard and cress can also be sown and grown outdoors, and in the USA this is more usual. Mustard is grown like spinach and cooked as 'greens'. Since it is very hardy, it is grown all winter in the South and in mild climates, but in the North the seeds are sown in early spring and late summer for fall cutting. In the small garden, a row of spring mustard can be followed by a row of snap beans for summer. Cress takes up even less space and can be sown in short rows among radishes and lettuce or the seeds can be scattered in patches. Both the curly and plain cresses also grow best in cool weather.

WATERCRESS
Site and Soil

Fresh water in a running stream is the ideal site. Check with your local water authority to see the water is free of health hazards before planting.

Sowing Instructions

Raise young plants from seed sown in boxes indoors, then prick off seedlings into more boxes to produce plants 3–4 in (7·5–10 cm) high. When the plants have 4 in (10 cm) long shoots they can be planted in streams, 4–6 in (10–15 cm) apart. You can also sow direct in the garden soil in April. Or take cuttings from watercress bunches you buy in the market.

How to Grow

Once planted the only treatment is to make sure they have plenty of water. If you are not growing in a stream, dig a shallow trench and add compost to the base. Once planted, keep very well watered.

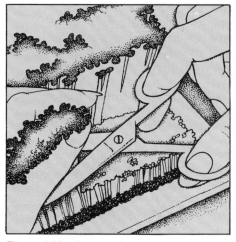

Figure 108: Cutting Cress.

Harvesting

Cutting can begin in the fall on beds planted in the spring.

Possible Problems

None to worry about.

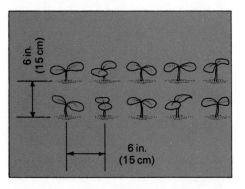

Okra

The slender green seed pods of okra (*Hibiscus esculentus*) are delicious for flavoring soups and stews. They may also be cooked and served on their own – fried for instance. Given treatment and conditions similar to those for outdoor tomatoes, okra is easy to grow. The plants do require space – perhaps more than most small gardens can afford. Okra plants, with their yellow typical hibiscus-like flowers that precede the pods are attractive enough to be given a place in the flower garden. (See Useful Tip below.)

Site and Soil

A warm sheltered site is essential in cold areas and a southerly facing plot, against a fence or wall is best. All reasonably well cultivated soils are suitable, but light, sandy soils improved by the addition of well-rotted compost to help water retention are the ideal. Warm situations and goods soils will produce vigorously growing plants 4 ft (120 cm) high.

USEFUL TIP

Like various other vegetables – eggplants and tomatoes for example – okra grown in containers make attractive as well as productive plants for patios, balconies or terraces.

Okra growing, showing the yellow flowers.

Sowing Instructions

Sow indoors in spring and then plant outside once there is no more possibility of frost. Alternatively sow direct in the growing site after the weather and soil have warmed in late spring. A

Okra seed pods shown gathered ready for cooking.

single row is ample for the ordinary family's needs.

How to Grow

Thin out the seedlings and space plants 20–24 ins (50–60 cm) apart. Hoe between the plants occasionally to control weeds. Water well in dry weather and give liquid fertilizer every

Figure 109: Okra growing in a container of synthetic soilless mix.

fourteen days or so from the time the first yellow flowers open.

Harvesting

Once the fruits are 2–4 in (5–10 cm) long you can begin harvesting. Plants raised from a May sowing are likely to be ready for picking in mid to late August. If you pick the fruit regularly, not only do you have a constant supply of succulent pods, but the plants will continue to fruit up to the first frost.

Possible Problems

There are none to worry about. Very strong growing plants may need a cane or stake to hold them upright.

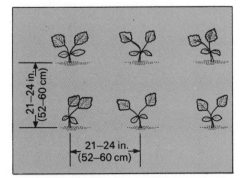

21–24 in. (52–60 cm)

21–24 in. (52–60 cm)

Onions and Shallots

To grow massively big onions (*Allium cepa*) fit for exhibition at vegetable shows from seed is quite a test for the gardener's skill, but to grow onions for everyday use is easy. The challenge and difficulty of growing the giants has perhaps tended to mask the ease of cultivating onions for culinary purposes.

ONIONS FOR SALADS

All varieties of onions may be sown to pull young as salad onions, but if you want them specifically for this purpose the special varieties like 'White Lisbon' are best. Good alternatives are the silver-skinned varieties like 'White Portugal' (which really is a silver color in comparison to the white of 'White Lisbon'), or 'Barletta'. If you leave some onions from these two cultivars in the row after pulling those you want for salads, they will grow into 'mouth-sized' onions. For scallions, select 'bunching' varieties.

Site and Soil

Any cultivated soil is suitable in full sun, but the best onions come from humus–rich fertilized soil.

Spring onions just starting to form bulbs.

Spring onions pulled very young.

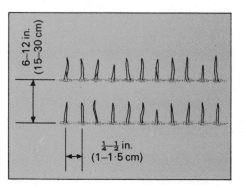

Sowing Instructions

Sow the seed in very shallow drills and just cover with soil. Rows can be as close as 6 in (15 cm) although a 12 in (30 cm) spacing will make inter-row hoeing easier. Sow once a month from March to September to give salad onions the year round – (the September batch will provide them through the winter). The best crops of bulbs for pickling will be those you gather twelve to sixteen weeks after the March/April sowings.

How to Grow

Hoe between the rows occasionally to control the weeds. The thin grassy leaves of the sowings may take a little time to show and it helps to mix a little fast-germinating radish seed in with the onions. This acts as a guide when you hoe to destroy weeds early in the year, and also gives you an indication of where the onions will follow. Grow spring onions sown in September/October in a cold frame or try them under polyethylene tunnels, and you will get a very good winter salad crop. This applies even in cold districts.

Harvesting

Pull the green onions as soon as they are large enough to eat, taking the largest first and leaving the smaller ones to grow some more. Lift small bulb onions for pickling when the bulbs have reached pickling size and then leave them to ripen in the sun. Onions which are green when lifted will shrink back as they dry.

Possible Problems

Plants may be affected by the disease white rot, which causes yellowing of the leaves and white fluffy mold at the base of the bulb. To prevent the build-up of this disease in the soil it is essential to follow a strict rotation plan, in which you avoid cropping the same land with onions year after year. As another cultural aid, avoid sowing too thickly. Once in the soil white rot will persist for years. If you have to use soil which has been proved to contain it, check with your local county extension agent for latest controls.

Small maggots attacking the roots are likely to be the larvae of onion fly, a pest which is most prevalent on dry, light soils. Lift and burn any infected plants and treat the seed rows with chemicals such as diazinon granules.

MATURE ONIONS FROM SEEDS

The cheapest way to make sure you have a continuous supply of cooking onions to bake, boil, fry or use raw is to raise them from seed. Given reasonably fine, crumbly soil at sowing time they are quite easy to grow. There is a choice of shape – either globe onions or flat-bottomed bulbs. The slightly milder-flavored scarlet-bulbed onions are attractive for use raw.

Site and Soil
A well-cultivated garden soil and an open sunny site are the requirements: the better the soil the bigger the onions are likely to grow.

Sowing Instructions
Most onion varieties require about 90 to 130 days from seeds to produce mature onions suitable for storing. In most Northern regions this means seeds must be sown early – outdoors just as soon as the soil is workable and can be raked to make a suitable seed bed. Although frosts will not injure the seeds or seedlings, they will slow germination and growth, so sowing seeds and growing indoors (under lights) or in a cold frame will speed the growth process. Of course if you just want onions to use fresh or at any stage for salads (see opposite), this early start is not critical.

However, any seedlings grown indoors must be 'hardened off', that is, they should gradually be exposed to outdoor conditions for a few hours each day for about a week before being planted in their final garden positions.

If growing onions for storage from seeds seems too complicated, you have two alternatives: growing from sets (see over page) or buying seedling plants, available in bunches from mail-order seed houses and nurseries

Globe onion.

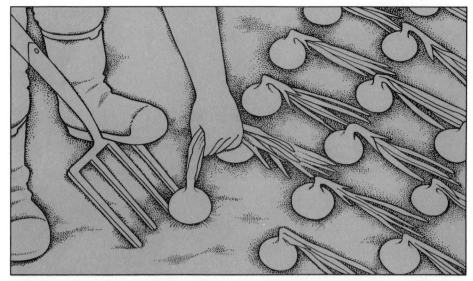

Figure 110: Ease onions gently out of the ground before drying in the sun.

or locally at garden centers. These plants are well along in growth since they have been growing all winter in the South. Their top growth is not 'soft' as is the case with your own indoor-grown seedlings, so they should be set out as soon as available or received – even if frosts are still prevalent. Plant seedlings 5–6 in (12·5–15 cm) apart. Onion seeds can be sown in late summer and fall in the South and in mild climates.

How to Grow
Once seedlings are showing and established, the onions need spacing to 4–5 in (10–12·5 cm) apart. Thin them first however to 2 in (5 cm) and then thin again about a month later to 4 in (10 cm). This ensures you have a full row of plants and also provides a succession of salad onions from the thinnings. Gaps can be filled by transplanting thinned out plants. Space the rows 9–12 in (23–30 cm) apart, so there are six to eight plants per square foot (900 sq cm) in order to give the maximum yield.

Harvesting
When the plants are fully grown, bend over the tops to prevent further flow of sap. After a week or two lift the onions by easing them out of the soil after loosening with a fork, and put them base up in the sun to ripen off completely. Then either tie them to a rope to hang up – Brittany onion-sellers' style, or place them in trays. Store them in a dry, airy, cool but frost-free place. If they do get frosted be especially careful to avoid knocking or bruising them as in this condition rot spots will quickly develop.

Red onion.

Possible Problems
Swollen, distorted and bloated leaves are symptoms of attack by nematodes – tiny creatures which are not easily seen with the naked eye. Avoid growing onions for at least two years on land which has been shown to contain this pest. Modern seed treatments should reduce the chance of this pest occurring at any stage.

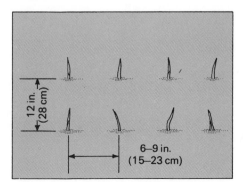

Onions and onion sets.

ONIONS FROM SETS
There really is no easier crop to grow than onions from sets. Just push these small bulbs into cultivated soil from early spring or hoe occasionally to control weeds and then harvest the bulbs. This method of growing is especially valuable in colder climates where short growing seasons and wet conditions are not favorable for seed-raised bulb crops.

Site and Soil
As for seed-raised onions.

Planting
Trim the wispy strawy piece on the top of the set either with scissors or by pinching off with your fingers. If you leave these the birds will pull the sets up by this wispy piece and the worms will pull the bulb into the ground. In fact this does no more than misplace the set in the row, but if you remove

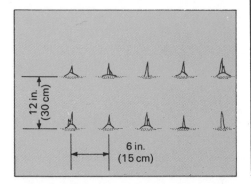

the wispy piece, there is no future need to replant pulled-out sets.

To plant, either draw out a very shallow drill, space the bulbs along it and cover with soil, or push them very gently into the soil until they are just covered. Space the bulbs 6 in (15 cm) apart and the rows 9–12 in (23–30 cm) apart. A ½ lb (0·2 kg) of average size sets plants a 30–45 ft (9–13·5 m) long row.

How to Grow/Harvesting
The procedure for these is the same as that for bulb onions from seed. Lift onions from sets once the leaves turn yellow and start to ripen. If you leave them in the soil and a heavy rainfall follows dry sunny weather, there is the chance of the onion starting to grow again and the base of the bulb splitting as a result.

USEFUL TIP
If some of your onions form a flower bud prematurely (known as 'bolting') rather than developing a good bulb, break out the bud as soon as it appears. Use these poorer onions first. You can avoid bolting in seed-grown onions by sowing the seed a week or two later, and in onion sets by selecting and planting smaller sizes of sets. Smaller onion sets are not only less likely to run to seed but also give you more for your money as you are buying by weight.

SHALLOTS
Shallots are much larger than onion sets, but they require exactly the same treatment. Very easy to grow, they store longer than many crops of onions and to the gourmet are the perfect seasoning for many dishes. Each planted shallot will grow and multiply to produce four to eight new shallots.

Siting, Planting and Growing
All exactly the same as for onion sets.

Harvesting
Lift once the leaves have yellowed and are beginning to die down. When the shallots are really dry and fully ripened, tie them in bundles or store them in trays. Select a few of the smaller shallots – 1 in (2 cm) diameter – of good shape and keep these for the next year's planting.

Possible Problems
All bulb onions are open to attack by neck rot, a soft brown rot which starts

Shallots.

at the stem in storage and quickly spreads through the onion. Reduce the likelihood of attack by treating seed and spraying crops in June with fungicide like Benomyl.

Note
The Welsh onion, *Allium fistulosum*, raised from spring-sown seed, is a perennial plant producing green leek-like shoots which can be pulled to use either green for salads or cooked for flavoring all the year round. Established plants need dividing every few years. It is usually listed as 'Japanese Bunching' or 'Evergreen Long White Bunching.'

Parsnips

The parsnip (*Pastinaca sativa*) is one of the hardiest of root vegetables and actually improves in flavor after exposure to frost. Although this vegetable is one of the earliest to be sown in spring and produces larger roots with the longest growing season, the current tendency is to grow smaller roots which some people find easier to cope with in the kitchen.

Site and Soil
Grow in full sun. All ordinary garden soils will produce worthwhile crops, but those which have been well dug in the fall and have had rotted organic matter added for previous crops are the best.

Sowing Instructions
Sow seed any time in early spring when the soil surface is reasonably dry and crumbly. In the South and other mild-climate regions, the seeds are usually sown in fall for spring harvesting. Space the rows 12–15 in (30–38 cm) apart and choose a calm day for sowing, otherwise the large flat seeds blow everywhere! Always use new seed as the germination life is short, (see chart, page 21).

Parsnips.

How to Grow
Thin the seedlings in two stages, firstly to 2–3 in (5–7·5 cm) apart and then, when these are well established, to the final spacing distance of 4–6 in (10–15 cm). If you want large roots (which are in fact the quickest to peel and give a more edible vegetable) space the rows 15–18 in (38–45 cm) apart and grow two plants per square foot (900 sq cm) of garden. For smaller

Figure 111: Thin seedlings in two stages to get parsnips of varying size.

roots of a similar size to those purchased prepacked in supermarkets (rather like big carrots), grow four per 12 in (30 cm) row.

USEFUL TIP
Lift a few roots in early fall and leave on the surface of the soil to get the full benefit of the first 'flavor-improving' frosts. Others can be stored in clamps or in peat or sand.

Parsnips need little cultural treatment, except for hoeing between rows and plants to control weeds.

Harvesting
Dig up the roots as you require them. Parsnips can be left in the ground throughout the winter, but as it is difficult to get them out of solidly frozen soil, lift some earlier and store them for your winter supply. You should certainly lift the remaining roots in early spring and store them in peat or sand, otherwise they will start to grow again. This spoils the roots for culinary use.

Possible Problems
None to worry about. The rusty brown marks, usually close to the shoulders of a root are caused by a canker disease. It just needs peeling off when the roots are prepared for cooking and eating.

Plants producing several twisted roots are difficult to prepare for eating. Avoid sowing in freshly manured soil to reduce the chance of producing these awkwardly forked or multi-rooted specimens. Try to prepare the soil about 18 in (45 cm) deep. Rocky soil will also cause malformed roots.

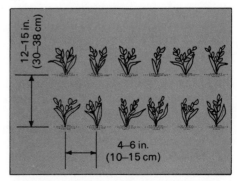

Peas

Second only to salads is the growing of garden peas (*Pisum sativum*) as a must for the small home vegetable garden. Young peas picked fresh from the garden and cooked with a flavoring of mint in early summer are a delicacy which, for me, surpass the more exotic flavor of asparagus or globe artichokes.

The early and late sown pea crops are usually the most successful for everyone and certainly for gardeners who have to contend with hot dry summers. The smooth-seeded varieties are the most hardy and resistant to cold wet soil conditions but the very wrinkled and somewhat larger-seeded varieties are heavier yielding and better quality, especially when picked a few days past the very young succulent pea stage.

Varieties

Seed catalogs usually list peas under the headings: 'Early' and 'Midseason' or 'Late'. These headings indicate the period of time from sowing to harvest, which for an early sowing of the 'Early' types is within 55–65 days, and up to 79 days for 'Late' types. Hot weather will give premature and lighter crops. Varieties from the three groups can be selected to give a succession of crops, but as well as variety, the weather is an important factor. If the weather is warm, growth will be rapid and sowing once every ten days will provide successional crops. If the weather is cold after sowing, growth will be slower, so the period between sowings will have to be extended. Or choose three or four pea varieties that have different harvesting times, but plant all three at the same time.

Site and Soil

All garden sites and soils will produce acceptable crops. In my experience, soil that is cultivated for the first time in a number of years will produce very good crops, be it old grass left undisturbed for a long time or a mixture of top and sub-soil left by builders on a new house site. It is worthwhile remembering that peas will take nitrogen from the air and convert it to nitrogenous plant food, leaving the soil richer than before. A slightly alkaline soil will encourage the activity of bacteria which work with pea roots to convert the nitrogen, so add a dusting of lime to acid soils. Round pin-head sized globules on the roots of all peas and beans denote the presence of bacteria.

Peas ready for picking.

Figure 112: Various ways of supporting peas as they grow.

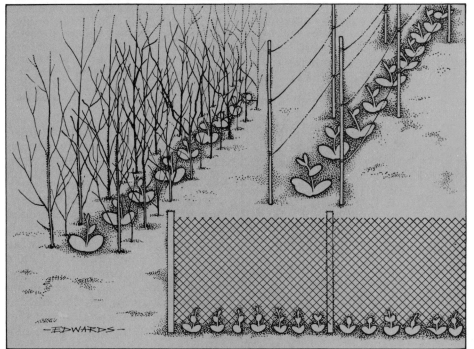

92

You can increase the growth of peas and thus get a larger crop, by adding organic matter to the soil. This will hold moisture, so is particularly valuable in the event of hot dry weather.

Sowing Instructions

For the earliest crops, sow directly into the growing site, either in late October/early November (in the South and mild climates) or in early March. Crops from this sowing will be ready for picking in late May/early June. You can also sow in peat pots indoors in late January/early February, planting them out under Hotkaps or polyethylene tunnels to get an early crop. After these sowings, sow successionally in the growing site through the spring and into early summer (see chart for more details).

Sow seeds in a V-shaped drill 2–3 in (5–7·5 cm) deep, spacing them to give 11 plants per square foot (900 sq cm). Sow dwarf varieties to give 16 plants

birds. When the seedlings are 2–3 in (5–7·5 cm) high they will need some form of support. For the simplest and minimum form of support, push a few sticks or canes into the soil on either side of the row, and tie horizontal strings between them at 6–12 in (15–30 cm) intervals from the ground. A better alternative is to fix plastic or wire netting up one or both sides of the row. The netting can be used for a number of years. Personally, however, I prefer to erect twigs like a neat fence on each side of the row, with the tops of the sticks trimmed off in a line to the height stated for each variety.

After providing some form of support, no other cultural treatment is needed apart from occasional hoeing to control weeds. In dry weather and where slow growth occurs you can improve crops by spraying with a liquid foliar fertilizer. Plants take this in through their leaves and it is known as a foliar feed.

An example of late peas.

that no gardener ventures forth to plant. When the peas finally reach the ground, the hot weather of summer rushes in, spoiling the pea crop at a critical growing stage. Other problems come from the soil, including two diseases, wilt and root rot. The only cure here is crop rotation, an observance that has been emphasized many times in this book and one that is very important for healthy peas.

Sowing in cold soil may result in seed losses and a smooth-seeded variety such as 'Alaska' is supposed to reduce such losses. Dusting all seeds with the fungicide captan is a help. You can sow a few extra seeds at the end of the row to provide some extra plants to transplant into any gaps, should they occur.

PEAS – less common types

There are three main types of pea other than the best known garden varieties. Firstly, the very small, neat and round 'Petit Pois', so popular on the continent of Europe, especially in France. The gourmet will tell you these peas need to be steamed in the

PEA VARIETY CHART		
Variety/Type	**Days to Maturity**	**Remarks**
Alaska (early)	55	Smooth-seeded variety supposedly more tolerant of cold, wet soil
Alderman (late)	74	Long-season bearer of high quality peas. Vines grow from 4–6 ft (120–180·5 cm), so staking is necessary. Highly productive.
Fordhook Wonder (late)	79	Sweet, dark green peas in large pods. Fine for cool summer regions.
Frosty (early)	64	Productive, high quality peas.
Green Arrow (midseason)	70	New variety from England with long pods 4–4½ in (10–11·5 cm) borne in pairs.
Lincoln (midseason)	67	Exceptional quality and sweetness.
Little Marvel (early)	62	Vigorous dwarf vines bear deep green, sweet peas.
Sparkle (early)	60	About the earliest pea of high quality. Vines only 15 in (38 cm) high.
Wando (midseason-late)	69	Adaptable variety recommended for South or for Northern regions in summer. Vines 2½ ft (75 cm).

per 12 in (30 cm) of row, spacing the rows 15–18 in (38–45 cm) apart, i.e. the same distance as the likely height of the plants. Seed packets and catalogs will give the approximate height for each variety, some of which grow to 5–6 ft (approximately 2 m). The richer the soil the taller and bushier the peas are likely to grow, so it is advisable to choose the dwarf varieties for the 10 ft × 12 ft (3 m × 4 m) vegetable plot!

How to Grow

It is a good idea to cover the young seedlings of early crops with polyethylene tunnels or Hotkaps as protection against the weather and

Harvesting

As soon as the peas in the pods are large enough to eat, gather them by holding the stalk in one hand and pulling the pods off with the other. Pick over the row several times, taking the plumpest pods first. Peas are ideal for deep freezing but they must be gathered before the pods start to wrinkle up near the stem. If you leave them to reach this stage, the peas will be old, mealy and starchy.

Possible Problems

The major problems with peas are usually involved with the weather and with the climate. Some years in the North spring can be so cold and wet

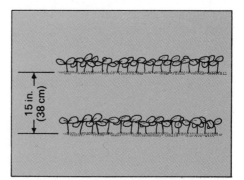

15 in. (38 cm)

Above left and right: Two kinds of edible podded peas.

pod and then shelled ready for eating to retain the full flavor. They are actually very similar to the ordinary peas which have been picked and cooked very young.

Secondly, there is the 'mange tout', commonly called edible pod which is not only cooked in the pod, but both pod and peas are then eaten. As the name indicates, 'mange tout', you eat everything! Ideal for busy cooks with no time to shell the ordinary kinds, these must be gathered while still young. If allowed to age, the pods become stringy.

The third type, the asparagus pea, is possibly more unusual and, as indicated by its Latin name *Lotus tetragonolobus*, it is not a true pea but more of a vetch. It has clover-shaped leaves, grows 18 in–2 ft (45–60 cm) in height and spread, and has reddish-purple, attractive flowers. The pods are winged or perhaps better described as 'deeply grooved' and they are cooked whole like the edible podded or snap bean.

Petit pois and edible podded peas are grown in exactly the same way as the better known pea varieties, so follow cultural instructions given on the previous pages. The following instructions are for the Asparagus Pea which needs different treatment.

Site and Soil
This is the same as for the better known varieties of peas.

Sowing Instructions
Sow indoors in late March/early April and set out plants in the growing position 18 in (45 cm) apart in mid-May. You can also sow directly into the ground from April to June.

USEFUL TIP

If a row of ordinary peas produces more pods than you can gather either to eat fresh or freeze for future use, they can be left on the plant and allowed to ripen to be used as a vegetable after soaking in water for 24 hours. Select the green seeded varieties for this.

How to Grow
Keep the soil moist at all times to give the longer cropping period. Providing you do this and the weather is warm, you can gather pods regularly from mid-June up until the frost. No other cultural treatment is required, except occasional hoeing to control weeds in the early stage of growth. These plants will soon cover the ground, smother-

Asparagus peas.

ing any weeds, but in the small garden where space is limited, some support is recommended.

Harvesting
Gather the young pods when they are 1–2 in (2·5–5 cm) long. At this young stage they have lots of flavor, but if you leave them you will find the resulting older pods rather tough and full of fiber. Cook the pods by steaming them whole with butter for five minutes or so and then eat them rather like asparagus tips.

Peppers

There is a distinct difference between the sweet pepper, *Capsicum annuum*, and the very hot chili or cayenne pepper, variety *frutescens*. The fruits of the sweet pepper are large and rather square lobed and they may be cooked as a vegetable or used fresh in salads. The much smaller, more pointed fruits of the cayenne pepper are used fresh for flavoring or they may be dried and ground up to provide chili powder. They are more tender than sweet peppers in their growing state and need slightly warmer conditions.

There are not, as is often believed red and green varieties of sweet pepper. They all start off green, like tomatoes, and turn red as they ripen. If you want the maximum yield from each plant it is advisable to gather the sweet peppers while they are still green. If left on the plant until they turn red, the total number of fruits yielded by the plant is reduced.

The pepper is a relative of the tomato (also eggplant) and is as easy to grow, requiring very similar treatment. It is one of the major home garden vegetables and even the smallest plot has space for a few bushes.

Varieties
The recently introduced F₁ hybrid varieties of sweet pepper are both earlier and heavier yielding and are preferable to other varieties. Hot peppers have very much smaller leaves, and are more branched. The fruits are smaller – usually long, thin and tapering – and they bear lighter crops than the sweet – just as well since a few hot peppers go a long way!

Site and Soil
All well-cultivated garden soils will give reasonable results, but those containing plenty of organic matter will give the heaviest yields as they encourage root development.

A sunny site is essential to provide the warmth and exposure needed for the best pepper harvests. If garden space is limited, you can raise plants against south-facing walls and fences. Peppers are also suitable for the home greenhouse where they will thrive under the same conditions as required by tomato plants.

Special Siting
In addition to the greenhouse and sunny gardens, peppers are attractive plants to grow in large pots on patios, terraces and balconies. They are even worth a try in window boxes, and

Sweet pepper.

although the severe root restriction will have the effect of producing small fruit, they are however quite usable.

Sowing Instructions
Except in the South and other mild climate regions, pepper seeds are always sown indoors about two months before thoroughly warm weather has arrived outdoors, at which time it is safe to set them in the open ground. Young plants can be set outdoors a few weeks sooner if they are placed under Hotkaps. The quickest way to grow them indoors is in Jiffy 7 pellets, the peat disks that swell into little fertilized pots when wet. Sow two seeds per pot, pinching off the weaker one after germination. Grow in a warm, sunny window, in a greenhouse if you have one or under fluorescent lights. A second transplanting from the Jiffy 7 pots is usually unnecessary, but if you sow seeds in a flat, you will want to transplant the seedlings into 3½ in (9 cm) peat pots.

Ripe and green peppers may be harvested at either stage, but are sweeter at red.

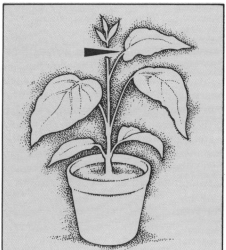

Figure 113: Pinch out growing tips on young plants.

Cayenne peppers.

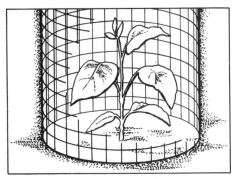

Figure 114: Support young plants with wire mesh 'towers'.

full size, leave one or two fruits on the plant until they start to turn red. At this point you will see just how large they are likely to get. Keep gathering the fruit once a week – remember the more you gather the greater the weight of peppers each plant will produce. Plants put out under Hotkaps in early May will bear from mid-June to early November given average to warm temperatures.

Possible Problems

If aphids appear, spray or dust with malathion, waiting three days before harvesting. Flea beetles puncture the foliage with tiny holes; spray or dust with Sevin (carbaryl), most only required early in season.

How to Grow

Pinch out the central growing point of the young pot plants when they are 6 in (15 cm) high. This produces a bushy, well-branched plant and improves bearing. After this either transplant the plants into larger (8–10 in (20–25 cm) diameter) pots, or plant them 18 in (45 cm) apart in the growing site. Growth is quite strong, and some gardeners like to provide a stake or cane to support the plants. Remember they can reach a height of 4 ft (120 cm).

Syringe the plants with water in hot dry weather to help the flowers set fruit. Give them doses of liquid feed every seven to ten days when the first fruits start to swell. It helps to give heavier crops. If you have to delay transplanting from indoors to outside for any reason, water the plants every five to seven days with a liquid tomato fertilizer so as not to check growth.

Harvesting

As soon as the fruits are large enough, cut them off at the stem with a sharp knife or pruners. One plant per person should provide enough for the average family, and both sweet and hot peppers are gathered green for general cooking purposes. If you want good large sweet peppers (perhaps for example to cut in half, remove the seeds from the centre and stuff before baking), and if you are not quite sure when they have reached

Decorative chilis to use in Christmas wreaths.

USEFUL TIPS

1. Try growing one or two hot peppers in flower pots on the window sill. While restricting the roots will reduce the crop, you will only want small quantities of this vegetable for flavoring and the pot plants should provide enough for the average family. If left to turn from green to red the fruits will provide an attractive display.
2. If growing plants in pots, allow a few flowers to set before pinching out the central growing point to get very early fruits.

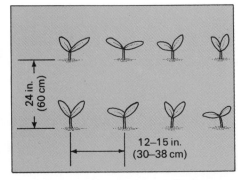

24 in. (60 cm)

12–15 in. (30–38 cm)

Potatoes

New potatoes (*Solanum tuberosum*) lifted fresh from the garden are – like tender young peas – a real early summer delicacy. It is possible that growing maincrop potatoes will take up too much space for their ultimate crop value in the average home garden, but every garden, no matter how small should be able to accommodate a few potato plants to supply those delectable early new potatoes. You should certainly have a few potatoes growing in the 10 ft × 12 ft (3 × 4 m) vegetable plot. Quite apart from the flavor, having a few potatoes which can be lifted from the garden whenever you want them guards against the inevitability of running out of those you have purchased, which always happens at the most inconvenient time! In addition, really freshly-lifted potatoes are much easier to scrape than those which have been lifted for a while, thus giving the skins time to 'set'.

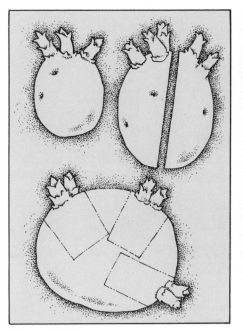

Figure 115: Cut seed potatoes to make planting pieces.

Potatoes can be stored in sacks for winter use.

Site and Soil

All gardens are suitable although crops will be light if grown in heavily shaded spots or where the soil is very light. You will get the heaviest yields from well-cultivated soil with plenty of well-rotted organic matter dug into it. You can clean up garden soil infested with weeds considerably by planting potatoes. The strong foliage smothers growing weeds and the earthing-up cultural treatment checks the weed root growth. Potatoes are therefore a good crop for a new piece of land which has just been dug, in preparation for vegetable growing. They are also useful to clean land in a new garden before planting lawns, perennial flowers and shrubs. The soil should be acid, about 4·8 to 6·5 pH.

Planting

'Seed potatoes' are not seeds as such, but tubers from the previous year's crop. Ideally they should be about 2–3 oz (55–85 gm) in weight, and about the size of an egg. If you save seed potatoes from your own crops there is a chance of virus diseases rapidly building up in the stock and progressively reducing future yields. It is certainly advisable to buy 'certified' disease-free seed potatoes.

Sometimes farmers save their own seed, planting what are known as 'once-grown seed' – in other words planting tubers grown once outside the aphis-free areas. Where seed potatoes are very expensive you may want to risk saving your own seed-tubers for one year, but generally speaking it is not worth the risk of viruses which will considerably reduce the yield. There are many varieties of certified disease-free seed potatoes which are sold grouped according to their speed of maturity as early, midseason and late.

If your seed potatoes are larger than the ideal you can cut them to make two or more planting pieces as long as every piece has its own shoot (see figure 115). Dust with captan.

A good way to increase the yield and get slightly earlier crops is to place the seed potatoes in trays in a warm (50°F (10°C)) light position for a few weeks before planting. During this time they will produce short dark green shoots.

Plant the tubers in rows with a trowel 4–5 in (10–12 cm) deep, 12–15 in (30–38 cm) apart, with 24 in (60 cm) between the rows. Begin planting outdoors in late March/early April – or four to five weeks before the last frost is likely to occur. Some gardeners prefer to pull out a 4–5 in (10–12 cm) deep U-shaped drill with a hoe, along which they space out the tubers and then cover them with the soil. Choose whichever system suits you best.

How to Grow

When the young shoots appear above the ground, draw up soil from between

Figure 116: Plant tubers in furrows and cover them with soil.

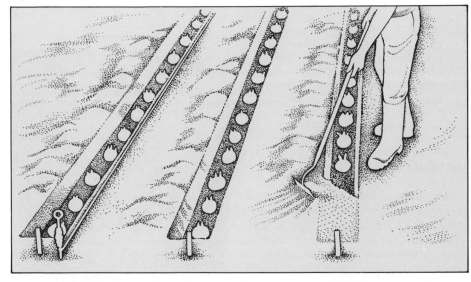

Figure 117: Earth up around the growing stems.

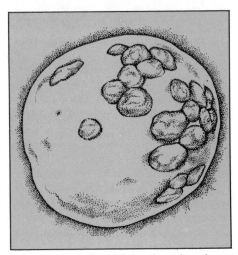

Figure 118: Soil which has been limed may produce tubers with scabs.

the rows around the stems. This is called 'earthing up'. If young shoots have come through and frosts are still likely, pull the soil right over them to give protection. Alternatively you can protect against frost by covering the rows with Hotkaps or polyethylene tunnels, but this is rarely necessary, or just covering with sacking on nights when frost is forecast.

Repeat the earthing-up process sev-

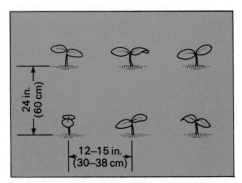

eral times as the crop grows. This increases the roots made by the potato stems and so gives a greater yield as well as helping to control weeds. It also keeps the developing tubers covered with soil and shaded from light which would turn them green and make them inedible.

USEFUL TIPS

1. For very early crops plant a few seed potato tubers in pots filled with potting compost and grow them in the greenhouse, sun lounge or glass-sided porch. Put one to three tubers in an 8 in (20 cm) pot—more tubers will give more small early potatoes.

2. An interesting way to grow potatoes on the 10 ft × 12 ft (3 m × 4 m) vegetable plot is to set the seed potatoes on the surface of the growing site and cover them with a 2 ft (60 cm) wide strip of black polyethylene. Bury the edges of the polyethylene to hold it in place and make a small slit in it above each tuber to let the potato shoots through. No earthing up is needed and the black polyethylene keeps the tubers from going green. The new potatoes are mostly produced on the surface and to gather them lift one edge of the polyethylene and pick the biggest potatoes.

Harvesting

Towards mid- to the end of July, move some soil away from the roots by hand to check the size of the new potatoes. When they are large enough to eat, start lifting them and keep the fork or spade well back from the plants to avoid cutting into the potatoes. Once

the foliage starts to turn yellow and die down it is best to lift all the potatoes. Leave them on the surface of the soil for an hour or so, then put them in bags and store in a frost-free but cool place for use through the winter.

Possible Problems

In very damp conditions in the fall the disease, potato blight, can be troublesome. This causes dark spots on the leaves and premature yellowing of the leaves. The spores drop from the leaves and infect the tubers which then develop soft brown rot in storage. You can prevent this by growing early varieties and lifting them early. Alter-

Sprouted tubers being covered with black polyethylene sheet.

natively, spray with maneb according to directions.

Reduce the possibility of potatoes getting 'scabs' (brown corky patches on the skin) by adding plenty of organic matter but *no* lime, to the soil before planting. If necessary, add sulphur to soil to increase acidity.

A heavy crop of potatoes.

Pumpkins and Gourds

Pumpkins (*Cucurbita maxima*) can be grown to eat as a vegetable or made into pumpkin pie – a favorite American dish. They are also traditionally carved into ghostly faces to provide Hallowe'en decorations. More decorative but not grown to eat are ornamental gourds which are now available in a great variety of shapes and colors. Both plants require the same cultural treatment, which is similar to that needed to grow squash, and they are also not altogether suitable for the 10 ft × 12 ft (3 m × 4 m) vegetable plot as plants need a lot of space to grow.

Site and Soil
Both types of plants grow vigorously and require at least a couple of square yards (1·6 sq metres) on rich soil for each plant. A warm sunny site is needed to grow the largest pumpkins but smaller fruits can be grown in partially shaded sites. Dig plenty of organic matter into the soil to supply the moisture needed for rapid growth. A well rotted-down compost heap provides an ideal site and rooting medium.

Pumpkins.

USEFUL TIP

Ornamental gourds look very effective trained up and over a trellis or fence. On terraces and balconies they can be grown in polyethylene bags filled with synthetic soil, or in soil-filled window boxes.

Sowing Instructions
Sow the seeds indoors about a month before last frosts occur outdoors, two seeds per peat or Jiffy 7 pot. When seedlings are big enough to handle thin out to one per pot. Plant out when there is no more possibility of frost, protecting with Hotkaps for faster

Ornamental gourds.

growth. You can also sow directly into the growing site in mid to late spring after frost danger has passed. Sow two or three seeds together at each point and thin down to one when the seedlings are big enough to handle. Sprinkle a little slug bait down after sowing out of doors as a precaution to prevent possible damage to the stems.

How to Grow
Keep the plants well watered in dry weather and give liquid feed every ten to fourteen days once the fruits begin to swell to obtain the largest fruit. Pinch out the growing tip of the main stem to encourage more fruit bearing side shoots to form. A pumpkin plant will carry four or five fruits, but reduce this number to one or two per plant if you want really big pumpkins. You can encourage roots to be made from the stem and increase fruit size even more by heaping fertile soil over the fruit-bearing side shoots.

Where flowers open but fail to set fruit, you should hand-pollinate them. Pick a male flower (it will have no immature fruit behind the flower), remove the petals and push the yellow pollen-bearing anthers into a female flower, (which does have an embryo fruit behind the flower).

Harvesting
This will be in the late summer or early fall. Leave the pumpkins on the stem to mature and ripen. If the fruit is not quite ripe and there is a possibility of frost, cover it with sacking overnight. If you want your pumpkins for Hallowe'en decorations, cut them a couple of weeks beforehand and just leave them on the soil. This really toughens the skin.

Gather gourds as they ripen and go hard which will be in late summer. Cut with pruners and leave them in a dry, sunny position to dry.

Possible Problems
Watch out for mice and rats which will eat the seeds at sowing time and also the fruits left outside to ripen.

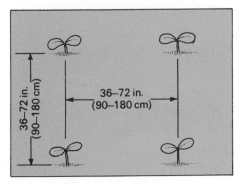

36–72 in. (90–180 cm)

36–72 in. (90–180 cm)

99

Radishes

Only mustard and cress are easier to grow than common radish (*Raphanus sativus*). All you have to do is scatter seed on the ground, rake it in and, miraculously, you will have succulent radishes ready for pulling within four weeks. The slight peppery flavor gives a spicy lift to salads and the bright scarlet skins of many varieties add color to the green of other salad vegetables.

There are two kinds of radish: the best known, which could be described as ordinary radish, can be grown from early to late spring. The other type – the winter radish – may be black or red skinned and is much larger than the ordinary radish. It looks rather like a small turnip, and as it is completely hardy it can be stored and used through the winter.

Varieties

For spring harvesting there are three main types – the globe-shaped, which may be scarlet or scarlet-tipped white; the oval or cylinder-shaped, which is red with a white tip, and includes one of the most popular varieties, called 'French Breakfast'; and the long-rooted variety, which includes the aptly named 'White Icicle'. This produces pure white roots like slender pointed fingers.

There are several varieties of the winter radish – probably the best known of which is 'Chinese Rose'. The 5–6 in (12·5–15 cm) long roots have white-tipped rose skin and grow up to 2 in (5 cm) in diameter. The other two varieties, 'Black Spanish Round' and 'Black Spanish Long', are about the same size as 'Chinese Rose'

Long black radish.

Globe radish.

but they both have black skins. The flesh of all three types is white and their flavors are comparable.

Site and Soil

Radishes will grow anywhere in all reasonably well-cultivated soils from early to late spring or so long as the weather remains cool. The crispest and best flavored radishes are those that are grown quickly on fertile soil in a sunny position. If they are grown in light, dry soils and during hot weather, the roots may be slow to swell and they tend to be very hot and rather woody.

Special Siting

Radishes grow so quickly there is no need to make special plans for them. Place short rows between slower maturing crops in the 10 ft × 12 ft (3 m × 4 m) vegetable plot; early in spring, for example, you can sow radish on either side of a row of emerging peas. Later in the year grow them between emerging beans and developing celery or brussels sprouts. This is known as 'catch-cropping', or the crop is described as an 'intercrop'.

You can grow small quantities in window boxes, and in greenhouses among lettuce and tomatoes. If you are growing tomatoes and other crops in containers and planters on a terrace or patio, you can also get in a quick crop of radish.

Sowing Instructions

In temperate areas start sowing the ordinary radish as soon as soil conditions allow. You should be able to sow very early in the North – just as soon as the soil is workable. Draw shallow drills 6 in (15 cm) apart and sow the seed thinly down the row. Sow in succession every ten to fourteen days from early to late spring to provide crops from spring to early summer.

Sow winter radish in July, *not* before, in rows 12 in (30 cm) apart. Thin out the seedlings as they develop, to stand 6–8 in (15–20 cm) apart in the row.

How to Grow

Radishes really are 'instant gardening', and once you have sown the seed there is very little more you have to do. In order to maintain a supply of succulent radishes, make sure they have plenty of moisture. If you don't sow the seeds too thickly, you may not have to thin the rows until you start the first harvesting (see below).

Harvesting

Start pulling up the roots as soon as the ordinary radish are large enough – about ½ in (1·5 cm) in diameter. Take out the largest ones first (you can see which they are by pushing the leaves gently to one side and selecting the thickest roots). The smaller roots that you leave behind will grow quickly to give a succession of radishes.

Start pulling winter radish in November and store the roots in peat or sand. You can also leave them in the soil and pull as you require them, but remember that in very hard, frosty weather pulling will be difficult. You should also protect them with straw.

USEFUL TIP
The radish is a very useful indicator crop to help you to plot slow-to-germinate items. For example, if you sow a mixture of radish and parsley seed in the same row, the radishes grow quickly and soon show just where the seed was situated. This allows you to hoe between rows to control weeds without disturbing the parsley seeds. The radishes will have grown and have been pulled to eat by the time the parsley is established and requires all the space. Sowings of onion, parsnip and carrot are good examples of where indicator crops are a help.

French breakfast radish.
Long white radish.

Possible Problems
Radishes are grouped in the same family as cabbages and all the brassicas, so they are susceptible to the same pests and diseases – for example clubroot. Try and plant on disease-free soil, but as the plants grow so quickly any subsequent signs of trouble are best cured by destroying the crop and making another quick sowing in fresh soil.

One problem which you may need to control is attack by flea beetles – small shiny black insects which eat neat round holes in the seedling leaves. Dust or spray with diazinon according to directions on the container. Cabbage root maggots can infest the roots but are most severe on early sowings, decreasing with successive sowings. So ignore – or dust diazinon over the rows after sowing.

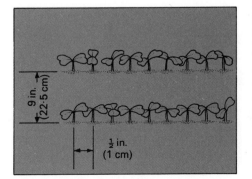

Rhubarb

There is heated debate in some horticultural circles on the classification of rhubarb (*Rheum rhaponticum*), which is grown very much like a vegetable and yet the bright pink stems are used as a tart acid-flavored alternative to fruit in many desserts. Because it features in the corner of many suburban vegetable plots, we include cultural details here. Remember, it is only the stems of the plant which are eaten – the green leaves contain poisonous oxalic acid. This should be borne in mind if small children have access to the vegetable garden.

Site and Soil
Rhubarb thrives in any site – however bad and all reasonably cultivated garden soil will give good results. The better the soil and the cultural treatment, however, the greater will be the yield of stems and those soils which retain moisture to support the rapid leafy growth in hot weather are the ideal. Once again you can help water retention by adding plenty of well-rotted compost to the soil. However, it should be noted that waterlogged soils are best avoided.

Sowing and Propagation
You can raise rhubarb from seed sown outdoors in spring in drills 1–2 in (2·5–5 cm) deep and 12 in (30 cm) apart, but plants raised in this way are almost certain to be inferior to named varieties propagated by division. They also take two or three seasons before they are large enough to provide leaf stems which can be pulled.

To propagate three- to five-year-old

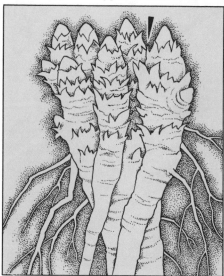

Figure 119: 3- or 4-year-old rhubarb crowns may be chopped to make sets.

Figure 120: Rhubarb set or root division. (Above) Rhubarb being prepared for the table.

plants of named varieties, lift them during the dormant period, November to March, and chop them with a spade to produce five or six planting pieces. These are called 'sets'. Each set must have one rounded pink bud and a fair share of root system; as a guide a planting piece should be about the size of a man's hand. It may be as well to cut through the very largest buds as these invariably produce a flower stalk the first year. Sets with one or more smaller buds will develop into strong plants the first year.

How to Grow
Dig the soil well and clear it of perennial weeds before planting the sets 2½ ft (75 cm) apart (October and March are good times to plant). Occasional hoeing to control weeds is the only other cultural treatment you need to do, but you can improve growth and yield by putting compost, manure and general fertilizer around the plants. Early spring is the usual time to apply rotted manure and/or compost as well as a good sprinkling of 5–10–5 fertilizer. Plants can remain in place for 20 years but in practice replacing in fresh soil every five or so years maintains good yields and keeps plants to manageable size.

You can get early crops by encouraging early growth (known as forced growth). To do this either cover the plants in the soil with boxes filled with straw or lift the whole crown, surround it with damp peat or soil and grow it in a warm dark atmosphere. Succulent bright pink blanched stems are produced by forced plants. All rhubarb crowns need a period of cold, frosty weather before forcing, so leave lifted crowns exposed to the frost before boxing and bringing them indoors to force. It is best to discard crowns after forcing.

Harvesting
Leave the plants for one season after planting. In the second year you can start to pull the stems, but don't denude the plant of leaves if you plan to harvest a number of years. Just pull up the leaf stems which are large enough to use and they will come cleanly away from the plant. Then cut off the leaves and the rhubarb stems are ready for use. Always leave a few leaves on the plant after pulling.

Possible Problems
None to worry about.

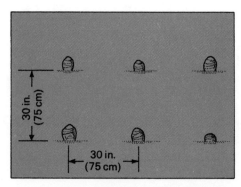

Salsify, Scorzonera and Seakale

These two less common root vegetables – Salsify, (*Tragopogon porrifolius*) which has rush-like leaves, and Scorzonera, (*Scorzonera hispanica*) which has broader strap-shaped leaves – are quite easy to grow. They require similar treatment both in the garden and the kitchen, but it is easy to distinguish between the two. Scorzonera roots have a black skin which can be removed by scalding and scraping. Salsify is a similar shape, but the roots are brown, not black. This vegetable is commonly called the Vegetable Oyster because of its flavor. The roots of both vegetables have a very subtle, delicate flavor and they are prepared for eating by either boiling in salted water or slicing and frying.

Scorzonera.

Salsify.

Site and Soil
Choose an open site and ideally a deep, well-cultivated soil to which you have added well-rotted manure for previous crops. The kind of soils which produce good carrots and parsnips are likely to produce good salsify and scorzonera roots.

Sowing Instructions
Sow in early spring in rows 12–15 in (30–38 cm) apart. A good long growing season is needed for plump roots.

How to Grow
Thin the seedlings to stand 6–9 in (15–23 cm) apart in the row when they are big enough to handle. Hoe occasionally to control weeds and water the plants well in dry weather.

Harvesting
Roots will be ready for lifting from mid-October, but be careful when lifting salsify as damaged roots will bleed

and lose their flavor. Lift the roots as you require them or lift them carefully in November and store in peat or sand. See that all lifted roots are adequately protected during storage so they remain plump and do not shrivel (which also reduces the flavor).

A few roots of salsify can be left in the soil to produce tender young shoots in spring. These shoots can be

---

USEFUL TIP

Seakale is unknown to most Americans but is worth seeking out and trying by those who enjoy good food and are willing to experiment. Seeds can be obtained from Thompson & Morgan, Inc., P.O. Box 24, 401 Kennedy Boulevard, Somerdale, N. J. 08083.

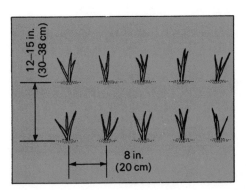

left green or blanched by covering them with a flower pot. Cut when they are 6 in (15 cm) or so high and cook them in the same way as you would asparagus. One row along the 10 ft (3 m) edge of the plot will provide enough roots for at least twenty, average-sized servings.

SEAKALE
Seakale (*Crambe maritima*) is another unusual vegetable which is forced in winter to produce blanched leaf stems.

Site and Soil
All sites for seakale need to be well-cultivated. Improve poor soils by adding well-rotted organic matter.

Sowing and Propagating
You can sow seed in March/April but plants grown from seed will not be ready to force for two years. The faster

Seakale.

method is to propagate from root cuttings (called thongs). These should be 6–8 in (15–23 cm) long and are cut from roots which have been lifted to force. Keep in sand, (tops uppermost) until spring planting time.

How to Grow
Thin seedlings and space thongs 18 in (45 cm) apart, covering the thongs with 1 in (2·5 cm) of soil.

Harvesting
Either cover the roots with straw or an upturned flower pot in situ to force, or put roots in deep boxes of damp peat.

Possible Problems
None to worry about.

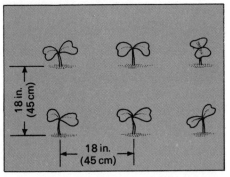

Sorrel and Spinach

SORREL

Common sorrel, which has arrow-shaped leaves and green, turning to red, flower spikes, may be found growing wild, but it is the larger-leaved French sorrel (*Rumex acetosa*) which may be cultivated in gardens. The leaves are paler colored and not so tart and make good flavoring for soups, fish sauces, omelettes and salads.

Site and Soil

Sorrel will grow in any well drained site in sun and partial shade. All lime-free soils are acceptable. The natural presence of sorrel indicates an acid soil. Add plenty of peat or flowers of sulphur to the soil to increase its acidity content.

Sowing and Propagating

Either sow seed outdoors in April or divide and replant established plants in March/April and September. Space the rows 15–18 in (38–45 cm) apart and the plants 9 in (23 cm) apart in the row. If you are growing from seed, thin the seedlings to this distance apart.

How to Grow

Pick out the flower spikes as they develop and hoe between plants to control weeds.

Harvesting

Gather the leaves young (after about six to eight weeks) for the tenderest and mildest flavor. Such leaves can be dried or deep frozen to provide year round supplies.

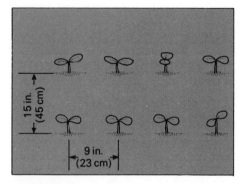

SPINACH

New Zealand spinach (*Tetragonia expensa*) is not botanically true *Spinacia*, but is grown to provide a leaf vegetable, it is usual to consider it with spinach, (*Spinacia oleracea*).

The annual spinach is one of the fastest maturing leaf vegetables and is ideal to grow as an intercrop between slower maturing vegetables such as

Spinach.

celery and leeks. The tender young leaves of spinach should be chopped and *steamed* to present an appetizing vegetable.

Varieties

Since in most regions of the North (in the South it can usually be grown all winter), spinach only thrives in cool weather, such as in fall or spring, some care should be taken in choosing varieties. 'Bloomsdale Long-Standing' is slow to bolt while 'Hybrid No. 7' is resistant to downy mildew. 'Winter Bloomsdale' (45 days) is recommended for fall and winter growing.

Site and Soil

Full sun or partial shade are both acceptable and the best soil is a rich, humusy moisture-retaining type. Light, dry soils and hot weather make plants run prematurely to seed.

Sowing Instructions

To get continuous spring harvests, sow spinach successively every 14 days from early to late spring and again in August and September. Sow the seed thinly in drills 1 in (2·5 cm) deep and 12–15 in (30–38 cm) apart. Thin the seedlings first to stand 3 in (7·5 cm) apart and then thin again after about a month to 6–12 in

(15–30 cm) apart. In the small home garden the closer spacing is quite adequate. Plants from the second thinning will be of edible size. Keep the seedlings well watered in dry weather to obtain the fastest growth.

How to Grow

Hoe to control weeds and water well in dry weather.

Harvesting

As soon as leaves are large enough start to gather them, picking the

Sorrel.

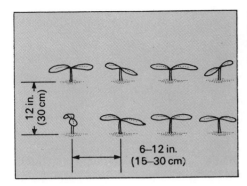

largest ones first. Don't strip the plant, in fact harvest no more than half the leaves at a time, leaving smaller leaves to develop, (although don't leave them too long, or the leaves will be old and tough). Gather leaves by pinching through the leaf stalks; don't pull them off as this may damage the roots.

USEFUL TIP

Spinach is an excellent quick crop for planter boxes on terraces. It will be ready to pick in seven weeks from sowing.

Possible Problems

The major problem with common spinach in most home plots is sowing the seeds too late in spring. Then warm weather arrives in a rush and the plants, which can't survive heat, quickly go to seed. The other problems that can occur also seem worse as the weather warms; leafminers and root aphids. In the home plot, spinach is such a short-season crop that con-

Figure 121: Pick the outer leaves of sorrel to encourage additional growth.

trol is hardly worth the trouble but malathion, used according to directions, is recommended at seven-day intervals for leafminers.

NEW ZEALAND SPINACH

The spreading plants of New Zealand spinach are often called 'cut-and-come-again' because they provide a continuous supply of leafy shoots. The photographs on these pages clearly show the difference in leaf shape between this and spinach – the New Zealand spinach has smaller and not such shiny leaves. Apart from its trailing habit, this plant is also different from ordinary spinach because it is *not* frost-hardy, but it will withstand dry soil conditions without forming premature flower spikes.

Site and Soil

Most garden sites and soils will give acceptable results but sunny positions and light well drained soils will give the best growth and heaviest picking.

Sowing Instructions

For the earliest crops, sow indoors in pots in late March/early April and plant out, after the possibility of frost,

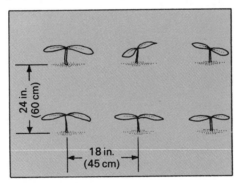

in May or June. Sow the main-crop outside in early May (only one sowing is necessary). Space the rows 2–2½ ft (60–75 cm) apart and the plants 18–24 in (45–60 cm) down the row.

How to Grow

Maintain rapid growth by constant watering in dry weather. Pinch out the growing tips, especially those that form early in the season, to encourage the development of side shoots. These will produce more leaves to harvest.

Harvesting

Leaves will be ready to gather in six to seven weeks from a May sowing. Try to pick the leaves singly to allow the development of further leaves along each stem.

New Zealand Spinach.

MALABAR SPINACH

Malabar spinach (*Basella alba*) is another spinach substitute and like New Zealand spinach does not mind summer heat. It is a vine-like plant and in the small garden may take up too much space unless trained on a trellis. Seeds can be sown in spring after the ground warms and harvesting of the foliage can start in about 70 days from sowing. Malabar spinach is a good subject for a city terrace or roof garden where it could serve a decorative function as well as culinary use.

TAMPALA

Tampala (*Amaranthus gangeticus*) is not a true spinach either, and is related to a genus that is more familiar to flower gardeners. Seeds can be sown in the open ground after both soil and weather have warmed and the leaves are ready for harvesting from six to eight weeks later. They can be steamed or used raw in salads and their flavor is slightly reminiscent of that of the globe artichoke. With any new vegetable, it is best to plant a small patch only the first year until the family has had a chance to decide whether the vegetable is to its taste.

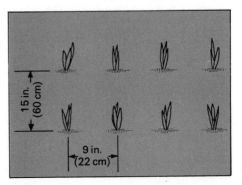

Sweet Corn

Sweet corn (*Zea mays*) is a very popular vegetable well worth growing in warm places. It is a perfect vegetable for deep freezing, but, particularly if you want it for this purpose, don't leave the cobs on the plant to get old and starchy. To freeze, pop the cobs into boiling water for seven to ten minutes, cool in cold running water. Either cut the grain from the stem or freeze whole ears. Put into plastic bags or deep freeze containers and place in freezer.

Site and Soil
Select a warm sheltered site in cooler districts – plenty of sun and well cultivated garden soil are the growing requirements. Add plenty of well-rotted organic matter to poor soils to improve moisture retention.

Special Siting
If you want a temporary screen in the garden plant strong-growing varieties like 'Silver Queen'. Plants will grow to 6 ft (180 cm) high.

Sowing Instructions
Sow indoors in pots (peat pots are the best) in late April/early May. Plant in the growing site under Hotkaps or unprotected when the risk of frost has passed. Alternatively sow directly into the growing site from mid-May, placing two or three seeds every 12–15 in (30–38 cm) down the row – the rows 15–30 in (38–76 cm) apart. If you are growing the tall, strong-growing varieties you will need the wider spacing.

How to Grow
Thin seedlings to one, once established. If you are growing them under Hotkaps, remove these when the leaves touch the top and the possibility of frost has passed. Pollen from the male tassels which form at the top of the plant floats down in the wind to pollinate the female cobs which are formed in a sheath of leaves lower down the plant. Complete wind polli-

Figure 122: Male and female flowers. (Above) Sweet corn cobs or ears.

nation is more likely if you grow plants in a block of several rows, rather than in a single row. Hoe to control weeds and as you do so, draw up some soil round the base of the stem. This encourages firm rooting. Remove basal side shoots to strengthen the main stem.

USEFUL TIP

Seek out the dwarf, early, F₁ hybrids for small compact plants to grow in the 10 ft × 12 ft (3 × 4 m) vegetable plot. Plant these 6–8 in (15–20 cm) apart.

Harvesting
A double or triple row of the dwarf 'Golden Midget' or 'Midget Hybrid' along the 10 ft (3 m) edge of the plot will yield more than twenty cobs which ripen through August and September. When the female thread-like stigmas protruding from the green sheath turn dark brown and black, ease the leafy bracts back gently to see if the grains of corn are ready. When ripe, a white milky sap will flow from the grain if you puncture it with your thumb nail. If the sap is clear and the grains small, the cob is not ready; if there is no moist sap, the grains have become too old and will be starchy. To gather, snap off the ripe cobs.

Peel away the husk and female

threads before cooking the cobs in salted water. Each plant should produce two or three cobs and you should restrict all but the strongest-growing plants to growing only this number.

Possible Problems
Poorly filled ears mean lack of proper pollination. Always plant in blocks. Control the corn borer and ear worm which attack the ears with Sevin. Consult local authorities for timing.

Figure 123: Grow sweet corn in blocks for good wind pollination.

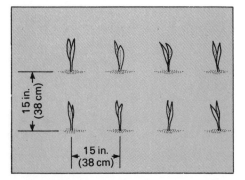

Tomatoes

The introduction in recent years of new varieties and new growing techniques for tomatoes (*Lycopersicon esculentum*) has meant that there is no reason why everyone should not have home – or even office – grown tomatoes from June to December each year. The only requirement is a window sill, fluorescent lights, or small terraced or paved area outside. If you have a garden and/or greenhouse as well, you will be able to grow masses of fresh tomatoes.

Varieties

The introduction of hybrid tomato varieties has made it easier than ever for the home gardener to be successful. In addition to their greater vigor, better quality and productivity, hybrids are more resistant to disease problems. Even if you don't start plants from seed and would rather buy them from local growers, most of whom sell only labeled seedlings, you will want to study seed catalogs for descriptions of the many hybrids, types and just standard tomato varieties available. Most tomato growth habits are now described in catalogs as indeterminate (vines with long stems that are best staked and pruned); determinate (bushy, compact vines that can be unsupported or grown in cages or containers); semi-determinate (vines that fall in between and grown in containers require some staking or, if in the garden, use of ring supports (see **How to Grow**).

Outstanding for gardens or growing in containers on terraces and roof gardens or indoors in pots in winter are many highly ornamental, early-bearing, small fruited varieties. They include 'Pixie', 'Tiny Tim', 'Small Fry', 'Tumblin' Tom' (for hanging baskets), 'Stakeless', 'Dwarf Champion' (rose pink fruits), 'Presto', 'Early Salad' and 'Patio'.

Among larger-fruited varieties are 'Springset' (67 days)' a cold-resistant hybrid of determinate habit; 'Supersonic' (79 days), a fine midseason hybrid for staking; 'Sunray' (83 days), a yellow-fruited plant for staking; 'Early Girl' (54 days), very early, and 'Roma' (75 days), a plum-shaped variety grown for paste and sauces.

Site and Soil

Sunshine is the one real requirement for good tomato growing. The brighter the light, particularly early in the year when raising young plants, the better the growth and the better the

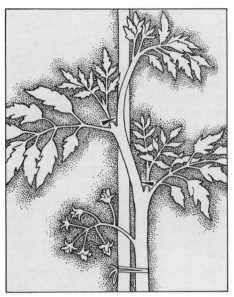

Figure 124: Remove side shoots as they form to direct energy into plants.

flavor. Tomatoes are tender plants that will not stand any frost, and if grown without protection they need a warm spot in sheltered gardens, such as a south-facing wall or fence. Cloche protection, glass-sided porches, home extensions and cold greenhouses will all lengthen the growing and harvesting season. Heated greenhouses extend the season even further, and if minimum night temperatures of 60°–65°F (15°–18°C) can be maintained, crops can be gathered more or less the whole year round.

Well-cultivated garden soils improved by the addition of well-rotted manure and other organic materials are best for tomatoes, although all garden soils are likely to give acceptable results. Use any of the proprietary potting composts to fill pots and similar growing containers. The richer the compost used, the longer will be the period before you have to give liquid feeding.

Special Siting

Use a little imagination and there is no end to the places where tomatoes can be grown – dwarf varieties in window boxes and hanging baskets use the variety 'Tumbling Tom' for example. (If you are using the smaller hanging baskets, regular liquid feeding will be necessary).

Very good crops will grow in greenhouse bed soil, but some crop rotation must be practiced. After two or three years of growing in the same soil, you must either change the soil or introduce another growing method or crop, if you are to maintain the same harvest rate.

Ring culture is a growing method that should interest tomato hobbyists. Stand 9–12 in (23–30 cm) diameter bottomless pots or rings on an isolated

Tomatoes – note the fresh green calyces.

Miniature tomatoes.

bed of aggregate (gravel, coarse ash, crushed stone) and fill them with rich potting compost (see figure 125). Plants grown in these obtain food from the ring, and water from the aggregate. After planting, water well and then leave for several days for the plants to root through the compost and out into the aggregate. Water the compost sparingly for ten to twelve days then water the aggregate regularly. Start liquid feeding once the fruit starts to swell.

Polyethylene bags filled with synthetic soil mix is an easier method and gives equally heavy cropping. Put the bags down on the cropping site, which could be a terrace, a greenhouse or a balcony for example. In England, where this method originated, special 'bags' are used, but the inventive gar-

dener can adapt any large plastic bag. Once you have got the amount of watering right, 'grow-bag' tomato growing is very easy, and you can check water requirements by tearing off a piece of newspaper and pressing this with your thumb against the surface of the peat. If moisture comes through no watering is necessary; if it remains dry, you must water.

Sowing Instructions

Although very good tomato transplants can be purchased from local outlets, it is satisfying and quite easy to raise a few plants from seed yourself. A sunny windowsill or fluorescent tubes are needed if the seedlings are to remain stocky and healthy during this indoor period. Allow about six to eight weeks to raise plants indoors, which means a late March-April sowing in most Northern regions. The process is vastly simplified by using Jiffy 7 peat pellets. Sow two seeds in each little pot, simply pressing the seeds into the growing medium. Keep warm and moist (but not soggy) and, after germination, pinch off the weaker of the two seedlings. Keep the seedlings about 4 in (10 cm) beneath the fluorescent lights. It may be necessary to shift the plants – pot plus plant – into larger peat pots filled with one of the synthetic soilless mixes, before it's safe to plant outdoors. Usually, though, the plants can remain in the Jiffy 7 pots.

How to Grow

Indoor-grown seedlings will need

gradual hardening off to toughen them to outdoor conditions. When planting tomato seedlings in their final garden positions, bury about half of the stem above the root ball in the hole. Roots will form along the stem to give the plant a firm footing to support its later burden of fruits. If spring weather remains cool and damp, setting the seedlings under Hotkaps is worthwhile and speeds growth. As the plants grow, cut a slit in the tops of the Hotkaps and remove them entirely when the weather is warm. You can then mulch the plants with compost, black plastic or whatever other material is at hand.

Planting distances depend on whether you stake the plants or let them sprawl. Staked plants can be set as close as 18–24 in (45–60·5 cm)

Pear-shaped tomatoes.

apart, but if space permits, allow more generous distances. Unstaked plants, except for the smallest and most compact varieties can consume 5–6 ft (150–180 cm) each way. So some sort of support is best in home gardens. The standard support is the single stout stake to which the main stem and one or two lower stems are tied with soft twine or cloth strips. All other shoots and suckers are removed. Easier are hoop-like wire supports obtainable at garden centers. The latest support method is to 'cage' the plants in 5 ft (150 cm) length of construction wire with a 6 in (15 cm) mesh, bent and tied to form a cylinder. Caged plants are not pruned; the fruit is reached through the wide meshes of the wire. Be sure the cages are firmly anchored to the ground.

Figure 125: Growing tomatoes in the ring culture system.

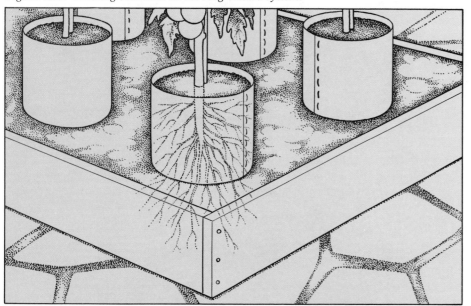

Golden tomato.

Giant fruited tomato.

Although tomato plants are heavy feeders, especially the new hybrids, too much nitrogen causes lush growth and fewer fruits. Begin feeding, about every 14 days, after fruit formation has started.

Give indoor tomatoes being grown for fruit, a shake or two to improve pollination.

Harvesting

The flavor will be best if you pick the fruit when it is red ripe, and eat it fresh from the plant! Lift the fruit, placing your thumb or finger nail at the little angled joint on the stem just above the green spidery calyx, and it will snap off easily without damaging the truss or the stem of the plant.

At the end of the growing season and before the possibility of frost, cut down the plants, leaving any ungathered fruit on the stems, and hang in a frost-free place to ripen. Alternatively, untie outdoor plants, place them on straw and cover with polyethylene to extend the ripening period.

Another method for late fall/early winter 'off-the-plant-ripening' is to cut off the trusses and place them in trays in a cool (45°–50°F (10°C)) dark position. Green fruit gathered in this way will provide you with a succession of ripening fruit through to Christmas.

You can speed up ripening by raising the temperature, but is also increases the risk of the fruit shrivelling.

Green or half-ripe tomatoes can be fried or broiled.

USEFUL TIPS

1. If you have difficulty in spacing the seeds evenly in a seed pan or pot (the creamy yellow, felty seeds tend to stick together and fall from the packet in clusters), damp the end of a wooden match and lift one seed at a time on the end of it.
2. The green stain on fingers from handling tomatoes is easily removed by rubbing with the juice of a green tomato.

Possible Problems

If the leaves turn yellow on plants soon after you have planted them out, or the stems turn blue and growth ceases, either the night temperatures are too low or the soil is too cold and too wet. Raising the temperature and planting later are the remedies.

Black patches on the base of fruit (a condition called 'blossom end rot') is caused by careless watering. Make sure your plants never suffer from lack of water, especially when they are carrying a heavy crop of fruit.

There are many other blights and bugs that can trouble tomatoes, but the truth is that few turn up in most home garden plots and even when they do, fail to spoil the entire crop. It makes good sense to buy a general purpose tomato dust and use it according to directions. It may foil early and late blight, aphids, whiteflies and flea beetles. It also makes good sense to follow a rotation of crops to foil soil-borne diseases and to select modern tomato varieties that are resistant to nematodes, verticillium and fusarium wilts. If you smoke, wash your hands in soap and water before handling tomato plants. And always avoid applying chemical weed killers anywhere near the plants which are highly sensitive to such chemicals.

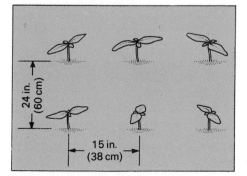

Turnips

The turnip (*Brassica rapa*) is one of those crops which need to be pulled young to give the most appetizing cooked vegetable. Plants which have grown quickly and are gathered in early summer are delicious and may be cooked and served whole or diced to complement other succulent root vegetables like carrots.

Varieties
There is quite a range of varieties to choose from, the main differences between them being in color and shape. The most popular types are those known as 'flat round' roots; the top and bottom of the root is flat but the remaining root area is globe-shaped. An example of this type is the variety called 'Just Right'. Flat-topped varieties in which only the top half is colored, such as 'Early Purple Top Milan' are also available. In addition to these there are the true globe-shaped varieties like the white 'Tokyo Cross Hybrid', which produces crisp roots in 35 days and the white and purple 'Purple Top White Globe' whose roots grow 4–5 in (10–12·5 cm) across.

Site and Soil
Any garden site is suitable, except those that are heavily shaded. All well cultivated garden soils are suitable, but the best shaped roots grow in soil that has been manured and enriched for previous crops. Plenty of organic matter in the soil gives the rapid root growth necessary for the production of succulent roots. They are fast growing crops and will be ready for pulling in seven to eight weeks, so use turnips as catch crops, i.e. sow a row on any spare

Flat round turnip.

Purple topped turnip.

soil before or after slower maturing vegetables.

Sowing Instructions
Sow successively outside from late March/early April, every three weeks to July. These sowings will mature in about eight to twelve weeks – the warmer the weather the faster the maturity – and the roots should be lifted to eat young and fresh. Late July/early August sowings will provide maincrop roots to lift in November and store for winter use. Sow the seed in rows 12 in (30 cm) apart and cover very lightly with soil.

How to Grow
As the seedlings produce the first rough leaves, thin them out to stand 4 in (10 cm) apart along the row. Pull some early roots so that the remainder stand at 8 in (20 cm) apart. This two-stage harvesting is very useful to obtain young roots in early fall, leaving the second for maincrop use. The only other attention that is needed is occasional hoeing in order to control weeds.

Harvesting
Start pulling the young turnips as soon as they are large enough to cook. This should certainly be before they reach tennis ball size, which is as large as quality will allow. You can check the size by pushing the foliage aside with your hands – part of the root will be above ground. If they are allowed to grow big and old, they will be coarse and woody and the mustardy flavor will be too strong. Lift the maincrop roots carefully in November, screw off the tops by hand and store in clamps (See Storage, page 119) and boxes of peat and sand.

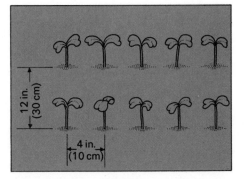

Possible Problems

As turnips belong to the brassica family, they can fall victim to the pests and diseases of cabbages and other green vegetables. Generally, however, they are very easy to grow and the only really likely problem is flea beetle attack. This pest loves hot dry conditions, so be particularly on the lookout if you are growing an early crop. Signs of attack are neat round holes in the young seedling leaves. Rotenone or pyrethrum dust will give quick control. Apply it to the leaves in the early morning.

Split roots may occur, particularly if heavy rain or watering follows a dry period. The splitting will be worse if the crop was large enough to pull ahead of the dry spell.

Very swollen and distorted roots will be produced on soils infected by the disease club root. If the soil has been proved to contain this disease it is best to avoid growing turnips.

USEFUL TIPS

1. If turnip roots are left in storage too long and produce blanched shoots, try cooking the shoots.
2. The fast-growing F₁ hybrid turnips such as 'Tokyo Cross' grow very well in deep planters and other containers on terraces and roofs. Very large roots can be produced, and if they have an ample water supply they retain the quality of small young roots grown in the open soil. After harvesting, another crop can be grown.

TURNIPS – grown for greens

Seedling turnips grown to provide a

Turnip tops.

A variety of golden turnip.

fresh green vegetable full of iron were popular in the past and used to be a major crop in country cottage gardens. For some reason they have fallen out of favor in recent years, but with fresh winter and early spring vegetables usually in short supply, turnip greens deserve a return to popularity.

Site and Soil

Any cultivated soil is suitable. Choose a spot that is sheltered a little from the hardest of winter weather.

Sowing Instructions

Either scatter the seed over the surface soil and rake it in, or draw shallow drills 9–12 in (23–30 cm) apart, where weed growth might be a problem in late August/early September.

How to Grow

Leave the seedlings as you have sown them, do *not* thin them out. Apart from hoeing between the rows to control weeds, no cultural treatment is necessary.

Harvesting

Cut the leaves when they are 6–8 in (15–20 cm) high and cook in the same way as spinach or leafy spring greens. You can begin to gather them eight to ten weeks after sowing, although early spring is the main harvesting period.

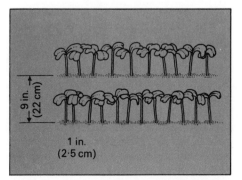

9 in. (22 cm)

1 in. (2·5 cm)

Pests and Diseases and their Control

The first and most important method of pest and disease control is to try to cultivate only strong, vigorously growing, healthy plants. Invariably it is the weaker growing specimens which fall first to the onslaught of pest and disease, and given this pocket of infection, the trouble will rapidly spread to adjacent, stronger plants.

This spread of infection emphasizes the importance of garden hygiene. Single diseased plants are, as a general rule, best removed and destroyed, either by burning, or better still, by burying in the trash that goes to the local dump.

Weeds as well as vegetables offer comfortable accommodation for pests and disease, so it is essential to keep the plot as free as possible from weeds. For the same reason the ground should be cleared of all crops once harvesting is complete. The dying remains of plants – be it leaves, stems, roots and seed pods are perfect pest and disease building spots and should therefore be cleared and placed on to the compost heap where break-down can begin as soon as possible.

Even where good growing and this kind of hygiene is carried out, the occasional pest and disease problem is possible and when this happens I see no harm in resorting to chemical control. It is very important, however, *to follow absolutely the instructions given by the manufacturers*. Be sure to keep concentrated chemicals and sprays away from children and out of fish ponds.

Chemicals will control the problem either by direct contact or systemically, which means the chemical is first taken up by the plant and then works its pest and disease destruction from the sap. As systemic chemicals are carried right through the plant system, the chance of missed spots, as occurs with inadequate spraying and dusting with contact chemicals, is less likely.

If you are using chemical dusts, early morning applications when the plants are still damp with dew, are the most effective as they give a better chance of the dust sticking to leaves and stems of the plants. Apply liquid sprays of contact pesticides and fungicides evenly over the tops and undersides of leaves and stems to get as complete control as possible.

There are a number of chemicals which can be applied close to harvest time, but it may be necessary to leave the crop for a given period after spraying and before harvesting, with some of them. You must observe these periods and also be extra careful when spraying plants in flower. Bees, as well as pests, can be killed by some sprays, so if it is unavoidable to spray flowering plants do so in the evening when the bees are not active.

There are also several chemicals which can be mixed into the soil to give a long period of pest control. It is wise in all cases, however, to use only the amount that is absolutely necessary – prevention may be better than cure in most cases, but you should still avoid using pesticides and fungicides continuously. If you do use them repeatedly, the chance of building up resistance to the control chemical increases, thus reducing or losing altogether the effect of a good weapon in the garden chemical armoury. Ringing the changes and using alternative sprays is the best way to avoid the build-up of resistance, where a pest or disease problem persists.

Aphids.

PESTS AND THEIR CONTROL

Aphids: A pest commonly called plant louse. There are black colored, gray cabbage aphis, rose aphis and several other types and shapes! Some of each kind have wings, others are wingless and they all breed at an alarming rate if not controlled. Some people recommend spraying them with soapy water, but all this does is wash them off the plant. Prompt destruction of the aphids is better, and can be achieved with materials like rotenone, lindane and malathion.

Birds: Sparrows and other birds can be kept from pecking seedlings by stretching occasional strands of black cotton thread over the rows of emerging seedlings. Large nets placed over winter green crops are the best way to protect them from pigeons. A cat might be kept to frighten the birds but their soil scratching and rolling can be more of a hindrance than a help. (Deterrents may be helpful to frighten off cats and dogs without harming them.)

Cabbage White butterfly.

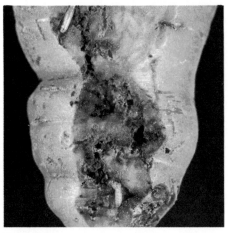

Carrot Fly.

Cabbage Root Fly: This produces small white maggots which feed on the roots of cabbage and other brassicas causing the plants to wilt. Destroy all the maggots you can find by crushing them and then either water the plants with lindane or dip the roots at transplanting time in calomel dust. You can also treat the soil with bromophos and diazinon.

Turn to page 60 for a simple non-chemical way of controlling cabbage root fly using a circular disk of rubber or similar material.

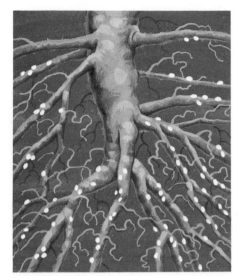

Eelworm.

ings while the earworm more generally attacks midseason and later crops. Many home gardeners would rather cut out the spoiled sections of ears – often minimal – than spray. Sevin (carbaryl) can control both pests. For borers, spray four times at five-day intervals, starting when plants are 18 in (45 cm) tall. For earworms, make five applications at two- to three-day intervals, starting as tassels form. Clean up in the fall.

Eelworm or Nematode: These tiny larvae drastically reduce crops of potato and other crops. Chemical control is difficult in the garden, but strict rotation of crops coupled with the using of certified seed potatoes only should prevent attack.

Flea Beetle: Small shiny black beetles which jump if you brush your hand

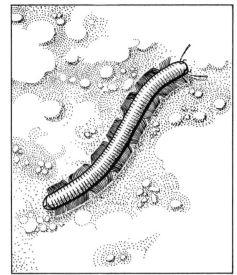

Millipede.

placing these on their sides down the rows.

Millipedes and Cutworms: Millipedes are slow moving and curl up when touched. Cutworms are lighter in color and look more like caterpillars. Both eat through the roots of plants and may be controlled with soil pest killers like lindane, carbaryl (sold under the name Sevin). Or, to control millipedes, add diazinon to the soil and deep dig. (Note that *centipedes* are not a pest.)

Onion Fly: The adult resembles a

Cabbage White Butterfly: Green caterpillars which rapidly eat the leaves of all greens. Pick them off whenever you can and destroy them. Dust or spray plants with lindane, carbaryl, rotenone or similar material.

Carrot Fly: These tiny maggots which look like small wireworms eat carrot and parsnip roots. Use seed treatments and treat the soil with lindane to get control. (Early carrot crops are not affected.)

Celery Fly: This is a kind of leaf miner which causes brown spots on the leaves of celery and may also attack beets. Crush the larvae between your finger and thumb and spray the plant with malathion. Give liquid feed after spraying to help plants recover.

Corn Borer and Earworm: The borer is most destructive in earlier plant-

Striped Flea Beetle.

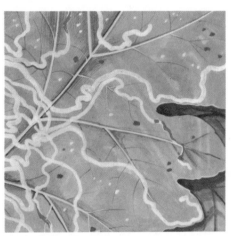

Leaf Miner

over seedlings. All brassica seedlings, including radish, are liable to attack in hot dry conditions, and indications are neat round holes appearing in the leaves. Lindane dust gives control of this beetle. Repeated evening watering will also help to prevent and control this pest.

Leaf Miner: Little white maggots which tunnel into the leaves of celery, beets and other crops – they can be killed by pinching with your thumb nail and by spraying the plant with lindane and malathion.

Mice: Will eat newly sown seeds, and are especially fond of peas and squash. You can control them quite efficiently by putting mouse bait in old cans and

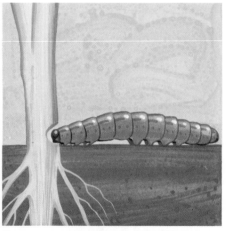

Cutworm.

house fly, but it is the small young whitish grubs which do the damage. Lift and destroy infected plants, making sure if possible that you capture all the grubs. Apply either calomel dust to the seed rows or diazinon granules to the soil, and calomel paste to the base of onion sets and shallots if this pest is a real problem. Attack is not all that

113

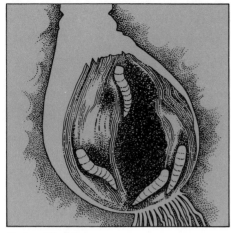

Onion Fly Maggots.

frequent, but the pest is most likely to occur in dry soil conditions.

Potato Beetle: Bound to appear as soon as potato foliage develops. Look for the yellow and black beetles and their fat red grubs. Dust or spray weekly with methoxychlor or Sevin.

Red Spider Mite: Very tiny red or yellowish-red creatures which feed on the undersides of the leaves, turning them a rusty color. Attacks from this pest are most likely in a hot, dry atmosphere and with severe infestations a fine webbing also occurs on the leaves. Spray infected plants regularly with water; in greenhouses spray with rotenone and malathion and use azobenzene smokes. Except in very hot, dry, weather, red spider is only a pest of crops such as tomato, peppers, melons, beans and eggplant, grown in greenhouses.

Colarodo Potato Beetle.

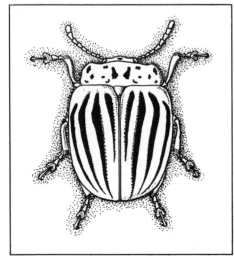

Slugs and snails: Signs of attack, which usually occur at night, are slime trails and plants with holes chewed in their leaves and stems. Both pests are easily controlled by using proprietary slug pellets or slug spray. Slug bait based on methiocarb will destroy slugs even in wet weather, but there is a chance that they will recover from metaldehyde-based materials in wet conditions, so repeat the application after a very heavy rainfall. You can entice and trap slugs by placing empty half grapefruit and orange skins upturned on the soil.

The small black slug which lives

Red Spider Mite damage.

Slugs and Snails.

below ground and eats holes in potatoes and other root crops is the most difficult to control. Growing early potatoes and lifting them early is the most effective way to avoid excessive damage. Improving drainage and watering the soil with liquid slug preparations will help too. Pieces of potato stuck on canes and pushed into the soil in spring make good slugtraps.

Squash Vine Borer: Also attacks cucumbers, melons and pumpkins. Difficult to control but try methoxychlor, spraying in early summer three times at ten-day intervals.

White Fly.

Whitefly: A light-colored fast moving insect and a persistent pest of greenhouse plants. It can be controlled by spraying with resmethrin, which allows the crop to be harvested within 24 hours of spraying.

Wireworm: The distinctive golden larvae of wireworm attack root crops such as potatoes, carrots and parsnips and will also eat through many seedling roots. This pest occurs particularly in turf so watch for it after digging up grass. Break larvae you find in half to destroy them and use soil chemicals like lindane for control. As with black slugs, a trap can be made using potatoes.

Wireworm.

DISEASES AND THEIR CONTROL

Asparagus Rust: Rusty brown powder on the foliage and black streaks on the stems in late summer. Cut the stems to the ground and burn. Plant resistant varieties. The 'Tree Onion', (rather like shallots but growing on a single stem 3 ft (90 cm) high), can also be infected with this disease.

Asparagus Violet Root Rot: Premature yellowing of the foliage and the presence of violet fungus strands on the roots. This condition is most likely to occur on old plants, but the disease will spread outwards to other plants in late summer so carefully lift and destroy those that are infected. Avoid planting root crops in infected soil; rotate with green crops, such as cabbage, which will be unaffected.

Black Leg of Potatoes: Plants turn yellow prematurely and will not develop fully. If you lift yellowing plants you will find they have a black shrivelled root and the tuber will probably be wet, slimy and have an unpleasant smell. Cold, wet soils encourage this disease which you can discourage by rotating crops and planting certified disease-free seed.

Botrytis: Commonly called 'Gray Mold' because of the fluffy gray mold which develops on the soft brown areas caused by this disease. Its brown-colored spots may appear on the leaves of lettuce in winter and, to a lesser extent, crops such as peppers in the fall and broad beans from late winter to early summer. Avoid cold, damp conditions for lettuce under glass and clear all old plant remains immediately. Control with dusts and sprays using materials such as benlate and thiram.

Blossom End Rot.

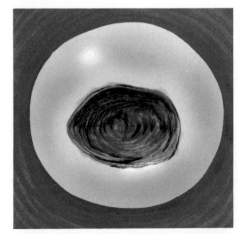

Buck-eye Rot and Blossom End Rot of Tomatoes: Buck-eye Rot causes concentric brown rings on the plant's lower trusses. It is splashed up from the soil, so be careful when watering with a hose. Blossom End Rot is much more common and is a dark green circular spot at the tip of the fruit which turns brown or black and is of a shrunken, leathery texture. It is caused by irregular watering, and it can be avoided by keeping the plants evenly moist – not subjecting them alternately to very wet and then very dry states.

Celery Leaf Spot.

Celery Leaf Spot: Brown spots on the leaves with tiny black fungus spores in the center are symptoms of this disease. Seed is treated to avoid initial infection and, you can use bordeaux and zineb sprays subsequently to give lasting control.

Club Root of Brassicas: Also called 'finger and toe' disease because of the plump round root swellings which result from this disease. The plants look sickly, are stunted and may wilt in hot weather. Don't confuse club root swellings with the swollen galls caused by turnip gall weevil; if you cut through club root swelling it is complete with a mottled appearance – the gall weevil swelling is hollow and often the maggot will be seen inside. Clubroot disease enters the root from the soil and heavy liming will control it. Add 4–5 oz per yd (100–125 gm per 0·8 sq m) immediately after clearing an infected crop. Burn all the diseased roots – if you just leave them to rot down, they can infect the soil for at least seven years. Pour one cupful of terrachlor mixed according to directions in hole when planting.

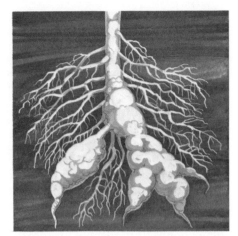

Club Root.

Damping Off: Sudden death of seedlings which keel over and on close inspection have shrivelled stems at ground level. This disease infects many seeds raised indoors in pots and the use of clean compost, clean containers and clean water is fundamental to control. Fungicidal seed treatment captan and synthetic soil mixes, are a help in controlling this disease.

Foot Rot of Peas and Beans: Early yellowing of the foliage and dry shrivelling of the root and base of stem, which become discolored reddish brown. Avoid replanting in infected soil and plan long rotations, i.e. three years or more between successive pea and bean crops. Applications of fungicidal seed treatment will reduce the problem.

Leaf Mold of Tomatoes, (*Cladosporium*): Yellow spots on the upper surface of the leaves and grayish mold beneath, occurring from June/July onwards under glass. Warm, humid atmosphere encourages this disease and although copper sprays can be

Leaf Mold.

used to help control it, it is better to grow disease-resistant varieties.

Mildew – Powdery Mildew: Powdery white and grayish-white patches which cover the leaves and other aerial parts of the plant. Attacks are likely on such plants as cucumbers, squash, rutabagas and turnips. Hot and dry conditions, especially if accompanied by heavy dew, encourage the spread of this disease and squash and rutabagas grown in the garden in early fall are likely to be subject to these conditions. Keeping plants well watered and dusting with flowers of sulphur or spraying with copper based fungicides such as bordeaux will help to keep the disease in check.

Mosaic Virus.

Downy Mildew: A grayish-brown or violet-gray growth on the undersides of leaves, with yellowish spots appearing on the upper surface. Young cabbage plants in a cold frame in winter where the atmosphere is damp are vulnerable to attack and cold wet conditions will encourage attack on spinach, lettuce, peas and onions. A dry atmosphere is death to downy mildew but garden hygiene is important for control, so remove any old crop remains which would otherwise allow this disease to carry over from one year to the next.

Mosaic Virus: Virus diseases are often transmitted by aphids, which suck the sap from an infected plant and carry it to others. Affected plants are dwarfed, the leaves turn pale and become mottled-dark and light green. It is important to sow only clean seed, and to destroy single infected plants immediately, so the disease does not

have a chance to spread. Also control aphids, (page 112). Crops which are affected by mosaic virus include lettuce, squash and tomatoes, but there are resistant varieties of tomato avail-

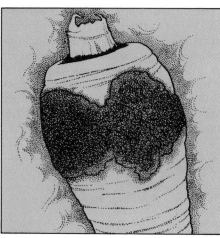

Parsnip Canker.

able. It is particularly advisable to use these specially produced varieties where the disease has occurred previously.

Parsnip Canker: Rusty brown marks and cracks, especially around the top of the root. Control carrot flies (see page 112) as they will encourage the spread of this disease. Grow resistant varieties and avoid excess nitrogen in the soil by being careful with fertilizer application.

Potato blight: Brown blotches on the leaves which spread, making the lower foliage turn yellow. The disease will also spread to infect the tubers, and appears as sunken areas of reddish brown which soon spread to turn the whole tuber rotten. Damp, humid weather from July onwards encour-

Potato Blight.

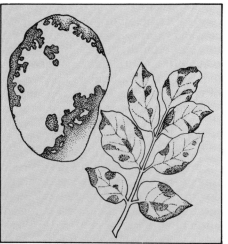

ages the spread of this disease. Spray every ten to fourteen days with copper based sprays, maneb or zineb fungicides. Outdoor tomatoes can also be affected with similar damage to leaf and fruit, and may be protected in the same way.

Potato Scab: Black, rough scabby, patches on the skin of potatoes which look unpleasant although they are peeled off before cooking. Add organic matter to the soil to help reduce the likelihood of attack. Make sure the soil is acid.

White Rot of Onions: Affects onions and also leeks, making the leaves turn yellow and die back while a white mold covers the base of the plant. This soil-borne fungus can remain in the soil for eight or more years so dig up and burn infected plants with the immediately surrounding soil. Con-

White Rot of Onion.

trol by crop rotation and weekly sprays of maneb or zineb. Note that the onion, 'White Lisbon', is particularly susceptible to this disease, so keep a careful watch if growing this variety.

In Conclusion
This list of pests and diseases may look formidable, but in fact it is seldom that the gardener is faced by many of them. More than half of those listed I have never personally encountered in twenty years of my home vegetable growing and none have prevented the cultivation of acceptable crops.

With judicious use of just a few chemicals – perhaps slug pellets, lindane, malathion, bordeaux and maneb dust, most vegetable problems can be kept at bay and will not present a serious threat.

Weeds and their Control

Although weeds tend to grow faster and more prolifically than anything else in the garden they are really only a difficulty when they are allowed to get the upper hand. Like so many other things, the answer is to keep them constantly under control. Picking out the perennial roots of such weeds as quack grass and dandelion, when digging, is the first essential. Removing the roots at that stage will relieve you of future problems.

The vast majority of weeds – that is, all those without persistent perennial

Figure 126: Hoe regularly between rows of vegetables to remove annual weeds.

roots – can just be dug into the soil at the end of each season. You can then easily control weed growth throughout the following spring by quickly and lightly hoeing over the surface every three weeks or so. Earlier in the

year, you can hoe over the plot less frequently, but as the temperature increases thus speeding up the growth of all plants – including weeds – you will find more frequent hoeing is necessary. Hoe even before you can see any weeds, as this destroys germinating weed seeds before they have time to become established.

MULCHES AND MULCHING

Along with hoeing and cultivating, mulches and mulching are an important means of weed control. If applied soon enough in the spring, mulches prevent weeds from germinating at all. A mulch should be at least 2–3 in (5–7·5 cm) thick and may require replenishing during the season as the materials begin to decay.

Mulching materials depend on what is available – rough compost, rotted or semi-rotted leaves, pine needles, sea-weeds, rotted sawdust (never use fresh sawdust), rotted animal manures, semi-rotted wood chips, grass clippings, partly rotted straw or hay and even newspapers. Peat moss, although often recommended for mulching, has some disadvantages for this use. Among them are its cost, its light weight (in strong winds it can blow away) and the way it forms an impenetrable crust that sheds rainfall and water. It is better used as a soil additive. A plus for organic mulches is that, as they decay, they add valuable humus to the soil.

A non-organic mulch is black plastic, sold in rolls in garden centers. The 'blackness' of the plastic prevents growth of germinating seedlings by

Figure 127: Use a dribble box for accurate placement of contact weedkiller.

keeping out light. Black plastic also has the advantage of retaining soil warmth, a decided advantage with those crops that need heat for the best results. They include watermelons, most kinds of muskmelons, snap beans, squash, cucumber, okra, tomatoes and eggplants.

WEEDKILLERS

Digging out perennial roots and repeated cultivation or using mulches are really all that is needed for nearly complete weed control, but if you have a large plot and feel you need additional help, there are several chemical weedkillers commercially available. The trouble with most chemical weedkillers, as far as the home garden is concerned, is that they have been

Figure 128: Although annual weeds do not present as great a problem as perennials, they should still be strictly controlled. Pictured here from l. to r. are Common Chickweed, Shepherd's Purse, Sun Spurge, Annual Meadow Grass, Annual Nettle and Groundsel.

Figure 129: Perennial weeds are often very hard to eradicate successfully. Pictured here from l. to r. they are: Dock, Quack Grass, Ground Elder, Bindweed, Bulbous Oxalis, Horsetail.

formulated for market gardens devoted to one crop. The important thing with all of them is to follow the directions on the container exactly. Also federal and state regulations differ and some chemicals can only be sold to and used by professional gardeners. Check with local authorities for the latest information.

A long-term weedkiller that should be effective against weeds germinating for a season is simazine. Apply to a clean, wet soil in early spring.

Other chemicals to consider are chloramben (a trade name is Vegiben) which can be used among tomatoes and peppers to control annual weeds and grasses before they germinate; DCPA (a trade name is Dacthal) which can be used among certain vegetables after being transplanted or

Figure 130: Perennial weeds may be controlled by pushing leaves into a jam jar of suitable weedkiller. This is an effective way of controlling bindweed.

seeded to control weeds before they germinate.

The complete long term weedkillers really have no place on the vegetable plot but the complete short term ones can be very useful. Short term weedkillers, such as *paraquat*, destroy all green plant material they touch but as soon as they reach the soil are rendered harmless. The sale and use of paraquat is highly restricted in many states and so it is not available to home gardeners. Check your County Extension Agent for information on its regulation. Be careful not to splash the vegetables with this material, however, because it will kill where it touches. Paraquat is very poisonous to human beings so keep the concentrate locked away and use all the dilute material once mixed (water any surplus onto spare soil where it will promptly be converted to harmless material). Never put it into harmless-looking bottles which may then provide a temptation to children.

One watering with paraquat will knock out the annual weeds. Repeated watering with paraquat will be necessary to wear down and eventually knock out persistent weeds with perennial roots like convolvulus, couch grass and ground elder.

Selective Weedkillers

Perennial weeds can also be killed by very careful applications of selective weedkillers. A good example is provided by the selective lawn weedkillers, which, when diluted and watered on grass, kill most broadleaved weeds yet leave the grass

unharmed. Diluted lawn weedkillers can be painted on the leaves of bindweed (convolvulus), docks and other perennial weeds in a vegetable plot. The weed leaves will take up the weedkillers and are destroyed, while the vegetables continue to thrive. Another way to destroy weeds selectively is to pull away several stems, for example of bindweed, and push these into a jar of diluted selective weedkiller. Spot applications in this way are useful to check perennial weeds in perennial crops.

A simple way of removing perennial weeds such as ground elder and quack grass is to cover the infested area with a deep mulch of 4 in (10 cm) or more of peat. The weed roots come up from the soil, run through the peat and may be lifted and shaken out.

Figure 131: These weeds grow commonly on poorly drained soil. They are from l. to r.: Common Sedge, Lady's Smock, Common Rush and Forget-me-not.

Storage of Vegetables

Brussels sprouts, parsnips and savoys are among the comparatively few vegetables you can gather fresh from the garden in winter. This does not mean, however, that you cannot enjoy your own home-grown produce throughout the year, for there are a number of crops which you can harvest in bulk and then use from storage as you want them. In addition it is not always practical or possible to gather the growing winter crops – parsnips will very often be frozen into the ground after a severe frost, which can occur even in temperate regions, and anyone who has gathered sprouts covered with hoar frost will not be in a hurry to repeat the experience!

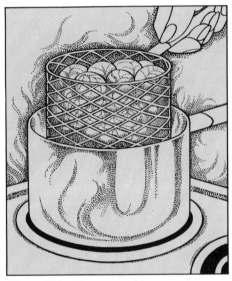

Figure 132: Most vegetables must be blanched before freezing.

FREEZING

There are various different ways of storing vegetables, and the useful life of most crops can be extended. More and more homes are now equipped with deep freezers which enable an instant supply of almost any type of vegetable throughout the year. Many vegetable varieties have been specifically bred to suit the commercial growers who are contracted to deep freeze processing factories and those varieties are also available in seed form to home gardeners.

Nearly all special freezing varieties have been so developed that the whole crop will mature at once. Fields of peas, beans and brussels sprouts for example are grown to be ready at all the same time, so that machine harvesting or complete field clearance may be done at one go. If one of your aims in growing your own vegetables is to make sure your deep freeze is well stocked up with garden produce to see you through the winter, you may well like to grow some of these specially produced freezing varieties. However, those people who would rather have fresh vegetables from the garden over the longest period will find it better to grow the ordinary varieties than the ones produced for the freezer.

The growing of vegetables can never be entirely predictable, owing to the vagaries of the weather and so on. If you do happen to get a sudden glut of peas or beans – perhaps more than the family can eat – you can freeze the surplus in polyethylene bags in the freezer section of an ordinary domestic fridge. Put them into the bags after you have prepared them for the table – and you will have the equivalent of a week or two longer supply of vegetables. Deep freeze owners will be familiar with the preparation of vegetables for freezing; most need to be blanched in boiling water for a minute or two, then cooled and sealed in plastic bags or plastic containers.

There are several vegetables that are suitable for freezing – the popular ones are found in the supermarket freezers and include particularly beans, broccoli spears, sprouts, peas, spinach and sweet corn. The succulent french or snap beans are the easiest green pods for freezing and are ideal for this kind of storage. Broad beans are excellent too, and best results will be obtained from the green-seeded varieties, which must be gathered while they are very young and succulent. In fact most crops are best gathered young but broad beans and garden peas really have to be picked at the earliest stage possible to give the best flavor.

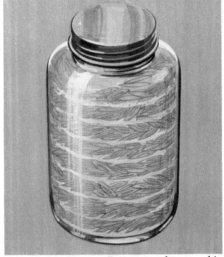

Figure 133: Runner Beans may be stored in common salt.

Root vegetables such as carrot, parsnip and turnip can be diced and frozen, but they break with the 'gather very young' rule, for the more mature roots are best. Some crops such as sweet peppers can be frozen fresh without blanching first. Try freezing cubes of fresh melon too, if you have some to spare – in fact, don't be afraid to experiment – most vegetables that are cooked before eating can be deep frozen. Asparagus, artichokes, eggplant, sliced cabbage, celery and squash, pieces of cauliflower and spinach are all good examples. Avoid only the water filled succulent salad crops like chicory, endive, lettuce, cucumbers and tomatoes (unless tomatoes are wanted for sauces and stewing in which case the tomatoes can be cut in wedges and packed in freezer containers). For directions consult cook books.

Figure 134: Stages of clamping vegetables.

Figure 135: Dry herbs by hanging in bunches or spreading on trays. Rub between hands when dry and sieve to remove large pieces. Store in labeled jars.

SALT STORAGE

Some blanched vegetables can be stored in a brine solution, and salt is also useful to store runner beans. Wash, string and slice the beans just as for cooking. Cover the base of a large jar or plastic container with ½ in (1 cm) or so of salt and put a layer of sliced beans 1 in (2·5 cm) deep on top. Fill the jar with alternate layers of beans and salt until it is full. Leave for a day or so, during which time the beans will settle and you will have to add more layers. When the container is almost full, cover with a last layer of salt, then seal and store it. When you want to use the beans, wash them several times in fresh, cold water to remove excess salt before cooking in the normal way.

Figure 136: Hold onions by the stems and string together firmly.

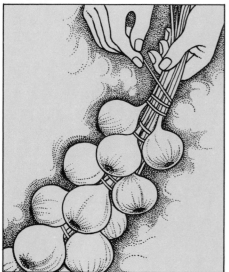

STORING IN CLAMPS AND IN PEAT AND SAND

Such methods of storage as freezing, salting, pickling and bottling are all more in the province of cooks than the gardener, and there are various ways in which vegetables can be stored in the garden. The traditional system for all winter-stored root crops whether potatoes, carrots, beets, celeriac or whatever, is clamping. For this you will need some straw and a patch of clear soil in the vegetable garden. Cover the soil with the straw and heap the harvested roots onto it. Surround the heap with straw and dig a ditch around the heap throwing soil from the trench over the straw. If you live in an area that is prone to heavy frost make sure you have a good layer of straw and a good deep layer of soil. However, if you are in a milder region, leave a small tuft of straw sticking out of the top of the clamp to allow air to escape.

Most gardens will not yield sufficient roots to fill large free-standing clamps however, and so instead make small heaps either in a shed or against a sheltered fence. Space the vegetables between layers of sand or peat and, if possible, cover with sacking and polyethylene to prevent the sand freezing.

The easiest way of all to store the small quantity of roots produced in most gardens each fall is in boxes of dry peat. Peat which feels dry to the touch, in fact contains quite a quantity of moisture, and if you use it to surround such roots as carrots, beets, turnip and chicory it will prevent them drying out and shrivelling. It is a good insulator and will protect the vegetables against quite severe frost. If it becomes frozen you can break through the outer frozen crust to get access to the roots which will remain unaffected. If, on the other hand, you store the roots in damp sand, a frost will seal them in, making it impossible to get to them until it thaws out again.

The lighter colored sphagnum peats are better for root crop storage than the black ones in my experience. Whatever peat you use can, of course be dug into the soil or used for some other garden purpose when you have used all the stored vegetables.

The laziest, but quite effective way of storing root vegetables is to lift them, place a layer of peat in the soil, and spread out a layer of roots and so on until all the roots are covered. Protect the heap from rain by a covering of polyethylene held down by burying the edges under soil.

If all these methods are just too much trouble for you, you can store roots in paper bags in a cool shed. Don't use polyethylene bags – they hold moisture and the condensation that collects on the inside of the bag is likely to make the roots go soft. Potatoes will store well in paper sacks in a cool frost-free building.

DRYING

Warm air drying, usually with warmth from the sun, is another method of extending the useful life of vegetables and herbs. Herbs in fact require somewhat special treatment but bulb onions and shallots, for example, if gathered when they are fully

Figure 137: Onions hanging in storage in a net (left), strung together (right).

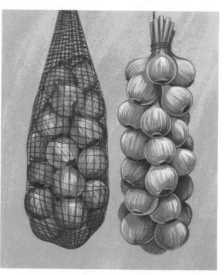

developed, may be ripened and dried in the sun for storage and used round to the next season's crop.

Drying and ripening can be done outside on the soil, or alternatively you can construct wire-netting-based racks as frames on which you put the onions and other crops. These are effective as they allow air movement from all sides. If crops are moved to the greenhouse or put under frames the drying will be even faster.

When they are quite dry and their skins crackly and brittle, onions can be stored by hanging in ropes or spaced out in shallow trays.

Drying herbs is an effective storage method that gives supplies of culinary flavorings the year round. Collect the foliage of parsley, thyme, sage and mint before the plants start to flower. This usually means you can take two crops – one in July and another in September.

Cut the leaves on short stems using a sharp knife or pruners for woody plants like thyme and sage. Group them in small bunches for ease of handling or drop the short sprigs into a fine mesh sieve. You can then either hang up the bunches or spread the stems in trays to dry. The secret of successful herb drying is to subject them to rapid drying in quite hot air, up to 100°F (38°C) out of direct sunshine. Although the foliage should be cut in full sun so it is dry and thereafter left to wilt in the sun for an hour or so, don't leave it in full sun to dry completely. This would take three weeks, and much of the flavor would be destroyed.

When they have reached the stage of being brittle, rub the sprigs between your hands to reduce them to usable size. You can sieve the rubbed herbs to take out the large and dusty particles, and then store them in sealed jars. Herbs treated in this way can be stored almost indefinitely. Remember they have a stronger flavor than their fresh counterparts.

If you want to dry dill, peas, beans and celery seed, for example, to store leave them on the plant to do most of the ripening and drying. You must then catch the crop just as the first few seeds fall naturally. Gather the heads of celery and pods of peas and put them in shallow paper-lined trays and paper bags to completely ripen. If you gather a few days before the natural release of seed, the crop will be quite all right, and the seeds will finish ripening in the pod and husk.

STORAGE AT A GLANCE CHART

Crop	Storage Method	Period of Use from Storage
ARTICHOKE (Globe)	Deep freeze	To the next crop
ARTICHOKE (Jerusalem)	Clamp or paper bag	October – May
ASPARAGUS	Deep freeze	To the next crop
AUBERGINE	Deep freeze	To the next crop
BEANS (Broad)	Deep freeze	To the next crop
BEANS (Snap)	Deep freeze	To the next crop
BEANS (Wax Snap or Butter)	Dry	The year round
BEANS (Runner)	In salt	The year round
BEETS	Clamp or in peat/sand	Almost to the next crop
BROCCOLI	Deep freeze	To the next crop
BRUSSELS SPROUTS	Deep freeze	To the next crop
CABBAGE (winter keeping)	In trays or on wire racks	November to March
CABBAGE – RED	Pickle in vinegar	The year round
CARROT	Clamp or in peat/sand	November to April
CAULIFLOWER	Deep freeze sprigs of flowering head	To the next crop
CELERIAC	Clamp or in peat/sand	November to March
CELERY (blanched stems)	Deep freeze	To the next crop
CHICORY	Store roots in peat/sand	Forced February to April
COURGETTE	Deep freeze	To the next crop
EGGPLANT	Deep freeze	To the next crop
MELON	Deep freeze	To the next crop
ONIONS	In ropes or trays	To the next crop
PARSNIP	Clamp or in peat/sand	November – May
PEAS	Deep freeze	To the next crop
PEAS	Dried	The year round
PEPPERS	Deep freeze	To the next crop
POTATOES	Clamp or in paper bags	To the next crop
RADISH (winter)	Clamp or in peat/sand	To the spring radish
RHUBARB	Deep freeze	To the next crop
RUTABAGA	Clamp or paper bags	Winter and spring
SALSIFY	Clamp or in peat/sand	Winter and early spring
SCORZONERA	Clamp or in peat/sand	Winter and early spring
SHALLOTS	In ropes or trays	To the next crop
SPINACH	Deep freeze	To the next crop
SQUASH	Deep freezer	To the next crop
SWEET CORN	Deep freeze	To the next crop
TOMATO	Hang up unripened trusses or store in boxes	October to December
TURNIP	Clamp or in peat/sand	To the next crop

Calendar of Garden Activity-Spring

Early spring

Harvest: Brussels sprouts, kale and cabbage and use as spring greens. Lift vegetables overwintering in the garden, such as Jerusalem artichokes, parsnips and leeks.

Sow – indoors: Broccoli, lettuce, celery.

Sow – outdoors: Cress, broad beans, peas, onions, radish and spinach. If you have a cold frame, sow lettuce in it.

Plant: Onion sets and shallots.

Cultivate: Put seed potatoes in shallow trays in a light frost-free place to develop short shoots. Start preparing the garden's soil generally, but don't overwork clay soil that is wet. Spread a general fertilizer such as 5–10–5.

Mid-Spring

Harvest: New green shoots from brussels sprouts as green vegetable, and spring cabbage as greens. Lift any remaining leeks and heel them in for use in next few weeks.

Sow – indoors: Tomato, eggplant, peppers using Jiffy 7 peat pellets or standard peat pots. Grow under fluorescent lights if sunny windows are lacking.

Sow – outdoors: Carrots, lettuce, cress, leeks, *onions, parsley, beets, *radish, *spinach.

Plant: Onion sets, lettuce and broccoli seedlings from indoors and cold frame. Use Hotkaps as cloches if weather remains cool.

Cultivate: Apply quick-acting fertilizer to cabbage and lettuce. Start collecting mulching materials, supports for tomatoes.

Late spring

Harvest: In many regions, it will be time to start cutting asparagus. Also ready: radishes, lettuce, cress, spinach.

Sow – indoors: Melons, squash, cucumbers in Jiffy 7 or regular peat pots.

Sow – outdoors: Beets, carrots, sweet corn, turnips and if the soil and weather are warm enough, snap and lima beans. Melons, squash, cucumbers can be sown under Hotkaps in most Northern regions.

Cultivate: Set out celery plants started indoors. Be sure to harden them off first. Check pea supports.

Protect: Seedlings from slugs which thrive in spring. Buy baits at garden center or try the beer in saucer method, sinking the saucer so slugs can reach the brew. Pinch out tips of broad beans if black aphids are present or spray with malathion.

*Successional sowings

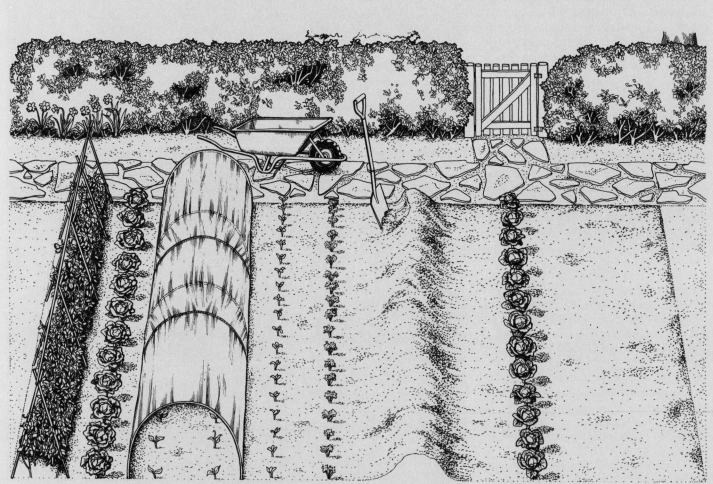

122

Summer

Early Summer

Harvest: Asparagus, spinach, cabbage, lettuce, radish, salad onions, peas and broad beans.

Sow – outdoors: Snap beans, *carrots, *beets, *lettuce (choose heat-resistant varieties), *sweet corn, rutabaga and brussels sprouts (both for fall harvesting).

Plant: Any indoor-raised plants. Transplant other seedlings such as brussels sprouts, lettuce.

Cultivate: Pull soil up and around potatoes, covering the young plants. Apply mulches 2–3 in (5–8 cm) deep to retain moisture and suppress weeds. Check tomato supports.

Protect: Keep a watch out for aphids and cabbage worms (on all brassica crops) and spray or dust at first signs of attack.

Midsummer

Harvest: Cucumbers, squash, snap beans, broccoli. Continue to gather lettuce, cabbage, onions.

Sow outdoors: *Beets, *carrots, *lettuce, *peas (for fall), kale, *turnips.

Late Summer

Harvest: Most crops – e.g. squash, snap beans, Swiss chard, cabbage, globe artichokes, carrots, turnips, lettuce, sweet corn, onion, tomatoes, early potatoes and shallots. Freeze the surplus!

Sow – outdoors: *Lettuce, *parsley, *radish and turnip.

Plant: Complete winter green transplanting.

Cultivate: Apply liquid fertilizer to beans, celery and tomatoes, every ten to fourteen days for the biggest crops. Water occasionally, (or well in hot, dry weather).

Protect: Potatoes in warm damp weather against blight by spraying with maneb every seven to ten days. Give some shade to emerging seedlings in very hot sunshine.

Fall

Early Fall

Harvest: Most crops. Lift onions and shallots and dry out in the sun before storing for winter use.

Sow – outdoors: In mild frost-free climates, a broad sowing program can begin.

Cultivate: Continue watering and liquid feeding where necessary.

Protect: Ripening onions and shallots from heavy rainfall to prevent regrowth and split bulbs. Harvest crops as soon as they are ready to prevent rapid ageing in hot conditions.

Mid-Fall

Harvest: Beans – snap, lima and runners, beets, cabbage, carrots, cauliflowers, cucumbers, lettuce, squash and turnips. It is a good time to lift potatoes (leave them to dry for an hour or two before storing for winter use).

Sow: Cover crops.

Plant: Spring cabbage from the late summer sowing.

Cultivate: This is a good time to start another compost heap as the fall clean-up is under way.

Protect: Be ready for frosts. A good time to erect plastic-covered structures, both cloches and greenhouses. They will then survive two winters and at least one full summer.

Late Fall

Harvest: Broccoli, cauliflower, the first brussels sprouts and the last of all crops likely to be destroyed by frost. Lift and store all the root crops as they mature. Complete lifting potatoes and put in storage for use through the winter.

Sow – outdoors: In mild climates: lettuce, peas and broad beans (towards the end of this period) to overwinter.

Cultivate: Cut down the old stems on asparagus. This is a good time to dig in well-decayed garden compost if you haven't sown a cover crop.

Protect: Endive to give blanched hearts and force chicory in pots indoors.

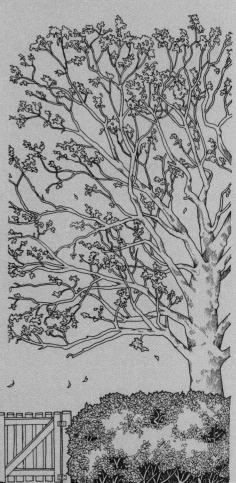

Winter

Early Winter

Harvest: Brussels sprouts, spinach, cabbage and the last of the cauliflowers. Start lifting celery (it will have more flavor after frost). Complete lifting root vegetables to store over winter.

Sow: In mild climates peas and broad beans.

Cultivate: Complete the big clear-up by storing canes and stakes, composting old leaves and plant remains.

Protect: Tender plants like globe artichoke by putting some old pea stems around the base and pulling soil up around them. Protect tender stored vegetables like potatoes from the frost.

Mid-Winter

Harvest: Check stored vegetables occasionally and remove any that show signs of rotting. Continue to gather brussels sprouts, winter cabbage and lettuce from cold frame.

Sow – indoors: Onions at the end of the period (but only if you want really big onions next year).

Late Winter

Harvest: Vegetables from storage. Continue to force chicory for winter salads.

Sow – indoors: Mustard and cress for winter salads.

Plan: For the coming year. Study seed catalogs. Select the varieties you wish to grow and secure supplies.

Cultivate: Have your soil tested. This is a good time to apply lime to dug soil which tends to be acid.

125

Index

Printed in the United States of America

Acknowledgements

We are indebted to the following organisations and individuals for permission to reproduce photographs:
Glasshouse Crops Research Institute
Murphy Chemical Limited
Richard Sharpe Studios
Sutton Seeds Limited
Syndication International
Thompson & Morgan (Ipswich) Limited
Michael Warren

Also to the United States Department of Agriculture for information, maps and charts used on pp. 28–31.